JEAN BAUDRILLARD

This uniquely engaging introduction to Jean Baudrillard's controversial writings covers his entire career, from his early theorisation of the consumer society, his contributions to social semiotics, his neglected masterpiece *Symbolic Exchange and Death*, to his later works on terrorism and 9/11. The book focuses on Baudrillard's central, but little understood, notion of symbolic exchange. Through the clarification of this key term a very different Baudrillard emerges: not the nihilistic postmodernist and enemy of Marxism and feminism that his critics have constructed, but a thinker immersed in the social world and passionately committed to a radical theorisation of it.

Baudrillard was a harsh critic of consumerism, of globalisation and of US foreign policy. He mocked the West's desire to unveil, to strip bare, to accumulate and to possess. He attacked pornography, advertising and 'reality' TV, as well as science and information technology, for exemplifying this naive and ultimately impossible 'dis-illusioning' of the world. Above all Baudrillard sought symbolic spaces, spaces where we might all, if only temporarily, shake off the system of social control. His writing sought to challenge and defy the system. By erasing our 'liberated' identities and suspending the pressures to compete, perform, consume and hate, that the system induces, we might create spaces not of freedom, but of symbolic engagement and exchange.

With lively critical discussion, this groundbreaking text is accessible to an undergraduate audience and will be an invaluable resource for those studying sociology, contemporary social theory, cultural studies and political sociology.

William Pawlett is a senior lecturer in Cultural Studies at the University of Wolverhampton. He received his PhD in Sociology from Loughborough University and is on the editorial board of *The International Journal of Baudrillard Studies*.

KEY SOCIOLOGISTS
Edited by PETER HAMILTON

This classic series provides students with concise and readable introductions to the work, life and influence of the great sociological thinkers. With individual volumes covering individual thinkers, from Emile Durkheim to Pierre Bourdieu, each author takes a distinct line, assessing the impact of these major figures on the discipline as well as the contemporary relevance of their work. These pocket-sized introductions will be ideal for both undergraduates and pre-university students alike, as well as for anyone with an interest in the thinkers who have shaped our time.

Series titles include:

EMILE DURKHEIM
Ken Thompson

THE FRANKFURT SCHOOL AND ITS CRITICS
Tom Bottomore

GEORG SIMMEL
David Frisby

MARX AND MARXISM
Peter Worsley

MAX WEBER
Frank Parkin

MICHEL FOUCAULT
Barry Smart

PIERRE BOURDIEU
Richard Jenkins

SIGMUND FREUD
Robert Bocock

ZYGMUNT BAUMAN
Tony Blackshaw

AUGUSTE COMTE
Mike Gane

ERVING GOFFMAN
Greg Smith

JEAN BAUDRILLARD
William Pawlett

JEAN BAUDRILLARD

Against Banality

WILLIAM PAWLETT

Routledge
Taylor & Francis Group

LONDON AND NEW YORK

First published 2007
by Routledge
2 Park Square, Milton Park, Abingdon, Oxon OX14 4RN

Simultaneously published in the USA and Canada
by Routledge
270 Madison Avenue, New York, NY 10016

*Routledge is an imprint of the Taylor & Francis Group,
an informa business*

Typeset in Times New Roman by
Graphicraft Limited, Hong Kong
Printed and bound in Great Britain by
MPG Books Ltd, Bodmin

British Library Cataloguing in Publication Data
A catalogue record for this book is available from the British
Library

Library of Congress Cataloging in Publication Data
Pawlett, William.
  Jean Baudrillard / William Pawlett.
    p. cm
  ISBN 978-0-415-38644-9 (hard cover) — ISBN 978-0-415-38645-6
(paper cover) 1. Baudrillard, Jean, 1929–2007—Criticism and
interpretation. 2. Sociologists—France. 3. Sociology—
France—Philosophy. I. Title.

  HM477.F8P38 2007
  301.092—dc22

                                              2007020950

ISBN10: 0-415-38644-6 (hbk)
ISBN10: 0-415-38645-4 (pbk)
ISBN10: 0-203-93736-8 (ebk)

ISBN13: 978-0-415-38644-9 (hbk)
ISBN13: 978-0-415-38645-6 (pbk)
ISBN13: 978-0-203-93736-5 (ebk)

For M

Table of Contents

Acknowledgements

I would like to express my thanks to the following people for their support and advice: Mike Gane, Mick Dillon, Gerry Carlin, Aidan Byrne, Victor Gazis and Meena Dhanda. Thanks also to Neil Iden and the Bodleian Library.

Introduction

I am definitively other.
(Baudrillard, 1993b: 173)

Rebel, provocateur, hijacker, outsider, trickster: Baudrillard was all of these.

It is a cold, blustery winter day in Leicester, UK, in 1998. It's Friday the thirteenth, an inauspicious day, and Baudrillard is giving a lecture at a weary municipal arts centre. I am writing a PhD thesis on Baudrillard. The theme of his lecture is 'Nothing'. This troubles me because my thesis, little more than a catalogue of his ideas, makes no reference to 'Nothing' and so even as a catalogue it is about to be rendered obsolete.

I am also anxious because, although shy, I have convinced myself that I will have to make contact with Baudrillard, introduce myself and attempt to ask intelligent sounding questions. I have seen Baudrillard lecture before and his physical appearance and demeanour surprised me greatly. Because he was a theorist seemingly obsessed with the power of appearances, of illusions and of seduction, I had expected a seductive, rakish man, imagining Baudrillard to look something like Antoine de Caunes, TV presenter of *Eurotrash*. Yet, as has been recorded elsewhere (Beard and McClellan, 1989: 61–2; Gane, 2000: 1), Baudrillard in the flesh was not this at all. He looked more like a retired trade union boss: dour and serious, tough-looking, almost pugilistic or soldierly. I remembered thinking that Baudrillard must never have been a handsome man, nor a striking one.

Yet Baudrillard, in giving his paper, did exert a seduction. The event was well attended, and there was excitement in the air. He spoke quietly, without any trace of showiness. He did not project the carefully crafted image of a successful celebrity intellectual; he was not, to use a term with which he is closely associated, a simulation. He did not attempt to dominate proceedings, even allowing mouthy and ill-informed postgraduates to rail against him with only a shrug of the shoulder or a muted 'perhaps'.

After the lecture I cornered Baudrillard and blurted out a few questions on simulation and its relationship to evil. He said that I spoke too rapidly for him to understand properly, but nevertheless he answered and clarified an issue that had been troubling me. I began to relax but at that point he was whisked away by one of the event organisers. Later there was a book signing and an exhibition of Baudrillard's photography entitled 'Strange World'. Baudrillard was even invited by a female undergraduate to sign her bra-strap, but instead he signed the strap of her shoulder bag. The book signing went on for some time with Baudrillard signing not only copies of his new book but, it seemed, any book that students brought to him: dog-eared copies of his older works, library copies of his works in translation, even a copy of Horrocks's *Introducing Baudrillard* (1996). I asked him if in this he was deliberately attacking the idea of authenticity and authorial status; he replied 'perhaps'.

I first encountered Baudrillard's ideas as a student of sociology in the late 1980s. Inspired by Mike Gane's rendering of his ideas, I rejected sociology almost immediately on contact with Baudrillard, seeking refuge in cultural studies. After I read Baudrillard, contemporary sociology seemed hopelessly slow and plodding, excruciatingly tame and stubbornly naive in its empiricism. Accessing Baudrillard's contribution to sociology is exceptionally problematic because his aim seems to have been to destroy it, or at least to observe its self-destruction.

Baudrillard's published writings span more than forty years and are concerned with subjects as diverse as poetry and economics, sociology and art, anthropology, architecture, film and photography, philosophy and literature. There are many changes of position and of methodology. There are changes of mood: harsh and softer moments. Baudrillard pursues themes raised by Nietzsche's attack on enlightenment and rationalist philosophy. Nietzsche, famously, announced the death of God and with it the collapse of notions of order, identity, moral

responsibility, truth and reality. Without God as foundation and guarantor these ideas have no access to ultimate, or even stable, meanings.
Baudrillard's work explores these themes in a highly original and
idiosyncratic manner through his notions of simulation and symbolic
exchange. Further, given the profound influence of Nietzsche on
Baudrillard's writings, we cannot expect a unified, coherent set of ideas
issued by a unified, coherent, identical self that is 'Baudrillard'.
'Baudrillard' is not a stable foundation that anchors the many ideas with
which he is associated. He immerses his position as thinker and writer
within his work, and within the paradoxical, radically uncertain world
that we inhabit: 'Since the world drives to a delirious state of things,
we must drive to a delirious point of view' (Baudrillard, 1990d: 1).
Baudrillard rejects rationalist, scientific epistemology that claims there
is an object – 'reality' – known by a subject, the thinker, and expressed
fully and truthfully by the medium in which the thinker works: words,
numbers, concepts, theories. In rejecting scientific objectivism, Baudrillard also attacks subjectivism or interpretivism. Loosely affiliated to
poststructuralism, Baudrillard rejects subject-centred claims to knowledge. The subject, the person or individual, in this approach is not the
source or foundation of representation or knowledge. Instead the subject is, first and foremost, a subject *in* language. The language code, its
rules of grammar and syntax, produce the fiction of a stable, centred,
identity as a ground for the accumulation of knowledge through
representation. 'The subject' is produced from 'outside': from society,
culture and language, from habits, norms and customs. This does not
mean that the subject is powerless or merely a puppet on the string of
language. Culture and language, norms and customs are not eternal
truths but power relations acting on subjects. And subjects can resist, refuse
and defy.

Yet Baudrillard is something of an oddity even within poststructuralism. While poststructuralism has become a recognised strand of
theory in the humanities and social sciences, a respectable body of thought
deftly summarised by Belsey (2003), Baudrillard remains marginal or
unacceptable. Belsey's (2003) overview makes no mention of Baudrillard, nor does Shrift's (1998) or Gutting's (2001). The name 'Baudrillard' continues to provoke suspicion, fear, resentment and ridicule:
discussion of his ideas is omitted or reduced to absurdity by hostile
readers.[1] Baudrillard's writings are certainly provocative and troubling.
After all, didn't he attack feminism at some point? Didn't he write something unpleasant about disability? Didn't he say that the Gulf War
didn't even happen and that we, in the Western world, wanted the World
Trade Center destroyed?

This book is required to provide readers with information on Baudrillard's ideas; to present a summary of his 'key concepts' in an accessible format. But this task is highly problematic given the specific nature of Baudrillard's writings. The problem is not one of complexity: Baudrillard's central themes can be summarised relatively easily. It is instead that Baudrillard's writings directly attack the very idea of the concept and its 'truths', the ideas of information and its dissemination, the possibility of explication and certainty. Baudrillard attacks the culture of mass communications, of the information economy, of capitalism, of globalisation, of pluralism and 'diversity'. These ideas and institutions are attacked not merely to provoke or offend, but because they dismantle, prevent or replace 'symbolic exchange', the central notion of Baudrillard's writing. But symbolic exchange 'is not a concept' (Baudrillard, 1993a: 115) and it cannot be reduced to information, or to a series or code of linguistic signs. Symbolic exchange 'is an act and a social relation' (ibid.), it is a space or relation established between people and is not separable or abstractable from that relation. Any abstraction from the dimension of reciprocal exchange is a 'simulation', a replacement of symbolic relations by coded, abstract signs. Symbolic exchange is communication, or better a communion; it cannot be expressed through 'bits' of information. This, of course, raises many problems for exposition and description. Nevertheless, I have tried to write a lively and accessible introduction to Baudrillard's thought. This is not 'Baudrillard for Dummies' but Baudrillard for anyone who is interested, anyone Baudrillard-curious. I do not assume prior knowledge of Baudrillard's ideas but I do hope to stimulate subsequent reading of them. We are surrounded by worthless information, but my conviction is that Baudrillard's books *are* worth reading.

My enthusiasm for Baudrillard's ideas was not dampened during the late 1990s when, needing a job, I discovered that university departments didn't want Baudrillard specialists. They wanted people interested in the sociological topics *du jour* (at that time 'identity politics' and 'globalisation') who might attract government research funding. Baudrillard's theory had, it was argued, gone 'badly wrong' (Ansell-Pearson, 1997: 34). Stuart Hall, with a shocking lack of precision, conflated Baudrillard's arguments on simulation with Francis Fukuyama's neo-conservative 'end of history' thesis (Hall, 1991: 33).[2] Baudrillard was, in any case, thought to be something to do with the 1980s and postmodernism (Callinicos, 1989: 86–7, 144–8; Kellner, 1989; Price, 1996: 448–51).

Everything changed on 11 September 2001. Everything. And this included Baudrillard's reputation. It was recalled that Baudrillard had written a great deal about terrorism and its relationship to the media. He had, in the mid-1970s, described the Twin Towers of the World Trade Center as a symbol of Western capitalism's arrogance, its exclusions, its fictions of invulnerability (1993a: 69–70, 82). Indeed, Baudrillard, chillingly, describes the Twin Towers as a spectacle of such self-satisfied hubris that the 'immanence of the catastrophe' haunts it and, quoting Walter Benjamin, suggests that such destruction might be received as an 'aesthetic pleasure' (1993a: 186). Baudrillard had warned, repeatedly, of the extreme vulnerability of Western societies and ideas to attack from Islamist fundamentalism from the late 1980s (1993b: 81–8, 1996c: 147). He had long opposed the drive of globalisation, warning of the increasing likelihood of violent rejections of and attacks against this fragile system of integration (1988a: 116–17, 1998b: 12–18).

The world, it seemed, was growing more and more Baudrillardian by the day. When, in the late 1970s, Baudrillard argued that party politics had become a meaningless exercise in images and promotion, and that wider political campaigning was assimilated into party politics without bringing about significant change, he was met with derision from the left. Today, with a pro-gay, pro-green Conservative Party in the UK, few would disagree that party politics functions as a promotional game of signs that has left 'reality' far behind. And now, after years of cursory rejection, Marxist theorists are lauding Baudrillard's work as 'an important contribution' to the critique of the capitalist system (Browning and Kilmister, 2006: 105).

When Baudrillard argued that the women's liberation movement risked worsening the social position of women if it 'liberated' them according to existing models of sexuality, he was denounced by uncomprehending feminists as a sexist creep who wanted to confine women to traditional roles. Yet in the age of size zero and models dying of anorexia, of omnipresent lap-dancing clubs and teenage lesbianism deployed in TV ratings wars, of pre-pubescent girls wearing 'Porn star' and 'Playboy' T-shirts and intelligent young women aspiring to work in the porn industry, Baudrillard's arguments have been reappraised. Victoria Grace's (2000) *Baudrillard's Challenge* dismisses early feminist readings of Baudrillard as puerile and makes the case that his work is an important, though eccentric, contribution to feminist thought, an outcome Baudrillard himself seemed to have hoped for (Baudrillard in Gane, 1993: 47).

After 9/11 US and Allied forces launched further virtual media wars against 'enemies' that had not attacked them. Conventional military engagement did not take place, but death and mutilation on a vast scale did, and Baudrillard's controversial *The Gulf War Did Not Take Place* (1995) was, at last, more fully understood. As Merrin argues, journalists such as Michael Ignatieff (2000) now publish their own 'sub-Baudrillardian ruminations' on the Gulf wars (Merrin, 2005: 96). The world's largest military and media machine has failed to win the war against an enemy it struggled to define or locate, and this time, has lost the propaganda war too, succeeding only in making the world a far more dangerous and uncertain place. This sounds like something from Baudrillard's fourth order of simulacra – and it is!

This book focuses on Baudrillard's ideas – and he had many. The most important is symbolic exchange in its many different forms and guises. The theme of symbolic exchange runs through all eight of the following chapters and beyond, in the provocation to think, to defy and to challenge.

1

The Object System, the Sign System and the Consumption System

> The description of the system of objects cannot be divorced from a critique of that system's practical ideology.
>
> (Baudrillard, 1996a: 11)

INTRODUCTION

Baudrillard's first full-length study, *Le systeme des objets/The System of Objects* (1996a), is rich and insightful, and is notable for worked examples and careful elaborations of position that are not present in most of his later works. Yet by no means is it a conventional sociological analysis. Baudrillard approaches everyday objects – clocks, cars, chairs, cigarette lighters – as an artist or photographer as much as a sociologist. This is both a strength and a weakness of the study. It offers a 'thick' or detailed description, almost a cataloguing, of the 'functionality' of the modern system of objects, but it lacks both the sustained critical force and experimentalism characteristic of later works. As a result the arguments of *System* are, at times, hard to distinguish from conservative denunciations of new technology and the state of 'modern life'. However, close attention to the text reveals far more interesting lines of argument, which are developed and reworked many times in later studies.

Only in the final section of *System* is the system of objects treated in a critical sociological fashion that emphasises their *ideological role within an integrated consumer capitalist system*. Earlier sections are empirical and descriptive, exploring the 'grammar' of objects just as Barthes had recently discussed the grammar of clothing in *The Fashion System* (Barthes, 1983). Section two deals with subjectivity and is a fascinating, but not truly distinctive, psychoanalytic reading of the processes by which people *invest* time, money and, above all, *desire* in the objects they possess. At many points Baudrillard's argument is recognisable as Freudo-Marxist: an intellectual synthesis in vogue throughout the 1960s and 1970s but from which Baudrillard would very quickly break. Indeed, what is fascinating in this early work is that Baudrillard is already clearly dissatisfied with Marxist and Freudian positions, and it is through *critical social theory* that Baudrillard opens up distance between his position and that of Freudo-Marxism. The most significant influences in this regard are the social anthropology of Marcel Mauss and the poststructuralist semiology of Roland Barthes. Also notable is the influence of the American popular sociological study *The Lonely Crowd* (1961) by David Riesman. Mauss's influential essay *The Gift* (1990, originally published in 1924/5) feeds Baudrillard's emerging notion of symbolic exchange. Barthes provides a means for interpreting the semiotic orders, and especially the central role played by fashion. However, Riesman's work plays an important role too in helping to focus Baudrillard's thinking on how the structures of the sign displace the symbolic order *at the level of the subject and lived experience.*[1] These influences enable a series of fascinating insights into the functioning of objects through the consumer system that moves beyond the confines of Freudo-Marxism.

THE PROFUSION OF SIGN-OBJECTS

> To become an object of consumption an object must first become a sign . . . it must become external, in a sense, to a relationship that it now merely signifies.
>
> (Baudrillard, 1996a: 200)

Baudrillard begins this study by noting that while 'mankind', as a historical category, remains relatively stable, there are rapid changes in the world of objects and technology. Baudrillard argues that increasingly objects have short life-spans: where pyramids and cathedrals saw the passing of many generations of human beings, today an individual will live through many generations of consumer objects. Objects are

increasingly disposable. They are highly valued, prized and cherished –
but only for a short time. We no longer seek a sense of the timeless in
our objects; instead our use of objects, and our objects' use of us, binds
us to a temporality of constant renewal. If modern man 'finds his soul
in his automobile', as Marcuse (1961: 9) claims, it is a transient soul
obliged to relocate every few years.

System inaugurates Baudrillard's career-long concern with the
object: as form, as image and as principle, initiating Baudrillard's
project to 'sweep away' the problematic of the subject (2004: 3). But
subject and object are not, of course, treated as a binary opposition.
Baudrillard's theories do not 'escape' but instead *displace* the problematic
of the subject, approaching it from the perspective of objects. The focus
of *System* is the way objects are possessed, arranged, consumed and
invested with meaning by the subject, which they, in turn, constitute
and define.

In *System* Baudrillard actually writes *in* the subject, criticising other
accounts of the new technological objects precisely because they
assume a 'consistent' level of analysis 'unrelated to any individual or
collective discourse' (1996a: 5). Baudrillard's interest is in objects,
technical and decorative, which form a cultural system of meaning. It
is the system of meaning that is given priority, not the subject's
interpretations and engagements with it. Indeed, Baudrillard contends
that humans increasingly appear 'irrational' in their desires, in comparison
to the functional 'rationality' of objects (1996a: 8). For Baudrillard,
influenced by structuralist theory, the system has constraining power over
individuals; indeed, it is only through the system that the notion of 'individual' is meaningful. Yet there is, for Baudrillard, something within
us that resists inscription within the system. The desires and emotional
investments of the subject 'surge back' through the object system,
finding means of expression: the subject is decentred in Baudrillard's
work – but very much alive!

The object system, organised by the codes of fashion and the imperative of functionality, operates as a principle of 'ideological integration'
(Baudrillard, 1996a: 9). The subject becomes 'person' through the process of 'personalisation', the terms of which are set by the sign-object
system. Of course individual choices are made and internal dialogues
are carried out, but always *vis-à-vis* objects, images or signs. The
process of personalisation is a site of contestation and active investment,
not a *fait accompli* determined from above the system. Personal and
emotional 'inessentials' are expressed through objects in unpredictable
ways, as in the case of the collector of objects, but whatever choices are
made, and whatever choices are resisted, the object system translates

drives, emotions and their ambivalences into *sign form*. Once rendered into signs they are managed and regulated by the system as commodities. All signs are exchangeable and, in a sense, equivalent with other signs: their differences are at the level of content and combination, which is made possible by their similarity at the level of form. Signs separate, abstract, order and render 'thing-like' the complex of ambivalent symbolic relations *between* people and objects.

The subject in Baudrillard's analysis is, at this stage, the subject as Freudo-Marxist theories portray it. Drives (*Trieb* in Freud), such as aggressiveness and erotic cravings, are *processed* through signs. Increasingly sexual and aggressive drives are promoted by the consumer system; we are encouraged to realise our desires, to indulge our cravings. In Marcuse's terms drives are 'repressively de-sublimated', or channelled into the consumer system. We are entreated to follow our desires but 'our' desires have been coded and mapped, in advance, to appropriate objects. For example, sexual desire is supposed to be something to do with busty young women and muscular young men: *sexual drives transcribed into signs*.

In *System* Baudrillard remains attached to a Marxist framework, arguing that physical toil and the visible bodily gestures of working hands gradually disappear, replaced by machinery and labour-saving devices.[2] In *The Consumer Society* (1998a) Baudrillard reworks the Marxist notion of alienation, while in *System* he admits that there are tangible benefits in the overcoming of constant toil simply for the purpose of survival; there are also, he insists, many costs. First, there is a profound effect on social character. The functional universe of sign objects is a world devoid of 'secrets' and 'mysteries' (1996a: 29). The social self exists in a state of anxiety, it needs to connect through technological means, to get close to others but not *too* close. Baudrillard develops what Riesman (1961) called the 'other-directed' form of social character. This refers to the individuated being, uprooted from tradition ('tradition-directedness') but also distinct from the 'inner-directed' individual that Weber (1992) famously linked to the morality of Protestant Puritanism. The 'other-directed' individual requires a social 'radar' (Riesman, 1961: 126–60) that enables constant self-monitoring and adaptation in terms of what others are doing. We each must become our own public relations officer, rather than our own priest or policeman. That is, we must define ourselves in relation to others both by conforming and crucially by introducing small or 'marginal' differences that we promote in order to define our distinctiveness, individuality or 'personality' (Baudrillard, 1998a: 87–98).

THE FUNCTIONAL SYSTEM AND THE END OF THE SYMBOLIC DIMENSION

It is very quickly apparent that Baudrillard regards modernity as an impoverished system that has lost 'the expressive power of the old symbolic order' and has nothing to 'replace' it (1996a: 17). Like workers and classes before them, objects are 'freed' from relatively fixed traditional meanings and symbolic ties. In the process, Baudrillard insists, many objects become banal or 'nondescript'. Several examples are given: traditional beds in solid wood are compared with modern, fashionable, functional beds (think Ikea). The latter are devoid of ritual or ceremonial meaning: a 'marriage' bed cannot be distinguished from any other double bed. The bed no longer has 'absolute' value, or value in itself. Instead it has 'combinatorial' value in that it is designed to complement other items in the 'bedrooms' range. The functional bed may well be *invested* with meanings in the course of experience and may come to *signify* love or passion. However, the meaningfulness of this process is predicated on the individual subject making choices based on 'needs' from a pre-coded range and then accumulating or accruing experiences to their 'identity'. Baudrillard develops a powerful critique of subject/identity as constructed through 'needs', themselves generated by the sign-code: 'personalised' or customised personalities are, he insists, *given* by the code. But surely traditional society was even more constraining, so what exactly makes the traditional bed different and more 'expressive'? Much of Baudrillard's argument, even at this stage, is based on such a distinction being possible without resort to mysticism or nostalgia, so it is very important to clarify this distinction.

To begin with, objects in the traditional order are craft-produced rather than mass or serially produced. To put it bluntly, they are produced by humans using tools rather than by machines using humans. According to Baudrillard there is an important relationship of human muscular effort and gesture (*le gestuel*) involved in the use of tools that disappears with the use of push-button technology. These very gestures symbolise sexual acts in an 'obscene' way, without shame, according to Baudrillard's soon to be revised Freudianism, and sexual desires are *sublimated through symbols*. Objects in the traditional order, then, are 'symbolic' in the sense that they symbolise the lived relations that exist between desires (primarily sexual) and culture (respectable, hierarchical, normative).[3]

Further, the form that these relations take is governed by rule and ritual – the marriage bed is only available to couples who have symbolically exchanged rings in a marriage ceremony. There is little freedom of choice concerning such ritual, the form is prescribed and the 'individual' must follow. They can refuse the ritual, or back out at the last minute, but if they do they cannot attain the status of married couple. In this sense the notion of the autonomous individual as master or mistress of their destiny, or as free and equal 'consumer' before a range of choices, is not meaningful in the symbolic order. Constrained by class and status hierarchies, dictated by ritual and ceremonial procedures, sublimated through toil and effort – there is no sense in which the individual self is 'free' in the traditional order. And for this reason Baudrillard argues there is little about which to be nostalgic (1996a: 54 n. 33).

The sign-object system offers a form of 'liberation', but, according to Baudrillard, this freedom is formal, not actual, and must be critiqued. The sign system offers relief, or even deliverance, from the ambivalences and restrictions of the symbolic order, from the constraints of ascribed status. Choices are offered: we become the designers of our own lives, or at least our own interiors! To pursue the example, functional furniture is often very affordable and not always of poor quality. The uses that furniture is put to are, at least partially, 'desublimated' as we see attractive models and young couples draped on new beds and sofas on our TV screens. There is nothing 'obscene' in this process, and we all have fun on furniture at one time or another, so what's not to like? Baudrillard's critique is directed at the *form* of the sign system, not at particular contents of signs. Considered as form, signs are the material of reification, they make living social relations into things, into units – they are, in a sense, the material of materialism. What this implies is that objects no longer possess essential values rooted in lived experience. The meaning of objects is dictated by the fashion cycle. For example, that special (meaning-rich) sofa from your student days is soon rendered unattractive by changes in fashion styling. If kept too long (for 'sentimental' reasons) it becomes an anomaly that could threaten the individual's positioning of himself or herself as a desirable and liberated modern person (i.e. their position within the sign-code). The old sofa is not charged with collective, ritual meaning, though it might be charged with individual, psychological meaning.[4] There is no obligatory ritual process to prevent you throwing it away and buying another; it is an autonomous commodity, your ownership is total and you dispose of it as you wish. And when do you wish to dispose of it? When it is ugly, aged and old-fashioned according to the terms set by the sign-code. So the sign-object system offers a sense of freedom, autonomy and sovereignty to consumers but only on condition that we accept the sense of individuality and personality that is given by the system.

Other examples of the shift from a symbolic to a functional order, discussed in this study, include the use of colour in domestic environments. 'Strong' colours tend to be replaced by pastels and thereby 'lose their unique value . . . the direct expression of instinctual life . . . and become relative to each other and to the whole. This is what is meant by describing them as "functional"' (1996a: 35). For Baudrillard, pastels are not living colours 'but signs for them'. Further elements of this transformation include the replacement of the grandfather clock with a number of smaller clocks, scattered about the house according to principles of tone and combination. The large centrally placed mirror, family portraits and wedding photographs also tend to disappear from modern interiors: time, space and (reflections of) self are literally decentred and disavowed.

The system constructs us as free consumers, as people who buy the products that are for sale because we want them as they satisfy our needs. Indeed, Baudrillard rails against the academic disciplines of sociology and economics for accepting the idea of 'the consumer' as a given: as an ontological fact. For economists such as the influential J. K. Galbraith, humanity consists of free and self-conscious individual beings with identifiable sets of needs and the desire to satisfy them. But needs are not freestanding essences; instead '*the system of needs* is the product of the system of production' (1998a: 74, original emphasis). Needs do not come about in response to particular objects, one by one, but are generated from a grid or code 'as system-elements', not within a unique relationship between individual and object. The code, then, is a collective and unconscious social constraint, a morality, an obligation. The tautology that Baudrillard seeks to expose is the mutually constructing nature of needs, desires and consumer goods – an unbroken circuit. Once we are convinced we possess 'needs' we have already consented to the consumer system because it generates the principle of abstract needs in search of satisfaction. We may recognise that the consumer system does not satisfy our needs 'properly' or fully, or that it rips us off in the process – but we tend not to question the existence of these freestanding, objective 'needs'. The principle of 'need' is, for Baudrillard, the crucial ideological construct of the capitalist system (1981: 63–87). And once consumers have invested value in the commodities they consume, these values are 'real', they cannot be dismissed as false or fake, though they are certainly ideologically structured (1996a: 153). To be a consumer is to be self-coding and is a considerable accomplishment demanding much time and effort. Consumers are required to act: to reflect, to decide, to choose – yet always within the particular, ideologically structured frame of reference that they exist within.

There is no question that the symbolic order and the modern semiotic system are both forms of social discipline. There is little in the way of genuine 'freedom' in either of them (though it is not an either/or situation because they are always found together). The key distinction is that the symbolic order does not purport to offer freedom, its constraints are cruel and manifest but the meanings generated are intensely charged, while the semiotic order purports to offer freedom, its constraints are (largely) hidden and the meanings generated are lacking in intensity. This is a rough summary of Baudrillard's key distinction in its earliest or least developed form, and his thinking on this distinction soon becomes far more developed, as I show in the following chapters.

The abstractness of signs, as lifted out of lived relations, makes possible their ever-changing combination and recombination in a limitless process of integration: 'no object can escape this logic, just as no product can escape the formal logic of the commodity' (Baudrillard, 1996a: 41). So the consumer society does not simply involve a shift in the economic sphere from the primacy of production to the primacy of consumption. Instead, Baudrillard argues, there has been a shift in the very nature of social reality that in scope far exceeds the confines of economic structures and institutions. Traditional objects 'tools, furniture, the house itself' (1996a: 200) were 'symbolic'. This means that as carriers of intense meaning they mediated social relationships as a living force binding human action and endeavour to durable and lasting sets of meanings. For example, the hearth and kitchen table express strong emotional bonds: family loyalty and conviviality, comfort and protection. Such symbolic values and sentiments are relatively inflexible; they tend to be binding rather than open to debate or questioning, although of course they do alter over time. Furthermore, they are, according to Baudrillard, characterised by *ambivalence* – that is, they tend to inspire opposed emotional attitudes within the same person, such as love and hate, fear and desire, attraction and repulsion.[5] The emotional-symbolic bonds of human relations are not, then, presented as the unproblematic 'positives' of a world now 'lost' or submerged by the 'evil' of the sign-system; Baudrillard privileges ambivalence, only ambivalence – and the related emotional intensities, not the norms or structures of a 'symbolic' society.

Symbolic relations are singular and unique, never abstract, never interchangeable, never equivalent to anything. However, symbolic and semiotic are not binary oppositions: to speak of an opposition between symbol and sign is a mistake. Signs 'stand in' for lived relations; they refer to and express them in abstracted, coded and therefore reductive fashion. Both symbols and signs (and symbols *are* signs) mediate human experience. The important distinction is that the system of signs 'bars' or disallows the rich ambivalence of symbolic expression (Baudrillard, 1981: 88–101). Signs actually replace the lived relation; they present a coded, stereotyped version of reality, one that is more manageable, less threatening but also less 'meaningful' or intense than the world of symbolic ambivalence. Signs suggest, claim or 'simulate' symbolic relations; they are abstracted from symbolic relations. The relationship between them is complex and it is as important to bear in mind the closeness or proximity of the symbolic and semiotic as it is the distance and distinction between them.

The process of replacing symbolic relations with coded signs is greatly accelerated by consumer capitalism, but it is not identical to it. From the early twentieth century onwards capitalism restructured itself around the consumption of goods rather than their production, creating a more manageable environment for commercial exchange, one less dependent on the productive force of organised, unionised labour. In a sense, of course, objects have always been produced, but they are produced for very different purposes. Objects were produced for worship or devotion long before they were produced for sale. Sacred objects were 'produced' through sacrificial ritual that could only be performed by the proper officiant; there was no 'freedom' regarding production and no 'economic' surplus was allowed to be produced. Any 'surplus' was social rather than 'economic' and was devoted to religious expression, often sacrifice (Clastres, 1977; Bataille, 1986; Mauss, 1990). Yet for hundreds of years, and in Western Europe on a considerable scale since the sixteenth century, objects have been produced in surplus for the purpose of sale for profit. The key distinction between this form of production and contemporary consumer capitalism is in the sort of objects, goods and services that are considered marketable. In the consumer society people seem to be willing to buy almost anything. According to Baudrillard we reach a situation where 'All desires, projects and demands, all passions and all relationships, are now abstracted (or materialised) as signs and as objects to be bought and sold' (Baudrillard, 1996a: 201).

But is the sign-code really this powerful? Are people really taken in, convinced by this 'reality'? And if so, in what sense is the notion of a symbolic order of ambivalence meaningful or distinct? These questions are answered by a close reading of Baudrillard's early texts. The sign-code takes itself to be this powerful, it functions *as if it is*, but, ultimately, it is not. People are not convinced by it. And, Baudrillard is clear, this refers to all people, not just a select band of vanguard intellectuals. Resistance to the sign-code does not follow a dialectical pattern, there is no revolutionary agency as Marxism conceives it, but there is refusal and defiance, rejection and withdrawal. Finally, the ultimate 'stakes' at play in consumer capitalism are symbolic. The sign-code is founded on principles of the symbolic order abstracted and put to use, as the next section shows.

ADVERTISING AS GIFT

Your happiness loves Cadbury's.
(Cadbury's Chocolate Advertising Campaign, 2001)

Towards the end of *System* there is a lengthy discussion of advertising, which opens with a starkly oppositional stance: 'Advertising in its entirety constitutes a useless and unnecessary universe' (1996a: 164). Advertising maintains the whole system of 'imposed differentiation' – the choice of coded differentials by which individuals are integrated into the system. The available range of choice offers 'personalisation' so that individuals define themselves in opposition to other individuals. The codes of fashion in advertising are a language in the Saussurian sense; that is, they are a system of arbitrary signs that derive their meaning from their position in relation to other terms in the system, *never by absolute, intrinsic or essential value*. How do we know how to look 'cool', 'trendy', 'wealthy', 'powerful', 'alternative', 'rebellious'? We do so by displaying signs or terms in the system that are not (yet) being displayed by those from whom we wish to differentiate ourselves and *are* being displayed by those whom we want to resemble. Thus the meaning of our sign displays are arbitrary, coded and only meaningful in *negative* terms. Any particular item of dress or furnishing is only fashionable while certain people *do not possess it*. There is nothing intrinsically cool or uncool about any particular fashion: objects draw their meaning from their relative position within the ever-changing system or code.

Crucially Baudrillard *does not present consumers as passive dupes of the capitalist system*. He is clear that capitalism, operating through the commodity system, is able to wield an immense degree of *social control*, but his interest is in the forms of refusal or defiance that emerge. Social control occurs, primarily, at the level of the *medium or form* of advertising, not through its specific messages or content. As Baudrillard indicates, we may well reject the hyperbole: the inflated or impossible claims made for certain products. We may reject the imagery of the 'chic' and 'successful' 'lifestyles' depicted in many campaigns for luxury items and we may be critical of newer trends in TV advertising where such 'lifestyles' are invoked only to be suddenly punctured by a 'get real' message: of course, the product won't make you look like a model but it's good anyway (Kellogg's Special K, Ocean Spray fruit juice) – or even, this *is* bad for you but we know you will enjoy it (Knorr Pot Noodles, varieties of chocolate). But this is merely to critique *content.* For Baudrillard the mechanism of control, at the deepest level, resides in the fact that advertising as form is a *free gift*: it is *for* us. It reassures us that society exists and that it is thinking of ways to satisfy *our desires*, solve *our problems* and assuage *our anxieties*. The consumer system, at the general systemic level Baudrillard theorises it, *need do no more than this*. The system is willing to suggest what 'type of person' we are, what we might desire and enjoy, what we ought to try. And it doesn't matter *what* we try, it matters only that we *do* try: 'Try something different today' (Sainsbury's Supermarkets Ltd, UK).

As individuated beings, with symbolic ties broken, we are ill-equipped to be 'social' animals, we need help – for example, in displaying 'our' fashion sense or 'our' social status – and *the system provides it*. According to Baudrillard it is a mistake to think that consumerism attempts to mould us to the demands and pressures of modern society: 'nowadays it is society as a whole which must adapt to the individual' (1996a: 169). Somebody, somewhere cares about your happiness – not for your deepest wishes or ultimate peace of mind, for these things are impossible, but simply about your day-to-day happiness. This is profoundly reassuring and it has a powerful integrating effect, because who can argue with happiness?

> We are taken as the object's aims, and the object loves us. And because we are loved we feel that we exist; we are 'personalised'. This is the essential thing – the actual purchase of the object is secondary. The abundance of products puts an end to *scarcity*; the abundance of advertising puts an end to *insecurity*.
>
> (Baudrillard, 1996a: 171)

Baudrillard has a point here. Imagine a young man on a shopping trip in a chemist's or drug store browsing the men's products. Lynx deodorant is marketed as if it possesses aphrodisiac qualities (women will follow strangers, undress and even spank each other when they detect its aroma) and many shampoos claim to thicken receding hair. The shopper does not really believe that the deodorant will confer sex appeal or that the shampoo will thicken his hair, yet he takes them to the counter. Such product choices position him as relatively affluent; as a thoughtful consumer who cares about his appearance and perhaps is the possessor of an ironic 'post-feminist' sense of humour. But imagine the horror, the speechless indignation, if our shopper were asked by the sales assistant to *explain* and *justify* these choices! That this could not happen is indicative of the social and ideological functioning of consumerism, because, as Baudrillard argues, consumption is not a passive process, it is an *active, self-aware, collective and social* one: a consensual myth, a language we speak to each other\ The mythic language of consumption forges the pact between shop assistant and shopper. The social act of understanding yourself and others as consumers, as beings who use products in an active and reflective way to satisfy needs and desires, inscribes us in the code. The consumer society delivers tangible benefits; it gives us *the gift of self*, suggesting not who we are but what we can *become*.[6]

Baudrillard does not, as is sometimes suggested, pit his notion of symbolic relations and exchange against the consumer system as its contradiction; his position is far more complex. Consumerism is described as a 'festival' that 'subtly renews links with archaic rituals of giving, of offering presents' (1996a: 171). The society of consumption is both orgiastic and circumscribed; it offers riches, dreams, and transformations but only through commodities. The 'festival' of buying is highly sexualised and not just because underdressed young women are used to sell many products. More than this, Baudrillard insists, buying involves us, personally, in an elaborate ritual performance, an 'amorous dalliance' (1996a: 172) involving much toing and froing, advance and retreat, seduction and abandonment. The buyer may lead the salesperson on to greater and greater demonstrations, only to abandon them and their product for a more coy and understated competitor. Consumerism, then, is sexual *in its form as well as in its content* and this is crucial to its ability to reproduce and expand, to enchant and compel. But, Baudrillard argues, consumerism is not simply driven by profit and by sex: its success, its ability to eliminate alternative forms of social organisation and to present itself as the highest form rests upon its ability to work at *the unconscious level.* It protects us like a mother, it tends to our every need, has solutions for our every problem:

> Whether advertising is organised around the image of the mother or around the need to play, it always fosters the same tendency to regress to a point anterior to the real social processes, such as work, production, the market, or value, which might disturb this magical integration.

> (Baudrillard, 1996a: 175)

In the absence of full and active participation in the social, which Baudrillard, following Durkheim and Mauss, associates with the earlier social forms (symbolic exchange, ritual and sacrifice) consumer society offers only 'a travesty of the social entity' (1996a: 174). But this is still something; it creates a 'superficial' yet 'vivid' sense of 'warmth' and belonging. We do not live in a world of atomised or fragmented individuals, constantly at war with one another for the best jobs and most desirable lovers – the system could not function if this was the case. We *do* belong, we *are* alike, but it is a belonging and likeness *of the code.*

THE SOCIAL LOGIC OF CONSUMPTION

> Consumption defines precisely the stage where the commodity is immediately produced as a sign, as a sign value and where signs are produced as commodities.
>
> (Baudrillard, 1981: 147)

Baudrillard's second major work, *La société de la consommation/The Consumer Society* (1998a), offers a greatly expanded treatment of consumption and is certainly Baudrillard's most recognisably sociological work. It is very important to emphasise from the outset that the French term 'consommation' does not translate as 'consumerism', but as *consumption.* Where consumerism is the idea or ideology of the consumer society, consumption is the act of consuming, or of being consumed. It implies being used, making use of and using up. For Baudrillard consumption is, fundamentally, the act of consuming, spanning conscious and unconscious levels, *the idea of the self as a consuming self,* or, as he terms it, 'the consumption of consumption' (1998a: 193–6).

The study begins, characteristically, by puncturing some of the myths of the consumer society. According to Baudrillard the consumer society does not entail any genuine progress, it does not attempt to alleviate poverty or generate greater equality between classes, sexes and ethnic groups and it does not seek to promote affluence or abundance. Instead its purpose is to maintain a system of social privilege, invidious distinction and discrimination; a vast game of customised or personalised identity types competing for status through objects.

First, two specific *myths* are tackled: the myth that growth promotes affluence and the myth that affluence leads to democracy. The 'growth' economy, Baudrillard argues, actually generates a structural poverty – a permanent 'underclass' or excluded minority. Contrary to the protestations of economists and politicians this class is not merely residual because it is never 'cleared up' by continued growth (and how much truer this is today). Baudrillard has already moved far from a Marxist position:

There is not in fact – and never has been any 'affluent society' . . .
whatever the volume of goods produced or available, wealth is
geared both to a structural excess and a structural penury. At the
sociological level there is no equilibrium. Every society produces
differentiation, social discrimination, and that structural organisation is based on the use and distribution of wealth (among other
things). The fact that a society enters upon a phase of growth, as
our industrial society has done, changes nothing in this process.

(Baudrillard, 1998a: 53)

Inequality drives the system, providing the underlying dynamic for
the games of invidious distinction. Baudrillard does not contend that
the capitalist system is 'deliberately bloodthirsty' (1998a: 56), simply that
it seeks to maintain privilege, domination and, through these, control.
It is simply that a new car for a private consumer is a more effective
means of social control than a new public hospital, while a visible 'underclass' of the marginal and rejected serves as a potent reminder of what
happens if you refuse to play by the rules.

It is important to emphasise that at this stage of Baudrillard's
thought there is a strong sense of 'determination by social structure': a
social level of causality that is quite real, although it is largely hidden
or unconscious. Baudrillard's analysis attempts to penetrate beneath or
beyond the 'metaphysical' notions of growth and affluence, of needs and
uses, to expose the workings of the system through 'a genuine analysis
of the social logic of consumption' (1998a: 60). This analysis reveals
fundamental inequality and divisiveness – a social status war. The level
of ideology, with its notions of equality, fairness and technological
progress, is secondary and offers *signs* of freedom that mask 'real' lived
inequalities (although the distinction between real and apparent is
abandoned in Baudrillard's next study, *For a Critique of the Political
Economy of the Sign*).

In a fascinating section of *Consumer* entitled 'Waste', Baudrillard begins
to develop a new position that will be elaborated and rearticulated many
times throughout his career – the comparison between cultures dominated by the principle of *symbolic exchange* and those dominated by
signs and simulations. In *The System of Objects* the notion of the symbolic *dimension* had played a pivotal role but it referred exclusively to
objects, gestures and lived relations characteristic of pre-industrial
Western societies: vestiges or remnants of which were fast disappearing. Symbolic exchange, by contrast, is a living, dynamic principle.

The methodology Baudrillard adopts in developing the notion of
symbolic exchange is, initially at least, paradigmatically sociological. He

opposes the common-sense view that waste is immoral and socially dysfunctional through an appeal to sociological sense that would bring out the 'true functions' of waste:

> All societies have wasted, squandered, expended and consumed beyond what is strictly necessary for the simple reason that it is in the consumption of a surplus, of a superfluity that the individual – and society – feel not merely that they exist, but that they are alive.
>
> (Baudrillard, 1998a: 43)

Baudrillard, drawing on Mauss (1990), develops a comparison between the restrictive frame of reference offered by economists and a more general 'total social logic'. From the latter perspective waste has a positive function. It is the site of the production of social values, the values of prestige, rank and status – symbolic values in Baudrillard's sense. Affluence is given expression through wastage: being able to spend the equivalent of a teacher's entire annual salary on a new car signals affluence; spending the same amount on a fur coat even more so. Here the economic values of pounds, dollars and euros are consumed: transformed into the symbolic values of status and power. The crucial difference between the consumer society and earlier forms of social organisation is that once collective, festive, ceremonial forms of wastage are now individualised, personalised and mass-mediated. This distinction is far more complex than it first appears:

> [W]e have to distinguish individual or collective waste as a symbolic act of expenditure, as a festive, ritual and an exalted form of socialisation, from its gloomy, bureaucratic caricature in our societies, where wasteful consumption has become a daily obligation.
>
> (Baudrillard, 1998a: 47)

This distinction is crucial to Baudrillard's project. In consumer society expenditure no longer erases or annuls the individual subject in a convulsive moment, an experience of sacredness or ritual festivity (Durkheim, 1961; Mauss, 1990); instead it seals the subject as an individual unit within the consumer system.

Baudrillard's third major text, *For a Critique of the Political Economy of the Sign* (1981, hereafter *Critique*), clarifies and develops the distinction between the symbolic and semiotic orders by presenting a systematic account of the different forms of social 'value'. Baudrillard even represents this as a table entitled 'general conversion table of all values' (1981: 123). There are four different logics: 'the functional logic of use value' is based on utility; the 'economic logic of exchange value' is based on equivalence; the 'differential logic of sign value' is based on coded differences; finally 'the logic of symbolic exchange', characterised by ambivalence, is neither law nor value strictly speaking but 'anti-value' or anti-economy.\The table is not a static typology but one of conversions, reconversions and 'transit'. Use, exchange and sign value operate together to bar or deny symbolic exchange. There is undeniably a theory of power relations here, although most commentaries fail to recognise it: 'economic exploitation based on the monopoly of capital and "cultural" domination based on the monopoly of the code engender each other ceaselessly' (1981: 125)/ The difference between sign-exchange-value and symbolic exchange is frequently missed, feeding the mistaken notion that Baudrillard has no theory of power. To clarify, sign exchange involves practices of waste or conspicuous consumption (*consommation*) in order to achieve and maintain social status differentials (value). However, symbolic exchange consists in the *consumation* or 'destruction of values'. There is no separable or autonomous 'value' that can be appropriated at the end of the symbolic exchange process: indeed, the process must not come to an end. Symbolic exchanges are obligatory and cyclical, dual or collective, not individual choices or expressions of status or wealth through possession of circumscribed or autonomous objects or values. In Baudrillard's words,

> In symbolic exchange . . . the object is not an object: it is inseparable from the concrete relation in which it is exchanged, the transferential pact that is sealed between two persons: it is thus not independent as such. It has, properly speaking, neither use value nor (economic) exchange value.
>
> (Baudrillard, 1981: 64)

But the relationship between signs/values and symbolic exchange is not binary or contrastive but highly unstable and volatile. All the forms of value must be suspended in order to achieve symbolic exchange, and inversely, all forms of value (use, exchange, sign or representional) work in unison 'breaking and reducing symbolic exchange' further; 'Once symbolic exchange is broken, the same material is abstracted into utility value, commercial value, statutory value' (1981: 125).\

Marxism enables a critical theorisation of the relationship between use-value and economic exchange-value, of sorts, by exposing the unequal social relations of ownership. However, for Baudrillard, Marxism fails to theorise critically the sign and representation, the field of language and culture. The economic or commodity sphere loses the power to determine social relations but this is not merely transferred to signs; instead the two levels merge, producing the political economy of the sign. In this complex, integrated system or code, only symbolic ambivalence has the power to challenge or suspend the system; it '*brings the political economy of the sign to a standstill*' (1981: 150). Baudrillard attempts a critical social theory of political economy *and* representation by proposing that 'exchange value is to use value what the signifier is to the signified', and, further, 'exchange value is to the signifier what use value is to the signified' (1981: 127). This involves a redefinition of the concept of ideology. The ideological nature of signs, of representation, is to be discovered *at the level of form not content*, not at the level of the meaning of the signified but in the mechanics of the sign itself. Ideology, for Baudrillard, 'is the process of reducing and abstracting symbolic material into a form . . . as value (autonomous), as content (transcendent), and as a representation of consciousness (signified)' (1981: 145). Ideology, then, resides not only in the content of particular signs but, more fundamentally, in the form or process of abstraction and equivalence.

The play of signifiers generates the illusion of a stable signified; the play of signs the illusion of reference; the play of commodities the fiction of use-value. For Baudrillard the signified (meaning) and the referent (the 'real' object out there in the world) are both a 'fiction' and are ultimately indistinguishable because their contents are 'assigned to them by the signifier' (1981: 152). Similarly, 'real' or 'natural' use-value is a fiction assigned by the system of commodity exchange-value. Use and need, the subjects or individuals who possess them and the representations they produce have, as their very condition of possibility, the breaking up of the world into sign units, the severing of symbolic relations into abstract 'things':

> The 'real' table does not exist. If it can be registered in its identity (if it exists), this is because it has already been *designated*, abstracted and rationalised by the separation (decoupage) which establishes it in this equivalence to itself . . . there is no fundamental difference between the referent and the signified.
>
> (Baudrillard, 1981: 155)

For Baudrillard, then, 'The process of signification is, at bottom, nothing but a gigantic simulation model of meaning', since the 'real' is 'only the simulacrum of the symbolic, its form reduced and intercepted by the sign' (1981: 162). 'Reality' is a 'phantasm by means of which the sign is preserved from the symbolic deconstruction that haunts it' (1981: 156 n. 9). Symbolic exchange forever haunts the sign, threatening to 'dismantle' all the formal oppositions on which it depends: signifier and signified; sign and referent; and the binary oppositions that flow from them – nature/culture, male/female, good/evil, black/white, adult/ child. Yet the symbolic cannot be defined, since this would render it semiotic and representational. The symbolic 'cannot be named except by allusion, by infraction': 'Of what is outside the sign, of what is other than the sign, *we can say nothing*, really, except that it is ambivalent, that is, it is impossible to distinguish respective separated terms and to positivise them as such' (Baudrillard, 1981: 161).

A THEORY OF THE MEDIA?

There is no theory of the media.

(Baudrillard, 1981: 164)

The Consumer Society (1998a: 99–128) and *Critique* (1981: 164–84) discuss of the effects of electronic media on human relations at length. Baudrillard wrote on electronic media long before 'the mass media' became a fashionable topic of sociological enquiry, and long before 'media studies' had attained the status of an academic discipline. Influenced by Marshall McLuhan's pioneering studies (see Genosko, 1999) and by the American sociologist Daniel Boorstin (see Merrin, 2005), Baudrillard argues that media are a central mode of social control and integration in consumer society. Contrary to some critics (the usual suspects) Baudrillard does not reiterate the Frankfurt School attacks on the 'mass' media as producing isolation and alienation (see Adorno and Horkheimer, 1971). In fact, Baudrillard takes issue with these very terms, arguing that they are inadequate to an analysis of contemporary culture (1998a: 187–96). Far from 'isolating' or separating people, the media integrate through solicitation, through the offering of the gift of 'self': the types and codes through which we are able to understand ourselves. The multiplied object/sign values disseminated by the media are invested with meaning to the degree that alienated and unalienated attachments to sign-objects cannot be distinguished. But such sign values do not float free of power relations, they are saturated by them. Baudrillard is clear that the system of consumption drives the sign productions of the electronic media. Signs are implicated in power relations, but as 'the caricatural resurrection, the parodic evocation of what already no longer exists' (1998a: 99). Baudrillard alludes here to Marx's 'The Eighteenth Brumaire of Louis Bonaparte' (1969: 394), suggesting the farcical nature of events that occur twice, the first time as meaningful and of historical import, the second time as a mere parody. Mass media signs refer to what is lost, what has disappeared or is disappearing, or they refer to other media signs in a closed circuit.

Baudrillard's initial example of this process is petrol service stations that insist on selling log fire and barbecue kits; the same oil companies that have rendered the 'real' log fire, and its symbolic meanings, obsolete. Extending Baudrillard's example, the growing fad for barbecues can be seen as a forced, parodic restoration in sign-form of the act of cooking as gift and communion. Cooking over the hearth or stove symbolically connects nature and culture through the burning of gathered wood and connects people through the coming together at table. With the barbecue, by contrast, we stand about in back gardens where prim lawns and patios merely *signify* nature, not nature as awkward, tangled 'reality' but nature processed and manicured, reduced to signs – a simulation of nature. And if it rains we give up and go back indoors; that is, if nature does intervene, it is as inconvenience.[7]

Modern communications replace the presence and 'communion' of lived relations with 'that modern, technical, aseptic form of communion that is communication . . . communion is no longer achieved through a symbolic medium, but through a technical one: this is what makes it communication' (1998a: 103). Baudrillard draws an important distinction here. Communion, meaning spiritual intercourse or contact, is replaced by technologically mediated social contact. Both communion and communication are derived from the Latin term *communis*, meaning common. Both communion and communication imply contact and exchange between beings via a form of mediation. Baudrillard is not bemoaning the loss of religious rituals of communion. Indeed, these have not *been* lost but endure in their traditional form as well as expanding into the technological sphere: the Internet offers many sites for virtual religious ritual. Further, Baudrillard's words suggest that some sense of communion is still present in modern electronic communications generally. There is a spiritual dimension in the 'form' of communication, a form of contact and commonality. There are, then, continuities within this shift from communion to communication. According to Baudrillard, mass communications *replace symbolic ritual with technological ritual*. Cultural practices of communion, in Baudrillard's Durkheimian reading, had marked the 'lived presence' of the social group or community. With the shift to communication symbolic practices are 'replaced' by signs. In order to do this, signs must be capable of fulfilling the role of symbolic exchange to some degree. And signs do, indeed, link people together – but as similarities and differences on a scale of value, as types of individual and as types of consumer.

There is a certain sense of communion in wearing the same brand or garment as your favourite celebrity, and there is no point in denying or scoffing at this. Nor is it new. For many years there has been a market for objects that were once owned by the famous. Yet symbolic practices, as Baudrillard theorises them, are distinct. In the practice of symbolic exchange communion annuls individuality, the group is expressed and affirmed in its communality. In this sense symbolic exchange is sacrificial. There is no scale or logic of value, at least not in the moment of communion. Symbols are fixed and unique, they are not commutable or equivalent as signs are. For example, in the Catholic communion the wafer and the wine are not signs of the flesh and blood of Christ, they are symbols. In the moment of communion they are said to *become* the flesh and blood, they do not signify it because the signified absorbs the signifier. With the communication of signs, by contrast, the signifier tends to absorb the signified. The replacement of symbolic practices of communion by semiotic practices of communication enables a shift from the symbolic act of consuming to the semiotic process of consumption: the very principle of the consumer capitalist society.

To exemplify his position regarding information, Baudrillard focuses on news reports where there is 'a discontinuum of signs and messages in which all orders are equivalent (1998a: 121). News reports on 'war, famine and death are interspersed with adverts for washing powder and razors' and, we might add, with the self-advertising of journalists, news organisations and TV companies. But this is not merely a chaotic, confused abundance of signs: 'it is the imposition upon us, by the systematic succession of messages, of the *equivalence* of history and the minor news item, of the event and the spectacle, of information and advertising at the level of the sign' (1998a: 122).

Not only events, but also the world itself, are 'segmented', cut up into 'discontinuous, successive, non-contradictory messages'. We do not consume a spectacle or an image as such, but the principle of the succession of all possible spectacles or images: 'there is no danger of anything emerging that is not one sign among others' (1998a: 122). Baudrillard engages with the theories of McLuhan and his infamous slogan 'The medium is the message', arguing that the really significant level at which media influence people is not that of the content of its messages. It is in 'the constraining pattern – linked to the very technical essence of those media – of the disarticulation of the real into successive and equivalent signs' (1998a: 122). Marxist attempts to theorise the effects of the media on audiences and consumers fail because such critiques focus on the ideological nature of content and the ownership of networks but pay little attention to the medium itself and to its possible affects on perception and social relations (1981: 166–72). In exploring the medium Baudrillard postulates a 'law of technological inertia', suggesting that the closer the medium gets to 'the real', through techniques such as documentary style film-making and live coverage, the greater the 'real absence from the world'. In other words, 'the world' as space of perspective – of seeing and knowing – is increasingly replaced by a sequence of images in which 'the primary function of each message is to refer to another message' (1998a: 122). In this way the medium, not the message, imposes a certain way of seeing the world on the audience. Rather than a space for reflection and critical distance we have information sliced and diced as a commodity-sign. This is no Luddite hatred of technology. Both McLuhan and Baudrillard note that the medium of the printed book, dating back to the fifteenth century, imposes a particular mechanics of perception, a form of constraint favouring solitary reflection and linearity. But the distinctive nature of the electronic mass media is, for Baudrillard, that they 'function to neutralise the lived, unique, eventual character of the world and substitute for it a multiple universe of media which are homogeneous' (1998a: 123). The electronic media are ideological in the sense that they declare through their form, and often also in content, '*the omnipotence of a system of reading over a world become a system of signs*'. The 'confused' and 'conflicted' world is transformed into an abstract, ordered one, a world of consumable signs where 'the signifier becomes its own signified . . . we see the abolition of the signified and the *tautology of the signifier* . . . the substitution of the code for the referential dimension defines mass media consumption' (1998a: 124–5). For Baudrillard the media are, in fact, 'anti-mediatory' (1981: 169). They prevent response, the reciprocal exchange of meaning, allowing only simulatory responses, responses drawn from a predefined range or code. Indeed, for Baudrillard 'the code is the only agency that speaks' (1981: 179). Today, 'interactive' TV is far more developed but the 'interactivity' on offer remains that of the medium or the code. We are confronted with a myriad of choices, channels, spectator angles and phone-in options, but all are generated from the medium: we merely complete the circuit. Human interaction is replaced by simulatory interactivity.

Baudrillard admits that his ideas concerning the recent transformation of society into one dominated by sign consumption apply only in limited circumstances; that is, in those parts of the world that consider themselves the most 'advanced'. Baudrillard acknowledges that 'traditional forms of praxis' have not disappeared, and indeed remain dominant such that the ideas he expresses only apply in very limited circumstances – those where a 'high technical level has been attained' (1996a: 29 n. 10). This is a very important clarification, overlooked by many of Baudrillard's critics despite being reiterated many times (1975: 121, 1993a: 115, 1993b: 5). As Baudrillard said much later in his career, 'theory must anticipate' (1998b: 24).

2

The 'Break' with Marxism

INTRODUCTION: BREAKING THE MIRROR OF PRODUCTION

> [I]f the system could function without feeding its workers, there would be no bread.
>
> (Baudrillard, 1981: 86)

> No fool this Marx.
>
> (Baudrillard, 2001b: 119 n. 1)

The notion of a 'break' with Marxism is misleading. From his earliest writings Baudrillard was clearly dissatisfied with both classical Marxism and the attempts at revision made by the Frankfurt School theorists and others. This is demonstrated in the important early essay 'Police and Play' (2001a: 61–9) and in other writings of the time published in the journal *Utopie*. Baudrillard never was a Marxist as such, yet he was deeply influenced by Marxism and retained a great admiration for Marx's theorisation of capitalism (1993b: 10). In what sense, then, can we speak of a 'break' with Marxism?

To investigate the relationship between Baudrillard and Marxism we must distinguish the writings of Marx himself from the vast body of theory spanning politics, economics and anthropology that can be labelled Marxist. Baudrillard's principal target in *Mirror of Production* (1975) is the latter, though he is also critical of the former.

In *Mirror*, Baudrillard develops many of what became his favourite tropes: the mirror, reflections, hauntings, illusion. He offers a sustained argument that Marxism is unable to challenge the system at anything approaching a fundamental level; indeed, that Marxist theory repeats, reiterates or fails to question some of the key assumptions of the capitalist system. Marxism *is the mirror of production*. Unlike Marx and the Frankfurt School theorists, notably Marcuse (1961: 4–5), Baudrillard does not claim that capitalism has produced a system of 'false' needs that have over-written and obscured genuine, concrete or objective needs. For Baudrillard *the principle of need itself is ideological*: 'true' and 'false' needs cannot ultimately be distinguished (1981: 63–97). This argument is explored below.

In *Mirror* Baudrillard begins to distinguish his theoretical position from that of critical theory generally, with which he had remained allied in *Critique* (see 1981: 29). Critical theory is rejected in *Mirror* because, according to Baudrillard, it questions only the *contents* of the mode of production and leaves 'intact' the *form* or *principle* of production (1975: 17). Further, production as principle insinuates itself into critiques of the capitalist mode of production such that would-be 'revolutionary' theories actually repeat and reinforce the system.[1]

Mirror and *Symbolic Exchange* involve the development and application of a new methodology in Baudrillard's work. Baudrillard develops what he terms an 'ethnological reduction' aiming 'to strip our culture, including its materialist critique, of the absolute privilege that it gives itself by the imposition of a universal code' (1975: 115). A code of signs, signs of truth, signs of reality – the entire representational apparatus of Western culture and rationality is attacked. *Mirror* is the last text in which Baudrillard seems willing to anticipate likely criticisms of his positions. The following is particularly important:

> The objection that our society is still largely dominated by the logic of commodities is irrelevant. When Marx set out to analyse capital, capitalist industrial production was still largely a minority phenomenon. When he designated political economy as the determining sphere, religion was still largely dominant. The theoretical decision is never made at the quantitative level, but at the level of structural critique.
>
> (Baudrillard, 1975: 121)

In other words, theory must not limit itself to description, to an empirical or 'realist' cataloguing, nor to taking a critical 'standpoint' in relation to an aspect of the system. In order to be analytical theory must depart from the existing state of affairs and the ideas it circulates.

What is clear is that the scope of Baudrillard's early work expands constantly, circling outwards from objects to the entire system of consumption, from the production of signs to the metaphysical system of production. At each stage Baudrillard seeks a mode of resistance to, or better defiance of, these systems, through a radical difference that cannot be assimilated. The difficulties involved in articulating a convincing mode of resistance show just how deep and pervasive the systems of power, control and regulation actually are.

LE MIROIR DE LA PRODUCTION/THE MIRROR OF PRODUCTION

The early 1970s was a time of major political upheaval and contestation in the Western democracies. In Paris the students' revolt and workers' strikes of May 1968 temporarily and locally suspended the capitalist system, but faded during the long summer months with students and workers split by government manoeuvres. The Conservative government in the UK was destroyed by strike action in 1974 and the USA suffered the Watergate scandal while the Vietnam war still raged, as did protests against it. At the same time there was a widespread escalation in 'terrorist' activities. Baudrillard's contentions in *Mirror* (1975), that Marxism was not capable of challenging the system, were untimely, awkward and provocative, and a number of Marxist-oriented critics have never forgiven Baudrillard for writing it.

Baudrillard's major contention in this work is that production is far more than a mode of creating goods for distribution and sale: production is, in Western culture, *a metaphysical system*. A 'metaphysics' is a system of thought that bases its arguments on an abstracted or 'meta' principle that cannot be shown to be valid and has to be taken on trust. The implication is that metaphysical principles are spurious and fanciful, and Baudrillard uses the term 'metaphysical' in the most derogatory sense to mean something like empty, abstract nonsense.[2] To produce goods to satisfy basic survival needs is very widely understood as the fundamental law of the human species. According to Baudrillard productionism, as metaphysical principle, functions as an abstract principle that codes all human practices, desires, aspirations and forms of exchange *as production*. Yet, following Durkheim (1961) and Bataille (1986), Baudrillard insists that very little human action can actually be understood in terms of production. Instead, profound meaning, joy and intensity are experienced in taking risks, in wastefulness and even in destruction. The metaphysics of production locks us within a system of the production of *value* – whether as goods, services or signs. Further, we are expected to produce and reproduce ourselves *as value*, we must maximize ourselves, exploit our potential, and this, for Baudrillard, is the most fundamental, insidious and developed form of social control.

According to Baudrillard, Marxism, though a powerful critical force in some respects, is confined within the metaphysics of productionism. Marxism departs sharply from liberal economic theory in that it emphasises the importance of the *social relations* of production, not merely the abstract forces or conditions of production (such as available technology, raw materials, markets for the sale of goods). Marx focuses on *the social relations* involved in any practice or process of production and asks awkward questions such as who benefits the most from such a system. Baudrillard still has a reputation as an anti-Marxist, forged largely by Marxist critics of his work, particularly Kellner (1989: 33–59) and Callinicos (1989: 144–54). However, there is no question that Baudrillard was inspired and deeply influenced by Marx even in the formulation of his notion of symbolic exchange and of sign-value, which, ultimately, Baudrillard deploys as a critique of Marx. Symbolic exchange and the logic of sign-value are developed to critique the integrating power of capitalism. It is therefore simplistic and misleading to suggest that these are anti-Marxist concepts and that by developing them Baudrillard entirely rejects Marxism (Kellner, 1989: 58; Callinicos, 1989: 147).

However, Baudrillard attacks Marxism explicitly on several related fronts. First, Baudrillard argues, Marx failed to see the interconnections between the system of political economy (of labour, the production of goods, the market) and the system of representation (language, the sign, meaning). For Baudrillard these two orders are parallel and 'inseparable' such that 'it becomes impossible to think outside the form production and the form representation' (1981: 43–63, 1975: 29). Other, more substantive criticisms flow from this principle. Because it does not question the abstract or metaphysical principle of production as a means of satisfying needs, Marxism tends to naturalise and universalise use-value. For the sake of clarity this point is explored in some detail.

In a section of *Critique* entitled 'The Myth of Primary Needs' (1981: 80–2) Baudrillard contests what he terms the 'bio-anthropological postulate' of primary needs. The notion of need is ideological in the sense that it is based on an insupportable abstraction: the separation of 'man as essence' from the social environment. One implication of this way of thinking is that the social system could be said to obscure the 'true essence of humanity', but Baudrillard denies that 'true', 'objective' survival needs can be identified, since 'it is always the production of the surplus that regulates the whole. The survival threshold is never determined from below, but from above' (1981: 81). That is, 'needs' and their satisfactions are always ideological, always implicated in power relations, never 'natural'. For Baudrillard needs are defined as:

> a function induced (in the individual) by the internal logic of the system: more precisely *not as a consummative force liberated* by the affluent society, but *as a productive force* required by the functioning of the system . . . there are only needs because the system needs them.
>
> (Baudrillard, 1981: 82–3, original emphasis)

Baudrillard attacks the very principle of needs, uses and wants. To speak of needs, uses or wants is already an abstraction because it covertly assumes a great deal. It assumes an already existing, taken-for-granted individual separated from other individuals and separated from the world. It assumes that this 'individual', itself an abstraction, will naturally abstract or break down the world into useful things (and less useful things) and make use of the useful things to survive and reproduce. This assumes a natural state of scarcity and of competition for these scarce resources. It assumes that all of these components – 'objects', 'individuals', 'scarcity', 'usefulness' and 'competition' – exist in nature or reality, independently of social or cultural meanings and representational practices. It suggests that these facts of reality or nature are the *cause* of cultural meanings and practices, which are merely a 'reflection' of them. Baudrillard's contention, and it is by no means an original one, is that these components are effects, not causes, of cultural practices. It follows that each of these contentions can be contested and, for Baudrillard, must be if the capitalist system is to be challenged. Crucially, the idea that the individual pre-exists society, culture or community is patently absurd – although it is widely held. Every 'individual' is born into a community with values, norms and a language, or rather the notion of the 'individual' is only constituted through relations with the community's values, norms and language. That an individual can be recognised, and function, as 'an individual' is a measure of the community's success in producing individuals. Moreover, what we refer to as an 'individual' is an idea generated by our cultural practices and meanings, which are capitalist, and which are built upon the 'barring' of symbolic exchange relations *between* people.

These points relate to Baudrillard's theories in two important ways. First, the notion of symbolic exchange invites us to think about social relations without the abstractions and separations we are accustomed to: symbolic exchange expresses a 'pact' that defies abstraction into separate poles, terms or individuals. Second, Baudrillard continues to explore the ways in which the individual – with his or her needs, wants and uses – are coded by the capitalist system. Capitalist exchange-value *represents* use-value as residing beneath or beyond it in a natural relationship of human beings to objects, but this is, for Baudrillard, a mirage on the horizon of exchange-value, 'a code effect' (1975: 25). The capitalist system of exchange-value claims to base exchange-values, or prices, on the solid reality of use-values. For example, a strong well made tin opener may cost twice as much as a flimsy poorly constructed one but it should last twice as long. But the relationship between use-value and exchange-value is not nearly this transparent. It obscures the fact that we live in a culture where people are unable to produce their own food and where they feel that they do not have time to prepare food. It obscures the appropriation of surplus-value or profit accrued by those who own the factories that produce tinned food. The Marxist critique enables us to theorise these relations, but it does not enable us to question the metaphysical principle of the individual with his or her needs and use-values because it accepts the reality of 'natural' needs and uses. Marxism allows capitalism this 'alibi' because it tries to locate and 'rediscover' a natural relation to use-value undistorted by capitalist exchange-value, but there is no 'natural' relation to use-value.[3]

Baudrillard focuses on the concept of labour, which is divided into two forms in Marx's *Contribution to a Critique of Political Economy* (originally published in 1857). The labour used to produce use-value is 'concrete, immediate and special' but the labour used in producing exchange-value is 'abstract, universal and homogeneous' (1975: 26). Yet this distinction has the effect of 'autonomizing and generalising labour as the essence of human practice'. This amounts to 'an incredible simplification of social exchange' (1975: 29), which, according to Baudrillard, actually 'intensifies' the abstractions and separations made by liberal theorists of political economy:

> Marxism assists the cunning of Capital. It convinces men that they are alienated by the sale of their labour power, thus censoring the much more radical hypothesis that they might be alienated as labour power, as the 'inalienable' power of creating value by their labour.
>
> (Baudrillard, 1975: 31)

At this stage in his argument Baudrillard refers less to the writings of Karl Marx and increasingly to 'Marxist' theorists of the twentieth century, particularly Louis Althusser and the Marxist anthropologist Maurice Godelier. Baudrillard's argument is that humanity, in all the richness of its relations of exchange, is circumscribed, contained and domesticated by Marxists because they 'generalise the economic mode of rationality over the entire expanse of human history' (1975: 33). The important distinction between symbolic and economic understanding of wealth is expanded in a chapter titled 'Primitive Societies' (1975: 91–6), where Baudrillard develops the notion of 'anti-production', which he perceives as operating within such societies. Baudrillard begins with the contention that the institutions of 'primitive' (meaning non-industrial) societies do not correspond to anything that can be recognised by the metaphysics of production. Such societies are not merely 'other' or different but radically other, inassimilable. According to Baudrillard they have no distinction between infrastructure and super-structure; moreover, they produce no surplus even though they are technically capable of doing so. The notion of symbolic exchange is immediate proffered as the principle that embodies this radical difference. Symbolic exchange 'excludes any surplus: anything that cannot be exchanged or symbolically shared would break the reciprocity and institute power . . . this exchange excludes all "production" . . . production appears nowhere as an ends or a means: the meaning occurs elsewhere' (1975: 79–80).

To clarify, it is not that culture or religion obstructs the potential for production or limits it to an underdeveloped state: for Baudrillard these are Eurocentric prejudices. Instead, social exchange is based on kinship ties of reciprocity, which are animated and maintained *through the ritual destruction of wealth*. The influence of Georges Bataille (1897–1962) on Baudrillard's theory is apparent at key points in the argument and is mobilised in the attack on Marxist anthropology. Following Bataille (1986), Baudrillard distinguishes between social wealth, which is material, and 'symbolic wealth', which is 'sacrificial'. The central distinction between productive economy and 'sacrificial economy' resides in radically different, 'irreconcilable' understandings of what constitutes wealth.[4]

Within 'sacrificial economy' the production of wealth is strictly limited and its destruction is an intensely meaning, expressive social practice. The rites and festivals of gift exchange cannot be considered forms of production, Baudrillard insists. To produce is not a spontaneous act of survival; production and even 'survival' are only meaningful in particular cultural contexts. In Western modernity it is thought desirable to maximize production, in other cultures it is not. In 'pre' or 'non'-industrial societies (there is no felicitous term) production is limited, and surpluses are not produced despite the 'potential' to do so. Surpluses or excesses are considered dangerous or disruptive because they carry the threat of a transformation of power relations, and an unleashing of violence and upheaval. Instead surplus is devoted to fest-ivity or sacrifice, where power and violence are expressed in symbolic form and limited by strict social rules. As we have seen, the relation-ship between production and wealth is not straightforward. Does production *produce* wealth? In this equation production is conceived as a force and wealth is defined in terms of an abstract equivalent – money. However, among what Baudrillard terms 'primitive' societies (a term he uses to offend academic anthropologists) the gift establishes reciprocity: the obligatory act of exchanging or circulating wealth such that one's possession of it is 'sacrificed', either to gods or spirits or to other human beings. The cultural meanings expressed and experienced through sacrifice are 'impossible', not reducible to an abstract equival-ent and therefore in a sense 'priceless' or 'absolute'.

Baudrillard's contention, apparent from the very structure of *Mirror*, is that Marxist theory is unable to understand 'primitive', feudal or capitalist society. With regard to feudal social systems, Baudrillard argues that the master–slave relation is a 'symbolic relation' (1975: 93) in that neither position is abstracted or autonomous. What is exchanged between them is not a commodity or 'value' as such but a status and role, and there remains, Baudrillard insists, 'an element of reciprocity' (1975: 95). The relationship is one of domination but not alienation or exploitation because the slave is not objectified in the process. The slave is obligated to fulfil a role but so too is the master. Of course, Baudrillard does not maintain that the relation is fair, equal or just. Symbolic relations are never equal, since 'equality' is a property of an individualised or autonomous unit in an abstract or integrated system. Baudrillard readily admits that slave trading, which he defines as slavery within a market economy, offers no such element of reciprocity. Ultimately, Baudrillard redefines the concept of alienation to refer not to the selling of labour but as the individual's self-conception as, fundamentally, a source of labour: 'The free worker finds his identity in the mirror of his labour power' (1975: 94). That is, we learn to *dispose* of ourselves as economic value, we become our own slave-traders. The feudal master, Baudrillard contends, had consider-ably less power over the slave than *we assert over ourselves*. Once separated from the network of symbolic ties we become our own mas-ter and our own slave through the 'interiorisation' of the master–slave dialectic, which becomes our internal psychological dynamic.

Within the symbolic relation, then, the distinctions between producer and product, producer and consumer, producer and labour power, user and needs and finally product and utility are not distinct. This is why symbolic relations cannot be analysed within a Marxist framework; the symbolic relation is 'irreducibly non-economic', since 'The symbolic sets up a relation of exchange in which the respective positions cannot be autonomized' (1975: 102–3).

BAUDRILLARD'S DEVELOPMENT OF A NEW METHODOLOGY: SYMBOLIC EXCHANGE AND THEORY

There are several important and interrelated themes to explore here. As I have indicated, Baudrillard was from his earliest writings unsatisfied with classical Marxist concepts, yet even in *Mirror* there is a strong sense in which Baudrillard attempts to 'complete' the critical tradition inaugurated by Marx: 'following the same revolutionary movement as Marx did, we must move to a radically different level that . . . permits the definitive resolution of political economy. This level is that of symbolic exchange and its theory' (Baudrillard, 1975: 51). Baudrillard critiques use-value as Marx critiqued exchange-value, in an attempt to delineate a position from which such value is revealed as contingent and particular, not natural and universal. Baudrillard's early formulations of the symbolic 'dimension' owed a great deal to Marx's concept of unalienated use-value, in that symbolic relations were deemed to be 'absolute' or 'unique' values. Yet in *Mirror* and *Symbolic Exchange* Baudrillard seeks to critique value itself, opening up a significant distance between his notion of symbolic exchange and anything conceived by Marx under the rubric of a communist utopia.

Symbolic exchange, for Baudrillard, expresses a 'rupture' with modern economic rationality and the values of utility, investment, accumulation and profit. *Mirror* pushes the rejection of Western rationality much further as Baudrillard seeks to locate the foundations of the code, to probe just how deep and pervasive the code actually is. The code is now defined not simply as the functional principle of consumption, it is also the governing principle of the modern system of representation and meaning: what Baudrillard terms 'the political economy of the sign'. In *Mirror* symbolic exchange appears as 'anti-value' and breaks or ruptures the code of value from within, albeit for a moment only. Symbolic exchange as the rupturing of codes is a theme developed a several occasions (1981: 159–63, 1993a: 195–242, 1993b: 81–8; 2003b) and these are discussed in the following chapter.

Mirror includes an important critique of the notion of universality that is much more than an attack on Marxism and will enable us to understand the shifts in Baudrillard's position during this very fertile period. Baudrillard's critique of the sign is a critique of representation and of epistemology: 'As soon as they [concepts] are constituted as universal they cease to be analytical . . . they become scientific [and] set themselves up as expressing an "objective reality". They become signs, signifiers of a "real" signified' (1975: 48). What Baudrillard suggests is that as soon as concepts (representations) take themselves for 'reality' (which they are not – they are representations) they lose their analytic power and lapse into simulation. Baudrillard is not claiming that there is a pristine reality 'out there' that cannot be captured by such crude things as concepts. Instead those who follow the 'surreptitious religion' of 'rational discursiveness' take their concepts for reality because their concepts actually construct the object(s) of their analysis as 'real'. According to Baudrillard all variants of critical theory, including Marxism, fall into this pattern, which is ultimately one of the repro-duction of their own terms of analysis and of the system of 'rational discursiveness' itself.

For example, Marxist thinkers, such as Godelier, claim to have described the mode of production and its dialectical workings in 'prim-itive' societies, just as psychoanalysis claims to discover the operations of the unconscious. For Baudrillard such societies and their people simply do not possess these things. In fact Marxism and psychoana-lysis have simulated the presence of these 'realities' through their own concepts; that is, they have exported their concepts and taken the effects of the application of these concepts for realities. Signs then construct the very idea of 'reality'. Baudrillard does not contend that 'primitive' societies possess a different 'reality' (such as a 'reality' simulated by Baudrillard's concepts!). His argument is that 'reality' as concept has no meaning in the context of pre-industrial societies because 'reality' is not the anchoring point or foundation of the system of rep-resentation in such societies.[5]

Let us examine these claims in some detail. In *Mirror* and in *Symbolic Exchange* Baudrillard does substantiate these claims in theor-etical discussions that are not repeated in later works. *Mirror* provides important arguments on the emergence of 'reality'. First, Baudrillard argues, during the eighteenth century 'Nature' comes to be under-stood in a new way: 'Under the stamp of Science, Technology and Production, Nature becomes the great Signified, the great Referent. It is ideally charged with "reality", it becomes *the* Reality' (1975: 54).

Nature as object constituted by science and technology is understood as a 'potentiality of forces' submitted to 'operational finality': the 'forces' of nature are put to use in order to achieve a particular goal or end, such as the fuelling of industry. The previous understanding of nature as totality, great law or principle did not lend itself to such operational ends. A scientific understanding of Nature that was suited to industrial society was required and was generated by scientists because they theorised from within the code or matrix of industrial society; that is, their thinking was dominated, at an unconscious level, by the metaphysical principle of production. Science, then, does not deal in 'objective', timeless truths but, to paraphrase Nietzsche, is always 'timely', always restricted by the socio-historic context and ideas about what constitutes the truth (epistemology) current at the time. This line of argument is directed at Marxism itself, with Baudrillard's mock incredulity that 'the *reality* of production enters the scene at precisely the moment when someone is discovered who invents the theory of it' (1975: 113). However it is also directed at other targets – particularly Western notions of Nature, Civilisation, Science and Progress.

For Baudrillard this new understanding of Nature realises a definitive split between the subject or person and the 'Nature-object'.[6] In this splitting Nature and Man become separate or autonomous, both are 'liberated' yet 'dominated' in the same movement. As separated elements both Nature and Man can be coded; that is, they are understood as subject to 'abstract, linear, irreversible' (1975: 56) processes of development or 'progress'. Once split, both are then split again as the unquestioned criteria of rationality erects a 'bar' or barrier separating rational and irrational, good and bad into binary oppositions. Good Nature (food, abundance and beauty) is separated from bad Nature (disease, catastrophe), just as good Humans (white, hard-working) are separated from bad Humans (black, lazy). Marxism, according to Baudrillard, sought to overcome 'bad' Nature by the increased effort to conquer and master Nature as the fundamental signified.[7]

Baudrillard also attacks science and history as they are constituted by Western reason. His theoretical manoeuvres here lead us to the first formulations of the concepts of simulation and the notion of the *revenge of the object*:

> It is only in the mirror of production and history, under the double principle of indefinite accumulation (production) and dialectical continuity (history), only by the arbitrariness of the code, that our Western culture can reflect itself in the universal as the privileged moment of truth (science) or of revolution (historical materialism). Without this simulation . . . our era loses all privileges. It would not be any closer to any term of knowledge or any social truth than any other.
>
> (1975: 114–15)

The recurrent and important theme of the revenge of the object is first developed in relation to Marxism. Because Marxist epistemology cannot question the primacy of needs, use-value and production, Marxist theory is ultimately, for Baudrillard, a 'simulation model' – a coding system that reduces all human activities to the model of production. Marxist theory tries to produce a general account of the course of human civilisation. It attempts this by sketching the respective modes of the production of goods that are said to characterise various historical epochs. However, in attempting to understand pre-industrial societies Marxist theory encounters, according to Baudrillard, cultures without the pretence of universality, without history, without relations of production, without a distinction between infrastructure and superstructure. In the attempt to analyse such cultures, by projecting its categories on to the Other, Marxism fails and *is actually analysed by its object*. This is the revenge of the object: Marxism's chosen object of analysis tells us far more about the state of Marxist theory than Marxist theory can tell us about 'its' object – 'primitive' society. The Marxist critique of political economy was, for Baudrillard, insufficiently radical because it was unable to perceive the operation of symbolic forces *within* the system of capitalist economy.

Baudrillard pursues the hypothesis that there has been an important shift from *competitive* capitalism to *monopoly* capitalism. While Marxism had considerable critical purchase on the workings of competitive capitalism it has little grip on the new phase. The dialectic, which had functioned in the phase of competitive capitalism, is undermined by the operation of the code as a system of 'total abstraction' where

the signified and the referent are now abolished to the sole profit of the play of signifiers . . . of a generalised formalization in which the code no longer refers back to any subjective or objective 'reality', but to its own logic. The signifier becomes its own referent and the use-value of the sign disappears to the benefit of it commutation and exchange value alone. The sign no longer designates anything at all . . . all reality becomes the place of a semiurgical manipulation, of a structural simulation.

(1975: 128)

According to Baudrillard there is no more dialectic of meaning, either in representation, the dialectic between sign and reference, or in economics, between supply and demand. The code absorbs these through 'predictive anticipation' and 'planned socialisation', which extends far beyond the production and consumption of goods and incorporates 'needs, knowledge, culture, information, sexuality' as terms of the code (1975: 126). All that once had an 'explosive force' (ibid.) is defused, deterred or contained; there may still be signs of the dialectic, but they are precisely that: *only signs*. Signs of revolt and 'liberation' abound: images of Che Guevara on T-shirts, spiky 'punk' hair on VO5 adverts, gay couples in soaps. But these are signs generated by the capitalist system and any 'revolution' they generate is at the level of the sign and of fashion. Content (of T-shirts and hair products for the young, of soap opera characters) changes constantly, it is always being *revolutionised*. There are, of course, healthy profits in niche and 'diversity' marketing, yet more important than profit margins, according to Baudrillard, is the level of form, of the sign as form and as code. The production and consumption of signs is the form through which we understand ourselves. The code sets all the terms in advance, of conformity and resistance, playfulness and seriousness. It promotes signs of revolt and signs of conformity because it constructs 'conformists' and 'rebels' as types of consumer, as alternative poles that structure patterns of consumption. The implication is clear: even 'pushed to the limit' Marxism is unable to critique the sign-form, the general principle of the code. The passage from the commodity-form to the sign-form or the political economy of the sign is one of 'the passage of all values to sign-exchange value, under the hegemony of the code. That is, of a structure of control and of power much more subtle and more totalitarian than that of exploitation' (1975: 121). The code is 'illegible', it cannot be read, it is instead the form that allows 'reading' to take place. 'Production' as metaphysical principle is the principle of the code: desire, sexuality, even knowledge is understood in terms of production. The code destroys social relations as *live* symbolic exchanges. It is far more destructive than ownership of the means of production, and, for Baudrillard, this represents a revolution as profound as the industrial revolution was two centuries earlier.

THE 'END' OF PRODUCTION: BAUDRILLARD'S THEORY OF CAPITALISM

> [T]he fundamental law of this society is not the law of exploitation, but the code of normality.
>
> (Baudrillard, 1993a: 29)

> The dialectic is definitively over.
>
> (Baudrillard, 2001b: 95)

According to Baudrillard we have now reached the 'end' of production. Production still takes place of course, but it leads an increasingly shadowy, obscure existence: banished to the third world, operating within closed and guarded compounds, non-unionised, off the radar (see, for example, Klein, 2001: 195–229). But Baudrillard's 'end' of production is not only geo-political but also epistemological. The sign-code or 'struc-tural law of value' signals the end of production:

> the structural configuration of value simply and simultaneously puts an end to the regimes of production, political economy, representation and signs. With the code, all this collapses into simu-lation. Strictly speaking, neither the 'classical' economy not the political economy of the sign ceases to exist: they lead a secondary existence becoming a sort of phantom principle of dissuasion.
>
> (Baudrillard, 1993a: 8)

So, for Baudrillard the logic of economic production, analysed by Marx, and the logic of representation, analysed by Saussure, follow the same form: they establish principles of equivalence. Equivalence estab-lishes regulated, ordered exchange, linear development and accumulation. In the economic sphere money is the abstract principle of equivalence: everything has a price and that price is directly comparable with the price for anything else. An academic, for example, is paid twice as much as a nurse, a doctor or lawyer three times as much as an aca-demic and so on. Similarly, in the sphere of language or representation a relation of equivalence between signifier and signified, and between sign and referent, enables 'meaning' to be produced, exchanged and accumulated. The signifier 'tree' invokes the same 'thing' whether it is used by a child, a horticulturist or a poet. This Baudrillard dubs the 'classical' representation or 'the second order of Simulacra' (1993a: 53–7). The spheres of economy and of representation are linked by the same underlying form, but at the level of content they are distinct, they can be distinguished, and Baudrillard terms this a relation of 'determinate' equivalence. The 'end' of production occurs with the shift from determinate to increasingly 'indeterminate' equivalence. Signs circulate in the code and are able to do so because they tend to become detached from determinate signifieds. As the relationship between signifiers and signifieds is weakened the 'referential dimension' of meaning is under-mined because it was the signified that supposedly 'captured' meaning out there in the world (the referent). Of course we do not live in a world of free-floating signs or signifiers that mean nothing, or alternatively anything (Callinicos, 1989: 145). This is a ludicrous misreading of Baudrillard given his emphasis on the constraining power of the code and his deconstruction of individual 'needs' and 'wants'. Signifiers *simulate* the effect of meaning and reference: a 'reality-effect' is crucial to the operation of the capitalist system. It might be objected that signifiers have only ever simulated the effect of meaning and reference. In a sense, this is not far off the mark, since Baudrillard insists that the world is illusion, is simulacrum (1996c: 16–19, 2005d: 39–46). But there are, he asserts, meaningful, qualitative differences within simulacra, different and distinguishable orders of simulacra that have direct, meaningful and theorisable effects on lived relations and social experience. Baudrillard's approach is, then, more sociological than is acknowledged, at least given a broad definition of the sociological![8]

With the phase of simulation, equivalence is established through the sign: it is internal to the play of signifiers. Signifiers circulate without the possibility of dialectical negation (or critique) because the signifiers refer to each other rather than to a 'real', or referent. A 'hyperreality' of simulations is far less susceptible to critique based, as it is, on contrasting the true and the false, the real and the unreal:

> signs are exchanged against each other rather than against the real
> . . . they do so *on condition* that they are no longer exchanged against
> the real. . . . Neither Saussure nor Marx had any presentiment of
> this: they were still in the golden age of the dialectic of the sign
> and the real . . . the 'classical' period of capital and value. Their
> dialectic is in shreds.
>
> (Baudrillard, 1993a: 7)

The tensions, contradiction, oppositions and sheer unpredictability of the dialectic tend to be neutralised by simulation, although Baudrillard is clear that the dialectic does not disappear, nor of course is it transcended or obliterated. It endures, as do aspects of the first order of simulacra, but in tattered, fragmented form in the firmament of ideas that have had their moment but do not die (see also Baudrillard, 1994b: 21–7). This, in itself, is a paradoxical, other-than-dialectical process because, according to dialectics, one state is supposed to be definitely raised, resolved and transcended by another state. The dialectic rolls on, but it no longer captures our imagination.

In a characteristic reversal strategy, directed at Marxist theory, Baudrillard argues that capitalism, rather than being 'transcended' by socialism, has actually leapt over the dialectic as it 'substitutes the structural form of value, and currently controls every aspect of the system's strategy' (1993a: 7). Given this metamorphosis, Baudrillard asks whether we are we still living within capitalism. 'Hyper-capitalism' may be a more accurate term, he suggests, but what is not in doubt is that 'the structural law of value is the purest, most illegible form of social domination . . . it no longer has any references within a dominant class or a relation of forces' (1993a: 10–11).

These are bold claims, yet Baudrillard, at this stage in his thought, does offer considerable substantiation in a discussion of the effects of the sign on labour, on wages and on strikes. Instead of labour we have *signs* of labour. In other words, labour as living historical agency, as force with the power to transform social relations, becomes a 'dead' abstraction in the economic calculations of capitalism. This process was well under way in Marx's time and Marx produced the concepts of abstract labour and commodity fetishism to describe the way in which the living force of labour is hidden behind finished commodities. But, for Baudrillard, the living agency of labour is not just hidden or reified into commodities, it is also rendered symbolically dead – it is less and less a living principle of exchange. In an age of structural, permanent high unemployment, labour cannot be exchanged for employment, for a salary or for a comfortable life:

> Labour power is instituted on death. A man must die to become labour power . . . the economic violence capital inflicted on him in the equivalence of the wage and labour power is nothing next to the symbolic violence inflicted on him by his definition as a productive force.
>
> (1993a: 39)

Labour, then, is a slow death; it is neutralisation by slow death, by 'total conscription'. Labour no longer possesses a determinate relationship to production, having no meaningful equivalence in wages. Further, production no longer exists in a determinate relationship to profit or surplus value. There is in political economy, Baudrillard contends, a general loss of representational equivalence: 'the monetary sign is severed from every social production and enters a phase of speculation' (1993a: 21). In this new reign of indeterminacy there is 'nothing with which to fight capital in *determinate* form' (1993a: 19; see also 1993b: 26–35). Capital flows in global, deregulated money markets without reference to labour, work, production – without equivalence in terms of a 'gold standard'. Similarly, Baudrillard contends, strikes once functioned within a binary system of equivalence held in dialectical tension, that of labour and capital, unions and management. But this notion of the strike is now 'dead' because striking cannot affect capitalism as 'the reproduction of the *form of social relations*' (1993a: 24). Capitalism can endure the lowering of profit margins, strike disruption and even the collapse of share values. These 'contents' are no longer fundamental to its operation. Capital need only impose itself as *form* in order to reproduce itself endlessly and it achieves this by investing all individuals with needs, wants and desires – the apparatus of the active consumer. Any 'gains' won by unions, such as pay increases or improvements in working conditions, are immediately realised as benefits to the functioning of the system;

for example, as wages poured into consumer spending or in proliferating signs of an attractive progressive workplace.

Baudrillard allows that new fractures and instabilities emerge. He gives the example of non-unionised immigrant workers destabilising the game of signs carried out by managers and unions. However, such instabilities are quickly neutralised by strategies of incorporation and assimilation. Increasingly management is able to appeal directly to workers without the intermediary of unions; such strategies, Baudrillard argues, were central to the events of May 1968 when unions backed down, compromising with management to maintain their role as representatives of labour. Nevertheless, Baudrillard never suggests that the integrated, coded system is complete or invulnerable. Quite the reverse! The system's construction of the person as individual, productive, rational unit never really convinces anyone and is 'beginning to crack dangerously'. Further, the system is constantly under threat from symbolic challenges, as we shall see in the next chapter.

Finally, wages, Baudrillard argues, do not measure the amount we produce in our jobs, as both liberal and Marxist theories proclaim; instead, they are now 'a sacrament, like a baptism (or the Extreme Unction)' (1993a: 19). They mark us as full and genuine citizens of the consumer capitalist system. Workers today are less producers of measurable, determinate value than consumers, and their wage is access to the world of consumerism. Moreover, achieving wage status makes one a 'purchaser of goods in the same way that capital is the purchaser of labour' (1993a: 19). We are, according to Baudrillard, invested, colonised, occupied by capital, and apply a 'capitalist mentality' to all affairs. Wages do not guarantee any 'thing' in particular – that you are able to support yourself, afford somewhere to live, afford to have children – they simply insert us within the system of consumption. Consumption – the understanding of oneself as consumer and of the system around us as consumerist – becomes 'obligatory' and so *is a symbolic relation*.

In *Symbolic Exchange* Baudrillard expands this argument, and in doing so moves further from Marx than he had been in *Mirror*: the supposed 'break' with Marxism. Baudrillard argues that the system of production has always depended, fundamentally, on symbolic relations. In a highly original theorisation of capitalism, Baudrillard argues that the system depends on political economy as 'internal critique', in order to maintain the fiction of its reality. Capitalism, as an integrated system, has so outmoded Marxism that the latter plays the role of a 'dialectical stimulus' to capitalism – providing the illusion of depth and difference. Political economy, then, is a 'simulation model' (1993a:

31–9) providing capitalism with an 'alibi' or a 'screen', and is kept alive or meaningful through the efforts of Marxist critics. The power and dominance of the capitalist system is not dependent on economics, it derives more fundamentally, Baudrillard insists, from the symbolic. Capitalism exerts a 'symbolic domination' over 'life and death, established by the code' (1993a: 31) and is not susceptible or vulnerable to Marxist critique. Any vulnerability of the system exists only at the symbolic level. The economic system, the systems of production, reproduction and consumption mask the symbolic level and thereby occlude 'the possibility of its symbolic destruction' (1993a: 31). According to Baudrillard, capitalism 'never confused itself with production, as Marx did':

> capital is content to extend its laws in a single movement, inexorably occupying all the interstices of life. If it has set men to work it has also impelled them to culture, needs, languages and functional idioms, information and communication; it directs them to rights, to liberty, and sexuality, it forces the instinct of preservation and the death instinct upon them; it has set them up everywhere in accordance with myths that are simultaneously opposed and indifferent. This is its only law: indifference.
>
> (1993a: 34)

For Baudrillard, the system is so 'indifferent' it is scarcely meaningful to call it capitalist. Asked in 1997 what capitalism had become, Baudrillard replied, 'I really don't know . . . a sort of dilution of the universal . . . purely operational . . . an automatic transcription of the world into the global' (1998b: 11). How might we oppose such a diffuse, indifferent yet 'automatic' system? The only possibility is to re-engage the symbolic level. The system operates through symbolic violence. The only genuinely defiant strategy, Baudrillard asserts, is the symbolic reversal or 'counter-gift' (*contre-don*). According to Baudrillard the events of May 1968 'shook the system down to the depths of its symbolic organisation'. The system responded to the symbolic challenge, the refusal of work and education, with another symbolic challenge by giving 'official status to oppositional discourse' (1993a: 34). The power of the system is based on the monopoly of gift giving, 'the exclusivity of the gift without counter-gift' (1993a: 36). The system gives the gifts of self and identity through advertising and consumption; it gives the gift of work and wage through the economy; it gives the gift of knowledge through the education system and the gift of information and interactivity through media and communication (1981: 164–84). These gifts are unilateral, they forbid response, they must and can only be accepted: they are, for Baudrillard, 'poisonous' gifts. The power of the system is completely dependent on 'the impossibility of responding or retorting' (1993a: 37).

The system might be shattered, or at least momentarily suspended, by a counter-gift of the rejection of the gift and a reversal of power relations through a symbolic challenge that forces the system to respond, to raise the stakes further. We might reject, or refuse to accept, the 'gifts' of self, career, status and information. However, the ultimate 'counter-gift' is, for Baudrillard, suicide – the rejection of the gift of life itself. Suicide as symbolic defiance is explored in Chapter 7, but first we must examine the relation of symbolic exchange to life and death in order to understand why suicide might be such a devastating weapon.

3

Symbolic Exchange and Death

> The symbolic is neither a concept, an agency, a category, nor a 'structure', but an act of exchange and *a social relation*.
>
> (Baudrillard, 1993a: 133)

> Everything which is symbolically exchanged constitutes a mortal danger for the dominant order.
>
> (Baudrillard, 1993a: 188 n. 7)

INTRODUCTION

Symbolic Exchange and Death (1993a) is widely considered to be Baudrillard's most important work. It presents a greatly expanded exposition of his notion of symbolic exchange, the scope of which becomes dazzling. It is a difficult yet very rich work but, as Baudrillard himself notes (in Gane, 1993), its arguments never received much serious critical attention. The failure to appraise this work critically has, particularly in the English-speaking world (translation was tardy and controversial), generated a great deal of unnecessary misunderstanding of some central themes in Baudrillard's work. These include the relationship of symbolic exchange to social power and economic production, its relationship to death, its role as act of subversion and, above all, its continuing impact upon everyday life *here and now*.

It is a mistake to interpret symbolic exchange as Baudrillard's attempt to describe the practices of 'other' or non-Western cultures. Kellner (1989: 42–5) reads it in this way, as more recently do Browning and Kilmister (2006: 105–29); but as Grace (2000: 26–9) argues, Baudrillard's purpose is deconstructive rather than descriptive. There is an element of description but it is minimal, as Baudrillard does not claim to discover an ideal society of unfettered symbolic exchanges in 'non-Western' cultures. Symbolic exchange is presented as a *form* or principle, rather than as the specific 'content' of cultural practices. At the level of form symbolic exchange is crucial to both Western and 'non-Western' societies, as it is to ancient and feudal social organisation. Symbolic exchange is, Baudrillard argues, an 'indestructible' yet 'cruel' principle, and in later works he describes it as 'unbearable': there is little in the way of an idealisation of the symbolic order or 'non-Western' in these constructions. By invoking anthropological notions such as the kula and the potlatch Baudrillard seeks to displace the 'priority' the West awards itself through self-generated comparisons with the 'under-developed' world. Kula and potlatch are deployed as deconstructive tools to explore the consumer system and to speculate on ways of defying the capitalist order.

Symbolic exchange emerges as a principle that attacks, undermines, annuls or suspends binary oppositions – the very structures of Western rationality, political order, law, logic and meaning. Symbolic exchange, for Baudrillard, is manifest in acts, gestures, rituals and behaviours that *demand a response* from the economic/semiotic system. These are grave threats to the system because the system thrives when it is able to operate as if it is complete, total and closed. The challenge of symbolic exchange reveals that the system is incomplete, partial and open – that it is vulnerable. Further, symbolic exchange appears, in this work, as immanent within the semiotic orders, not 'outside' them. It refers to a barred absence 'haunting' the orders of the sign (1993a: 1). The sign is the material of symbolic exchange, just as it is the material of the semiotic orders. Symbolic and semiotic are not, of course, binary oppositions: they are locked together in a twisting spiral of ambivalence, both sides of the bar.

Symbolic Exchange and Death includes an important definition and clarification of 'the real' or 'reality' as the product of binary oppositions. If this definition is overlooked, as it often is, the emerging notions of simulacra and simulation become very difficult to comprehend. Further, Baudrillard's later works, which confront what he terms the fourth order of simulacra, continue to develop the notion of symbolic exchange first elaborated in this work and, again, these works are often misunderstood because of lack of familiarity with this text.

THE POTLATCH: READING ANTHROPOLOGY AGAINST ANTHROPOLOGY

> [P]ower belongs to the one who can give and *cannot be re-paid.*
> (Baudrillard, 1981: 170)

The potlatch ceremony as discussed by Marcel Mauss plays an important, even pivotal, role in Baudrillard's formulation of the notion of symbolic exchange. The issue of how convincing Baudrillard's reading of anthropology in general, and Mauss in particular, is, is an important one and will be explored in some detail here.

As is widely recognised, Baudrillard's understanding of the potlatch relies heavily upon Mauss's influential study *The Gift: The Form and Reason for Exchange in Archaic Societies*, first published in *Année Sociologique* in 1924/5. However, other, less well known works by Mauss and by other anthropologists such as Bronislaw Malinowski, Maurice Leenhardt, Robert Jaulin and Marshall Sahlins were also important influences on Baudrillard at this time. Baudrillard's relationship to anthropology as an academic discipline is complex because sometimes he will refer to accounts, such as those produced by the above, as 'facts' or truths (1983: 81), while at other times he will denounce or belittle the discipline as a whole for dealing in simulation (1994a: 7–11). This has led to a curious situation where those critics who are receptive to Baudrillard's ideas politely ignore what he has to say about social anthropology (Gane, 2000; Hegarty, 2004), whereas those who seek to discredit Baudrillard's ideas argue that his approach to 'other' cultures is inadequate, offensive or contradictory (Kellner, 1989: 181–5; Lane, 2000). Baudrillard's position seems to be that anthropology as a discipline is now defunct, having passed into simulation (1994a: 7–11), but that the insights of certain of its practitioners remain important.

Baudrillard's position on 'non-Western' societies is relatively consistent though certainly contentious, and is crucial to an understanding of the trajectory of his thought. Baudrillard's basic assumptions regarding 'non-Western' societies seem to be as follows. First, forms of social organisation radically different from Western modernity do exist. Second, some of the practices, particularly ritual practices, of such cultures cannot be understood through the categories and concepts of Western rationalism. Third, the practices of 'other' cultures are not incoherent or unknowable and some understanding of them can be reached through the critical or deconstructive reading of accounts produced by anthropologists.[1]

To play anthropological accounts 'against themselves' is vital, for Baudrillard, because anthropology as an academic discipline is constituted by Enlightenment thought (as, of course, is sociology). This means not that Enlightenment thought is invalid or false, but that it encounters particular difficulties in understanding or accepting the operation of symbolic forms that Baudrillard takes to be central to the organisation of many non-Western societies, and always implicit in Western societies. Baudrillard, like Mauss before him, emphasises continuities and resemblances between 'self' and 'other', modernity and 'pre-modernity', between West and 'non-West'; indeed, the gift is a vital form of cultural expression in Western modernity, as it is in 'non-Western' cultures.

Baudrillard, clearly, is not a cultural relativist, let alone an 'absolute relativist', as his Marxist critics Kellner (1989), Callinicos (1989) and Norris (1992) suggest. Baudrillard does use the term 'primitive', even 'savage', to describe non-Western cultures and Lane (2000) is right to question just how 'deconstructive' Baudrillard's radical anthropology actually is.[2] But the answers are in Baudrillard's work if we look for them. The terms 'savage' and 'primitive' are used by Baudrillard to achieve a number of objectives. First, they draw attention to the disreputable past of anthropology, to its roots in colonialism and economic exploitation. Second, he offends liberal and humanist sensibilities; for Baudrillard such people feel guilty about their own positions of power and wealth and seek to assuage this by insisting on politically correct or 'sensitive' terminology, while jealously guarding the power they have (2001b). Finally, by using such terms Baudrillard signals that the practices of non-Western cultures are not merely 'different' from the West in the pluralist sense of similar objectives or ends (survival, reproduction, expression) being satisfied in a different way. This is the 'culturalist platitude' he despises. Instead they are, he insists, radically and fundamentally different: 'the term "savage" conveys this foreignness better than all the later euphemisms' (1993b: 148). This is an otherness or foreignness more radical than can be understood within the 'mirror' of the self/other binary opposition, an otherness that is not merely the fantasy of the Western self but the annulment of its binary codes, thus challenging Western models of social organisation and knowledge.

GIFT AND COUNTER-GIFT

[B]y giving one is giving oneself, and if one gives oneself it is because one 'owes' oneself – one's person and one's goods – to others.
(Mauss, 1990: 46)

The term 'potlatch' is generic and imprecise: indeed, the use of the term has been the subject of an entire study (see Bracken, 1997). Marcel Mauss uses the term very broadly in his study *The Gift*, and Baudrillard uses it still more generally. I will outline what this important term implies, how it is developed by Mauss and the impact it has on Baudrillard's theory of symbolic exchange.

The term 'potlatch' is derived from the Nootka language of the indigenous or first nation people of North-West America. The Nootka 'patlatsch' means 'a gift'. The colloquial term 'potlatch' is Chinook, a hybrid or 'pidgin' language composed of English, French and various first nation languages and formerly used by traders and settlers in these regions. The Chinook 'potlatch' means both 'gift' and 'to give', and as both noun and verb it gained a wide currency by the late nineteenth century (Bracken, 1997).

'Potlatch' ceremonies are a particular case of gift exchange once practised by indigenous people living along the coastal regions of North-Western America, from California to Canada and Alaska and including the Nootka, Haida, Tlingit and Kwakiutl peoples. The ceremonies, which were of course varied and complex, have been studied extensively by social anthropologists and ethnographers (Boas, 1890; Rosman and Rubel, 1972; Mauss, 1990). There are indigenous accounts available (Clutesi, 1969), as well as philosophical and deconstructive readings of different kinds (Bataille, 1988; Derrida, 1992; Bracken, 1997). Mauss himself did not travel to the region and was dependent on accounts produced by Franz Boas, Maurice Leenhardt, Bronislaw Malinowski and others.

Mauss's study *The Gift* focuses on the potlatch and other ceremonies such as the kula, practised traditionally in the Pacific islands, which he argues to be similar in form and function to the potlatch. Recognising the imprecision of the terms 'gift' and 'potlatch', Mauss proposes his own term: 'total services and counter services' (*prestations et contre-prestations totales*'; Mauss, 1950: 187). This term describes systems of exchange including presents, but also loans, entertainments and hospitality in the widest sense. What Mauss refers to as 'potlatch' refers to 'total services of an agonistic kind' with 'very acute rivalry and the destruction of wealth'; such ceremonies, Mauss declares, are 'rare but highly developed' (1990: 7). There is, then, among such tribes, *honour in destruction*:

> Consumption and destruction of goods really go beyond all bounds. In certain kinds of potlatch one must expend all that one has, keeping nothing back. It is a competition to see who is richest and also the most madly extravagant. Everything is based upon the principles of antagonism and rivalry.
>
> (Mauss, 1990: 37)

There are a number of related themes, drawn out in Mauss's study, that are vital for understanding Baudrillard's thought.[3] The first is that there is no independent or autonomous logic of the economic – and this is central to both Mauss's and Baudrillard's rejection of both liberal and Marxist thought. It follows that the notion of economic man (*Homo economicus*) – man existing in a state of nature for immediate survival – is a fabrication of economic theory. This fabrication has been able to present itself as common-sense fact because it is shared by liberals, neo-liberals and Marxists; by both left and right.

Several other themes in Mauss's study are crucial for Baudrillard: the obligatory nature of reciprocation and particularly the power of 'counter-prestations' (or what Baudrillard prefers to call the *contre-don* or counter-gift) *to challenge existing power relations*. This theme is not highly developed in Mauss although it is hinted at by his emphasis on the establishing of honour through 'humiliating others' in potlatch ceremonies (Mauss, 1990: 39).

There are further Maussian influences on Baudrillard, neglected by commentaries on Baudrillard's thought. Important here is the notion of the 'spirit of the thing given', which is developed in Baudrillard's *The Spirit of Terrorism* (see Chapter 7). Moreover, the exchange of 'life' and 'death' in potlatch ceremonies, discussed by Mauss (1990: 14–17, 38), provides support for Baudrillard's assertion that death is a symbolic relation rather than a biological event (1993a: 125–94). Further, Mauss's theorisation of the 'individual' as only meaningful within wider kinship ties, as a 'channel' along which gifts circulate, and of ritual agents or personae (1979: 35–94, 1990: 9, 41, 46) is a profound influence on Baudrillard's notion of individuality, agency and the 'passion for rules' (see Chapters 6 and 8). But Baudrillard does not merely *follow* Mauss. For example, Mauss strongly suggests that obligatory gift-exchange ceremonies function to avert war between clans, tribes and cultures (1990: 7, 13, 25), Baudrillard does not take up this theme and we will enquire as to why this is in Chapter 7. Moreover, Baudrillard rejects Mauss's conclusions concerning the re-emergence of generosity in modern welfare systems (Mauss, 1990: 65–71; Baudrillard, 1998a: 37–9).

The fundamental concern for Mauss is the obligatory nature of the gift exchanges and what he calls its 'total social' character, meaning that the ceremonies involve all aspects of the society at once, immediately or simultaneously. The gift-exchange ceremonies are 'total social phenomena' because 'all kinds of institutions are given expression at one and the same time – religious, juridical, and moral, which relate to both politics and the family; likewise economic ones . . . production and consumption [and] aesthetic phenomena' (Mauss, 1990: 3). Gift-giving ceremonies, Mauss asserts, are far more complex phenomena than has been appreciated. The ceremonies are 'both practical and mystical' (1990: 73). Participation is both 'self-interested' and obligatory: social hierarchy, honour and prestige are at stake and are contested, but participation is constrained by an enforced obligatory nature (1990: 33). For Mauss the gift-giving process consists of three interlocking moments: the obligation to give gifts, the obligation to receive gifts and the obligation to reciprocate gifts (1990: 13–14). These definitely are not societies of communistic equality, Mauss asserts, but nor is there a notion of individual freedoms and rights. Such cultures cannot be fully understood by either Marxism or liberalism: to put it very crudely these peoples are neither sharing, caring hippies nor budding capitalists. They have no money in the sense of an abstract system of equivalence, nor do they barter. In fact, Mauss argues, such cultures demonstrate that the notion of credit and loan predate the emergence of barter and money, so the attempts of both liberals and Marxists to understand the 'development' of economy from barter to money to credit are quite simply wrong (1990: 36, 72–3).

Mauss is particularly keen to understand what force compels the obligatory reciprocation of gift-giving in these 'primitive' societies, the traces of which, he insists, are found very widely and persist into modern capitalist societies. The answer for Mauss is *in the spirit of the thing given*. The gift carries within it a moral force, it has a spirit and it carries something of the 'soul' of the giver (Mauss, 1990: 10–13, 43–4): 'to make a gift of something to someone is to make a present of some part of oneself . . . to accept something from somebody is to accept some part of his spiritual essence, of his soul' (Mauss, 1990: 12). Wealth is circulated such that the participants 'did not emerge any richer than before' (1990: 9), and Mauss assures us specifically that there is no economic advantage in the ceremonies even for the chiefs (1990: 29–30). There is no ultimate end, purpose or destination for the gifts other than their return and constant circulation.

'Hau' is the spirit of the thing given in traditional Maori culture (Mauss, 1990: 10–13). The things exchanged are not inert or inactive. The Hau, it is said, wants to return to its 'place of origin', to the earth or forest from which it came. The 'ownership' of things is temporary, lasting only until the point when they must be returned. Gifts are in no way a neutral medium of equivalence. They are not an 'underdeveloped' system of money or of barter because they carry spirit or soul with them, they have stories that change and develop as they are exchanged, which increases their prestige – which is not an abstractable 'value'. In other words, 'persons and things merge' (Mauss, 1990: 48). Possession and gift are undifferentiated: things ultimately belong to the gods or, better, are *of* the gods and must return to them.

The sanctions for failing to observe ritual rules are grave and include loss of honour and authority and even, in traditional Maori culture, death – apparently self-willed and brought about by feelings of sickness and disgrace (Mauss, 1979: 35–56, cited by Baudrillard, 1993a: 134). 'Death' appears as a relation of social exchange rather than a biological event in the life of an individual because life and death are reversible. The disgraced may die and be brought back to life at a later date by the renewal of their inclusion in the ceremonial expressions of their community. Further, according to Mauss 'the chiefs . . . represent and incarnate their ancestors and the gods, whose names they bear, whose dances they dance and whose spirits possess them' (1990: 38–9). The participants in ritual are not 'themselves', not individuals, but are masked incarnations of the dead. The living die so that the 'dead' may live, and the 'dead' return to the beyond so that the living may go on living: 'life' and 'death' are reversible, indeed the meaning of the terms is annulled in exchange. Further ritual acts are enabled by the wearing of spirit masks, not chosen by the 'individual' participant: ritual agency is the agency of the *persona* rather than of the individual (Mauss, 1990: 39). Baudrillard's later work, I will argue, develops a closely related sense of agency within the ritual or rule (Baudrillard, 1990b: 134–6, 2001c: 67–73).

Mauss's discussion of the kula ceremony of the Trobriand Islands, which draws on Malinowski's monumental study *Argonauts of the Western Pacific* (1922), is also influential on Baudrillard. His discussion of the kula in *Critique* (1981: 30–1, 64–5) bears the imprint of both Malinowski and Mauss. Baudrillard writes of the gift being thrown at the feet of the recipient, and the anxiety and difficulty of giving and accepting gifts, which recalls Mauss (1990: 22) and Malinowski (1922: 173–6).

Mauss's account suggests an alternative anti-liberal and non-Marxist means of theorising 'the economy' and the position of the individual within it. The 'economy', Mauss contends, does not exist as an auto-nomous or separable sphere or institution. Indeed, there is no such thing as 'natural economy', Mauss insists; even so-called 'primitive societies' do not live in the 'state of nature', a raw and unending quest for survival (Mauss, 1990: 5). On the contrary, these societies are tradi-tionally very wealthy, with vigorous trading practices. Such people are perfectly capable of striking hard bargains and accumulate very large surpluses even as measured by Western standards (Malinowski, 1922; Mauss, 1990). As the natural economy of hand-to-mouth survival can-not be located, it is for Mauss, as for Baudrillard, a mythical construct of capitalist modernity. There is no locatable economic infrastructure; instead the 'total social' practice of gift exchange, an endless cycle of giving, determines the course of social hierarchy and authority, kinship relations, religious practices and the 'aesthetic' phenomena of dance and performance. Gift exchange is the expression of societies without the demarcation into the spheres we recognise as politics, economics, religion, sexuality and culture.

It could be objected that a form of power does indeed emerge in such ceremonies. However, prestige or honour do not necessarily translate into political power or authority (see Clastres, 1977, cited by Baudrillard, 1993a: 43). There is a double sense in which power could not be 'owned' or accumulated by individuals. First, prestige is accrued through the loss or giving away of wealth, rather than its accumula-tion: chiefs may live in destitution. Second, prestige is a temporary effect determined by gift-giving within networks of kinship relations, it is not the *property* of individuals.

Mauss's study also suggests what we might hesitatingly call a 'psychology' of gift-giving (bearing in mind that these are 'total' social phenomena, not quasi-autonomous features of the psyche). The processes of gift-giving tell us something about the nature of indi-viduals and their actions, particularly if we accept Mauss's (and Baudrillard's) assertion that the principles of kula and potlatch persist 'hidden below the surface' of 'our own societies' (Mauss, 1990: 4).[4]

BINARY OPPOSITIONS AND DEATH

Power is possible only if death is no longer free . . . the economic consists in life taking death hostage.

(Baudrillard, 1993a: 130)

The social begins by taking charge of death.

(Baudrillard, 1993a: 178)

What could be more natural than the separation of life and death into a binary opposition? Surely death is death, when life is no more we encounter death. Death is inevitable, it is final, it is brutally obvious. All objects can be separated into animate and inanimate, living and non-living. Even animals recognise these differences. Yet Baudrillard wants to 'deconstruct' this opposition. Why?

The separation and opposition of life and death, Baudrillard contends, creates power: the hierarchical structures of authority that are the fundamental mechanisms of social control. When life and death are seperated time becomes linear rather than cyclical, religion becomes repressive rather than expressive and death becomes *the final, irreversible event in the life of the individual*. The separating of life and death, then, is the founding condition of binary thinking. Once binary thinking becomes dominant it is difficult to think of otherness or difference as anything other than a relation of binary opposition to what is known or similar. The linear calculation of time produces the 'cyclical' as no more than its binary opposition: as imaginary, phantasmal, irrational or lost rather than real. Or, to take the example of religion, the ritual practices of polytheist or 'pagan' religions are not *opposed* to monotheistic religious codes but come to seem so from the perspective of the latter. Other binary oppositions – the opposition of male and female, of good and evil, order and disorder, individual and society, workers and their labour – flow from the separation of life and death, Baudrillard asserts. The production of the binary opposition of life and death is nothing less than the foundation of Western civilisation. Baudrillard attempts, on many occasions, to elucidate a sense of otherness or 'radical difference' that is not contained or pre-structured by a binary opposition and that does not exist in a dialectical relation. The symbolic is not the opposite of the semiotic, seduction is not the opposite of production: these are what Baudrillard later calls 'dual forms' and are discussed in this and the following chapters.

Baudrillard begins his task of deconstruction by acknowledging the importance of Foucault's *Madness and Civilisation* (1967). Foucault's genealogical study argued that 'madness' is constituted by Enlightenment thought as it erects a division between the normal and abnormal. Whereas in the medieval period a far wider spectrum of behaviour was permitted, enlightenment thought judged human experience in relation to scientifically defined 'norms', thereby actually producing categories of 'abnormality'. The 'abnormal' were then confined to asylums and subjected to further scientific scrutiny. Yet Baudrillard aims to outflank Foucault's genealogy of modernity by arguing that the fundamental exclusion enacted by Western civilisation is not that of the mad, but that of the dead. The dead are 'thrown out of the group's symbolic circulation . . . no longer beings with a full role to play' (Baudrillard, 1993a: 126). In Western societies the dead are removed further and further away from the living: they are no longer buried in village churchyards but banished to out-of-town municipal cemeteries or 'ghettos', increasingly inaccessible to their kin:

> there are no longer any provisions for the dead, either in mental or physical space. Even madmen, delinquents and misfits can find a welcome in the new towns . . . only the death-function cannot be programmed . . . we no longer know what to do with them, since today, *it is not normal to be dead, and this is new.* To be dead is an unthinkable anomaly: nothing else is as offensive as this.
> (Baudrillard, 1993a: 126, original emphasis)

The emergence of the notion of the immortality of the soul, according to Baudrillard, ruptured symbolic exchanges between living and dead. Immortality first appeared in ancient Egyptian society (approx. 3000 BCE) and at first only the elite were said to possess a soul; indeed, it was the pharaoh's possession of a soul that made him 'Man-God'. In other words, a vast degree of social power accrued to the Pharaoh and his priesthood by their severing of collective social exchanges between 'living' and 'dead'. How do we know that collective exchange rituals between living and dead occurred before the great dynasties of ancient Egypt? We don't. However, the anthropological sources that interest Baudrillard – Mauss, Leenhardt, Clastres and others – explore societies that had not developed the settled agriculture, literacy and city states that characterised ancient Egypt. Societies such as the Canaque of New Caledonia, studied by Leenhardt (1979), appear to have no strict opposition between 'living' and 'dead', or between the 'body' and the 'soul'. Indeed, Leenhardt argues that the Canaque have no word for 'body' and no concept of a biological body. Traditionally their art makes no attempt to suggest depth or perspective, so 'bodies' or 'physical properties' are always presented in two dimensions. Further, their term for death, dead, dying and ill – 'boa' – is also their word for god (Leenhardt, 1979: 24–42).

Leenhardt suggests that the distinction 'men and gods' is more appropriate to Canaque society than 'living and dead' because persons who possessed 'do kamo' (translated as 'which living') became gods when their 'costume' was worn out. Of course, there were inequalities among the Canaque: the possession of do kamo was not an automatic 'right' for all members of the tribe but was conditional upon 'honourable' behaviour. How this was judged is not clear from Leenhardt's account.

The status of women was certainly different from that of men, although women, like men, were considered sacred and acceded to the god-like status of tribal ancestors upon what we would term 'death'. Certainly inequalities in status and power were not of the order of those of the first 'civilisations', such as ancient Egypt where pharaohs used their divine status to rule absolutely.

In time the immortality of the soul was distributed democratically, becoming the property of all men under Christianity. It was later extended to include women but was never officially conferred to animals. The fundamental rupture of symbolic exchange between living and dead, then, enables the emergence of social and political power, first of the priesthood and later of the secular state. The rupturing of symbolic exchange is, for Baudrillard, the foundation of social power.

As modern, rational standards of normality and abnormality are applied, life and death become binary oppositions, separated out across linear time as the beginning and end of biological existence rather than being enclosed within cycles of exchange (the 'life cycle').[5] What is now termed 'death', as an event that happens to the body, is for Baudrillard 'ultimately' nothing more than the social line of demarcation separating the 'dead' from the 'living' (1993a: 127). That is, society and its systems of knowledge attempt to define what constitutes 'death'. There are a number of conflicting and irreconcilable definitions of what precisely constitutes death. Is it when the heart stops beating? When the brain stops functioning? When the soul has left the body? How are these criteria affected by life support technologies? The binary opposition of life and death is unable to progress beyond the simplistic logic of life equals not dead, and dead equals not living. When one is confronted by 'reality', matters are not always so simple. To be alive is to be mortal, as we live we are also dying, as we die we are also alive. Once we are dead we are no longer dying. We die only as we are living. Life and death are not either/or categories, are not binary oppositions.

Baudrillard's theoretical manoeuvres with binary oppositions owe a considerable debt to Lacanian psychoanalysis. The concept of the bar (*la barre*) is taken from Lacan's reading of Saussure (Lacan, 1977: 149) and the concept of the Imaginary flows from this. Where Baudrillard is original is in his rejection of the Lacanian notion of the Real, and in his contention that Real and Imaginary function as binary oppositions, each implying the other in a tactical, coded relationship. In other words, the 'real' is produced through the binary opposition, it does not precede or pre-exist it as ontological essence. Baudrillard, following Nietzsche, completely rejects the notion of essential things-in-themselves, the so-called brute physical nature of things supposedly existing independently of any particular perspective. Instead the Imaginary – the perspective of the human self, its self-identifications through images and objects, and its capacity to represent – produces the 'illusion' of the real world.

Baudrillard pushes further. Life and death are separated by a 'bar' or 'line of social demarcation'; the bar actually constitutes understandings of *both* life and death, of the properties on both sides of the bar. Life and death are still conjoined, contiguous: the bar of their separation also joins them. The barred symbolic exchange (of life and death) is present in the very process of its barring. Death as symbolic exchange with life is barred, but separated out from symbolic meaningfulness death is devoid of meaning, an 'unprogammable' horror, an 'unthinkable anomaly'. Yet life too, separated from death, loses its meaningfulness, reduced to 'the indifferent fatality or survival' (1993a: 126). In other words the separation of life and death does not result in a profit accruing to life. Although life is shielded from death it must end in death; moreover, a death now devoid of symbolic meaning. Life, then, is reduced to survival, not living but literally 'living-on', not (yet) dead. No matter how we deny or hide death it touches life. Similarly, it is possible to define sanity only by separating it from insanity, so the meaning of sanity depends upon the existence of insanity. The 'excluded', negative or demonised term exerts a certain power over the positive term. So, according to Baudrillard, the spectre of death haunts life, just as the spectre of madness haunts sanity, disorder threatens order and Evil stalks the Good. The excluded or 'pathological' term casts a shadow over 'normality' because, in the terminology Baudrillard borrows from Lacan, it become its Imaginary, its phantasy.

Capital and economic power are, for Baudrillard, ultimately only the 'fantastic secularisation' of the power to separate living and dead. Humanism, democracy and even revolution alter nothing fundamental because they do operate at the level of symbolic exchange – that is, they do not challenge the bar of binary oppositions. Indeed, by aiming for equality they actually nourish the systemic or structural nature of binary oppositions, Baudrillard suggests. Political movements based on improving matters for the repressed term, in terms set by the dominant term, cannot, for Baudrillard, ever be revolutionary: on the contrary, 'the revolution can only consist in the abolition of the separation of death, and not in equality of survival' (1993a: 129).

THE EXCHANGE OF DEATH

Symbolic exchange is halted neither by the living or the dead.
(Baudrillard, 1993a: 134)

The *effect of the real* is only ever therefore the structural effect of the disjunction between two terms, and our famous reality principle, with its normative and repressive implications, is only a generalisation of this disjunctive code to all levels.

(Baudrillard, 1993a: 133)

Baudrillard develops these themes with great audacity. He insists that the biological conception of death – accorded the status of objectivity in modernity – has no meaning in 'primitive' societies. Death, he argues, like disease and other 'natural' phenomena, is brought 'under control' by symbolic exchange rituals. Death, then, is understood not as biological event but as social relation:

the real materiality of death . . . lies in its form, which is always the form of a social relation . . . initiation is the accented beat of the operation of the symbolic. It aims neither to conjure death away, nor to 'overcome' it, but to articulate it socially.

(Baudrillard, 1993a: 131)

Initiation rites make death a symbolic relation; initiates 'die' symbolically and are 'reborn' in new or transformed social roles. As initiates 'die' they are said to join ancestors, conjoining the living and the dead, then the ancestors give back the living in a reciprocal movement such that 'death can no longer establish itself as end or agency':

the initiation consists in an exchange being established where there had been only a brute fact: they pass from a natural, aleatory and irreversible death to a death that is *given and received*, and that is therefore reversible in the social exchange . . . the opposition between birth and death disappears.

(Baudrillard, 1993a: 132)

What exactly is Baudrillard claiming? There seems to be a significant equivocation in his argument here. Does symbolic exchange ritual merely disguise the 'brute fact' of biological death? Is ritual exchange nothing more than a comforting pretence, a sham? Baudrillard warns against mystical interpretations: death is not 'conquered' (as, for example, is claimed in the Christian notion of resurrection). On two occasions (pp. 132 and 134) Baudrillard seems to suggest that symbolic exchange rituals are a response to the 'natural' or 'real' event of death, as if the 'reality' of death precedes symbolic exchange. But such a position would amount to conventional Freudo-Marxism. Although Baudrillard does not make this particularly clear he appears to be using the terms 'real' and 'natural' here not in the scientific or objectivist senses but in a sense adapted from Lacan. 'Death' is a construction of the Imaginary, not an objective biological reality, and symbolic exchange 'puts an end to the opposition between the real and the imaginary' (1993a: 133). In other words, symbolic exchange disrupts and overturns binary oppositions, since for Baudrillard all binary oppositions are based on the real/imaginary distinction. For him, 'each term of the disjunction excludes the other, which eventually becomes its imaginary' (1993a: 133), so death is only the imaginary construct of the living, women is only an imaginary construct of men, nature is constructed by culture and the idea of the soul by the experience of the limited, biological body. Moreover, according to the principle of symbolic reversibility, 'every separate term for which the other is its imaginary is haunted by the latter as *its own death*' (1993a: 133).

Nevertheless there is a temporal problem here. Which comes first, the symbolic order or the real/imaginary opposition? In other words, do symbolic cultures develop symbolic exchange to overcome their conception of the brute fact of death (albeit real/imaginary rather than simply biological)? If so, then how does this primal conception or experience of the 'brute fact' of death come about? One response would be to argue that there is always a tension between symbolic exchange and binary structures, that it is meaningless to suggest that one 'precedes' the other in a historical fashion.

What does emerge is that Baudrillard does not adopt a strong constructivist or culturally relativist position on death. Death is horrifying and threatening to the social order in both 'primitive' symbolic cultures and capitalist modernity. For Baudrillard all societies, 'primitive' and modern, share a necessary 'thanatopraxis'. This means that any society must do something to ward off or make meaningful the 'sudden loss of signs that befalls the dead, to prevent there remaining in the *asocial* flesh of the dead something which signifies nothing' (1993a: 180). *It is not 'real' biological 'death' but the asociality of signs that is most threatening.* The corpse of the recently deceased is rich with social meaning, the bleached bones of the ancestor are rich with meaning, but in between is putrefaction: a formless squalor of signs signifying nothing. It is, then, always a matter of signs and social meaning, not the biological 'reality' of death. As we have noted, the Canaque have no word that corresponds to 'body' and one term, 'boa', covering both dead and god. Nevertheless, the Canaque hasten the decomposition of the corpse by the sprinkling of water over it, and obscure the signs of decomposition by embalming (Leenhardt, 1979). All societies, it seems, deploy artifice or 'semiurgic practices' to avoid confrontation with the disturbing loss of socialised signs.

The distinction between 'primitive' and modern is, for Baudrillard, that modern semiurgic practices attempt to achieve 'naturalness' to make the dead look like the living, whereas 'the primitive concedes the dead their difference' (1993a: 181). Through their difference the dead remain partners and agents of social exchange; difference or heterogeneity enables symbolic exchange, sameness or homogeneity undermines it. Modern practices, then, are built upon the persistent, but nonsensical, binary opposition that life is natural and death is unnatural. Confined and naturalised as 'stuffed simulacra', the dead lose their social status.

So, in Western modernity, it seems the binary opposition life/death develops, whereas in 'primitive' cultures such an emergence is prevented by cycles of symbolic exchange. Yet Baudrillard's interest is not in documenting 'other' cultures but in interrogating the West:

> Throughout the entire system of political economy, the law of symbolic exchange has not changed one iota: we continue to exchange with the dead . . . we simply pay with our own death and our anxiety about death for the rupture of symbolic exchanges with them.
>
> (Baudrillard, 1993a: 134)

The operations of symbolic exchange suspend or annul binary oppositions and 'end' the dominance of the code. Symbolic exchanges are always breaches in the code because in the act of exchange the two terms of the binary oppositions lose their autonomy, lose their 'reality'. 'Reality' is revealed as a fabrication, an illusion.

NATURAL AND SACRIFICIAL DEATH

Socially programmed for survival, we are increasingly fascinated by death: 'If life is only a need to survive at any cost, then annihilation is a priceless luxury. In a system where life is ruled by value and utility, death becomes a useless luxury and the only alternative' (Baudrillard, 1993a: 156). Death becomes 'inhuman, irrational and senseless' (1993a: 162); torn from symbolic relations it is absurd and abnormal. In modern societies 'the social' is an abstracted, separated instance distinguished from and opposed to other spheres such as economic, politics and law. The social has its own structures, and institutions and social relations are further abstractions: welfare and security, the family and health, work and leisure (1983: 90 n. 7). According to Baudrillard these institutions 'annex' death by constructing the phenomenon of 'natural death'.

The construction of natural or biological death effects an 'equivalent neutralisation' of life such that life is understood as a quantity of linear time' – 'life capital' – while death is reduced to nothing. The retired and the old, Baudrillard argues, come to be seen as a 'dead weight', a burden on society capable of nothing but 'sliding' into death (1993a: 163). Increasingly they are packed off to care homes and hospices where they survive for a few years, out of view, no longer in any position to participate in symbolic exchanges – *already dead*. Rarely visited, tended by staff paid the minimum wage or less, surrounded by the stink of piss and excrement, they expire: a merciful release not only for the dying but for their embarrassed families too. The difference from 'non-Western' cultures, and the West in its pre-modern period, where elders, corpses and ancestors are venerated and central to social rituals, could not be greater.

According to Baudrillard, as 'natural' death becomes ridiculous, 'violent, accidental and chance death' takes on a macabre and fascinating interest – and surely he has a point. We moderns seem to be obsessed with the ghoulish figures of serial killers and suicide bombers, with so-called embodiments of evil. But why exactly do we find violent or accidental death so fascinating? Baudrillard warns against a simplistic 'blame the media' argument and again understands these phenomena through the severing or barring of symbolic exchange. Violent and accidental death is the closest form in modernity to the sacrificial deaths of the symbolic order. Violent and accidental deaths, like sacrifices, 'escape' natural or biological reason: they are in Baudrillard's language 'artificial' and so are a challenge to nature. Further, by their artificial form, such deaths are lifted out of the sphere of individuals and families, of science and medicine, which are equipped only for 'natural' death. Artificial deaths arouse collective passions and, by the rule of symbolic exchange, such deaths demand a collective symbolic response. Yet today there are no rituals 'for reabsorbing death and its rupturing energies' (1993a: 165), so what remains is the 'phantasm of sacrifice' and this is what fascinates.[6] Another example of 'willed death', which Baudrillard develops at some length, is hostage-taking. Willed or 'anti-natural' violence may be willed by the self, such as in suicide, or by others, such as an aggressor or murderer. In either case such violence brings about a collective shock-wave of fascination or horror, which, Baudrillard suggests, links modern and symbolic cultures. We are never convinced by the modern, rationalised, economic order, Baudrillard insists, so the 'collective imagination' always tends toward modes of symbolic exchange.

SUICIDE, SUBVERSION AND DEFIANCE

> [D]eath is perhaps the only thing that has no use-value, which can never be referred back to need, and so can unquestionably be turned into a weapon.
>
> (Baudrillard, 1993a: 176)

> Violent death changes everything, slow death changes nothing.
>
> (Baudrillard, 1993a: 40)

Our lives and our deaths seem to be separated out and neither 'belongs' to us. We lose ownership of these, apparently our most singular and personal experiences, to the state, science and medicine. As the juridical, medico-scientific and administrative dimensions of modernity extend, Baudrillard argues, we are all confined, figuratively speaking: 'we are all madmen and criminals . . . we are all Indians, Blacks, Palestinians, women or homosexuals' (1993a: 192 n. 34).

The 'ultimate aim of the system', of seizing 'control of death' (1993a: 48 n. 24), makes it highly vulnerable to any defiance of its control over death, since for Baudrillard the entire edifice of power is built on this foundation. Death, then, is the ultimate weapon against the system because it is capable of re-engaging the symbolic exchange of life and death. As we are condemned to a 'slow death' of labour and survival by the system, according to Baudrillard,

> We must therefore displace everything onto the sphere of the symbolic where the challenge, reversal and overbidding are the law, so that we can respond to death only by an equal or superior death. There is no question here of real violence or force . . . only the challenge and the logic of the symbolic.
>
> (1993a: 36)

Baudrillard clearly feels that 'real' acts of violence are pointless and counterproductive because they feed into the system, justifying its methods of control, and ultimately serve as commodity-sign or entertainment value for its media networks. To defy the system, Baudrillard argues, we must be prepared to 'die', in the sense of surrendering the 'life' (or living-death) that the system has given us. We must, he asserts, throw the gift of living death back in the face of the system and demand either an 'immediate death' or a new 'life' freed of the barring of symbolic exchange (1993a: 36–7). The self as *given* by the system cannot liberate itself from the system because it is *of* the system. This self must be annulled or sacrificed and the system is then put in the position of having to respond to this symbolic exchange:

To defy the system with a gift to which it cannot respond save by its own collapse and death. Nothing, not even the system, can avoid the symbolic obligation, and it is in this trap that the only chance of catastrophe for the capital remains.

(1993a: 37)

In modernity, suicide has such a subversive force: 'through suicide, the individual tries and condemns society . . . by inverting the authorities and *reinstating reversibility*' (1993a: 175, emphasis added). So, for example, the high rate of suicide in prisons is understood as a symbolic exchange, 'an infinitesimal but inexpiable breach' in the system of control. Suicide is a 'challenge that society cannot reply to' (1993a: 180), it seizes back control of (the individual's) death and, further, it subtracts 'capital' or value from a system based on the accumulation and realisation of value. In the act of suicide we remove ourselves as a quantity of capital. Moreover, Baudrillard insists, 'if every suicide becomes subversive in a highly integrated system, all subversion of and resistance to the system is reciprocally, by its very nature, suicidal' (1993a: 176).

Baudrillard does not only mean suicide in the literal sense, but any behaviour that challenges or opposes the maximizing of performance, growth, accumulation, success. He includes neurotic behaviours by which 'sufferers' can prevent their full integration into the code and also street demonstrations that have no other goal than to provoke the authorities to 'real' violence, to shame and humiliate them.

Baudrillard does not develop examples at this stage, but he cites briefly the student demonstrations of May 1968 where students 'sacrificed' their gift of a higher education, throwing it back at the system such that the system 'loses its footing'. The anti-Poll Tax riots of July 1990 in London seemed to undermine the Thatcher government as people rejected the secure life of (signs of) prosperity and instead risked life and limb in pitched battles with the police. But in both cases any fractures in the system were soon repaired, or at least papered over; particular politicians are removed but the system continues. Yet this does not necessarily undermine Baudrillard's argument as he asserts that the system has the power 'to displace the time of exchange, substituting continuity and mortal linearity for the immediate retaliation of death' (1993a: 40). In other words the system has time on its side, or rather linear time is the time of the system. Baudrillard's point becomes painfully obvious in cases where corporations are found by the courts, or increasingly by the media, to have risked the health of consumers by negligence. This occurred when Coca-Cola marketed 'Dasani' purified water as a health drink when it was in fact ordinary tap water with various pollutants added by the company, and when Cadbury-Trebor-Bassett UK sold chocolate laced with salmonella. On both occasions the companies' PR spokespersons announced that since the unfavourable findings were made their company had already introduced the most stringent safety improvements: in other words your critique is already long out of date, time is on *our* side.

To summarise, the system (political economy) has 'possession' of death such that it 'gives' us our natural, biological death, just as it gives us the gifts of a self and identity in consumer society. It gives us the gift of welfare, security and finally a painless 'natural' death in hospital. We may well try to resist these gifts, by driving fast without a seatbelt, heavy smoking, over-eating or starving ourselves.[7] We may deliberately refuse to maximise ourselves, to realise our potential, or our refusal may be beyond conscious volition as in Baudrillard's examples of impotence and anorexia (1990a: 119–28). In each of these cases failure is equal to symbolic death in our competitive, performance-obsessed societies. However, an effective 'counter-gift' of potlatch-style destruction can only occur through suicide. The system gives and dominates by giving unilaterally, its power is based in the cessation of the cycle of symbolic exchanges. According to Baudrillard 'the worst repression . . . consists in dispossessing you of your own death' (1993a: 177). Suicide gives back, returns or counters the gift of life/death given by the system: symbolic exchange is once more put into play, the cycle continues and unilateral power and authority crumble by lacking a symbolic response.

Domination is never total. The system cannot hunt down or neutralise every aspect, every fragment of our lives and thoughts; we remain 'free', at least free to challenge the system. We cannot and will not be made to identify fully with our individual interests, needs, desires and 'potential' that the system promotes as coded options within an integrated system. Baudrillard's conviction is that people will never acquiesce to the system and resign themselves to being merely 'the capitalist of their own lives' (1993a: 179–80).

SYMBOLIC EXCHANGE AND LANGUAGE

Symbolic Exchange and Death claims a site of resistance and defiance at both the socio-economic level and the level of language and writing. The principle of symbolic exchange, according to Baudrillard, operates at the level of words and meanings. 'Poetic language' is a site of the sacrifice or extermination of linguistic value, a place of the suspension and annulment of the fixed, referential meaning of word-signs. Symbolic or poetic language is, for Baudrillard, a non-expressive, anti-discursive 'beyond' of the economy of signification. Within the poetic or symbolic operation words do not signify or represent, signs are cancelled or 'sacrificed'. The ordered, regulated opposition between signifier and signified and sign and referent is dissolved in ambivalence by poetic resonances that play on both sides of the bar simultaneously (1993a: 198–205).

Here Baudrillard reads 'Saussure against Saussure'; not the Saussure of the *Course in General Linguistics* (1966), his well known study assembled posthumously by students, but the far less well known Saussure of the anagrams, termed Saussure's 'abandoned hypothesis' by Baudrillard. Briefly, Saussure's hypothesis , at least as Baudrillard renders it, consists of two 'hidden' laws of poetry. The first is that the numbers of vowels in a verse should be 'countered' by a given number of non-vowels in a fixed pattern. In other words, meaning is not free to be developed at will by the poet, it is constrained by a rule of composition that ensures there are no remainders, no leftovers; all must be *exchanged*. The second rule is that a 'theme word', such as the name of a god or hero, be generated by anagram through emphasised phonemes. Put simply, as the poem is spoken out loud (as poetry always should be) the sound produced by recital will suggest a name through the repetition of certain sounds. Such poems, found widely in ancient Greece and Rome, are thought to be offerings.

Baudrillard opposes Saussure's understanding of the anagrams secreted in ancient poetry in two main ways. First, Baudrillard criticises Saussure for ignoring the symbolic relations between poet and reader in his focus on the poet and 'artistic inspiration'. According to Baudrillard this understanding participates in the severing of symbolic relations, abstracting the greatness of the individual poet while ignoring the 'ecstasy' that can sweep over the reader of a great poem in a symbolic exchange. In other words, the greatness of a poem resides in the pact formed by reader and poem, not unilaterally in the figure of the poet.

Second, Baudrillard contends that the rule of no remainders does not merely reinforce the meaning or message of the theme words through repetition, but actually cancels the theme word by 'doubling' it. For Baudrillard such poems are sacrificial: the god is put to death, symbolically, through the poem by dispersal into phonemic elements. The signifier – the name of a god – is sacrificed by the splitting away of the signifiers, the word-sound from the supposed referent – the god in a dispersal into sound, a 'cancellation by the double' (1993a: 199).

The poetic form, according to Baudrillard, 'shatters' the equivalence of signifier and signified, it shatters the 'linearity of the signifier' (the accumulation of meaning) and it shatters the boundlessness or infinity of meaning, bringing it under strict regulation. But these principles of regulation, the laws of the anagram, are not a code. The poetic has a form but not a code – an important distinction. Poetry 'ruptures not only the arbitrariness of the sign, but also the Law of equivalence (signifier/signified) and the function of representation' (1993a: 214).

This is a complex point and must be dwelt on. The sign, as unit of meaning or value, acts as a 'stand-in' for reality. Representation works by requiring us to believe that the sign/stand-in actually emanates from a reality that, so to speak, 'makes signs at you' (1993a: 214). This Baudrillard terms 'the Linguistic Imaginary'. Representational meaning or signification takes place in the imagination of the science of linguistics, not 'out there' in the world. Poetry does not operate in this way, Baudrillard asserts, but linguistic science attempts, unsuccessfully, to *code* poetry. Poetry, according to Baudrillard, is generally misinterpreted as a 'better' or higher type of equivalence, as offering a more apposite expression of meaning – not merely arbitrary but artful in its ability to tie together signifier and signified. But this interpretation remains locked within the code of representation and equivalence. Baudrillard follows standard structuralist and poststructuralist theory here but also adds something distinctive in his insistence that the rule-bound or ritual-like use of language leads to a sacrificial annulment of referential value. The following of rules as a mode of breaking with coded models of subjectivity is explored in Baudrillard's later work (see Chapters 5 and 8 of this volume).

Taking the example of Swinburne's poetry, where Ss sound like s-nakes hi-ss-ing, Baudrillard argues that the 'Linguistic Imaginary' reduces poetry to an artful technique used to reinforce meaning, to bolster the metaphysics of representation. Without a logic of equivalence there can be no representational meaning, there is 'nothing': 'if the poem refers to something, it is always to NOTHING' (1993a: 209).

The something that is nothing cannot be coded, it cannot be rendered into equivalence. It is not a 'thing' but a 'no(t)-thing'; that is, it is not an abstract unit but a relation, an experience, a possibility. To clarify, a person can be given a number and treated as a number – indeed, this happens all the time in modern bureaucratic societies. A number is a thing, an abstract unit of coding, but a person is not a 'thing', to be a person is to exist in relations with other. Our sense of personhood, of who we are, cannot be separated from our relations to others. A person, then, is not a thing but a not-thing, not an abstract, isolatable unit but a relation, a form.

Poetry, for Baudrillard, or at least 'good poetry', is akin to gift-exchange and sacrifice. Indeed, poetry is to language what gift-exchange is to economics: its sacrificial annulment, its resolution without remainder, its 'anti-value'. Value, whether economic or semantic, is, according to Baudrillard, merely a residue that has escaped or 'not been exhausted' in the cycle of gift exchange. Such residues are the source of power struggles and conflicts.

The 'rational' economic, productivist worldview dominates when we believe ourselves 'free' to use words without 'ritual, religious, or poetic restriction of any kind' (1993a: 201). The illusory freedom to *use* words as we please to *produce* referential meaning enables, and is mirrored by, the later situation where capitalists are free to *use* labour as they please to *produce* profit. Baudrillard's argument here 'mirrors' Marx, even as he suggests that Marx mirrors capitalism, in that Baudrillard seeks to expose empty, formal rather than actual, freedoms in the sphere of representation, as Marx had done in the sphere of economics. Baudrillard's theories pass beyond Marxism, but, initially at least, by way of Marxism. The unlimited productivity of goods and labour, of words and meanings, does not deliver freedom or progress, Baudrillard insists. Instead modernity is 'caught in an endless escalation at every level' (1993a: 201), an accumulation and profusion of residues – of objects, capital, meaning and psychic debris.

For Baudrillard everything that is symbolically exchanged is a 'mortal threat' to the dominant order because the dominant order in all its dimensions – linguistic, economic and political – is built upon the expulsion, barring or denial of symbolic exchange. Systems of representation and meaning, systems of political economy and finance, systems of communication and mediation can only function as commodity-signs if symbolic exchanges are barred. Accumulation, hierarchy, social power and control occur when the cycle of symbolic exchange is brought to an end; during the cycle they are in a state of flux. The capitalist system has the distinction of effecting a permanent, though partial and always unstable, cessation of the cycle of exchange. Gift exchange continues in circumscribed form at the individual level, but is barred at the systemic level. Ambivalence is not an opposing or alternative 'code' but 'the incessant potentiality of the annulment of value' (1981: 210), nothing more, nothing less. The various forms of symbolic exchange – willed, suicidal, accidental, poetic – 'shatter' these systems.

4

Simulation and the End of the Social

INTRODUCTION: THE ORDERS OF SIMULACRA

Let's never forget that the real is merely a simulation.
                                        (Baudrillard, 1998b: 69)

Simulation is, clearly, an important term in Baudrillard's vocabulary, but it is not his 'key' concept or central idea as is often thought. Indeed, the term has largely disappeared in Baudrillard's work of the past twenty years or so. It does, nevertheless, play an important role in the unfolding of Baudrillard's ideas and will be explored in detail in this chapter. The relationship between 'real' and simulated and between simulacrum and simulation are among the most poorly understood of all Baudrillard's ideas; consequently their clarification is very important.

Simulacrum, from the Latin, means 'image', 'semblance' or 'likeness'. The *Oxford English Dictionary* emphasises the *material* nature of the simulacrum, the image *as thing*, as fashioned and constructed. Baudrillard theorises the orders of 'simulacra' (the plural form), exploring the phases or stages of the image in modern Western culture from the Renaissance to the present day. Influenced by Nietzsche and Pierre Klossowski, Baudrillard theorises the simulacrum as complete or total: every 'thing' is simulacral (2005d: 39–47). There are only images

or illusions; 'behind' images there are more images; the
at which the final illusion is stripped away to reveal . . . *reality.* The
notion of 'reality', then, is itself an illusion, moreover it is an illusion
of recent provenance; Baudrillard locates the construction of the idea
of 'reality' within the orders of simulacra (1998b: 23, 2005d: 39). The
idea of 'reality' is not, of course, a constant. It emerges with the first
order of simulacra and its distinctive binary oppositions of real/unreal
and true/false. The idea of the 'real' reaches its apogee in the second
order of simulacra, where life, sex, and work are understood as *the*
essential realities. After burning brightly in the second order, 'reality',
according to Baudrillard, is fading fast and is now kept alive by further
simulation. Simulation consists of coded, stereotyped signifiers that
refer to other signifiers in a model, not to an external referent or
'reality'. Simulation generates 'hyperreality', not the 'real' or 'unreal'
but the semiotic effect of a 'more real than the real'.

Baudrillard's usage of the terms 'reality', sign, illusion and simulation are often very badly misunderstood. He *does not* argue that signs
have replaced reality, since 'reality' for Baudrillard was only ever
generated through signs (1998b: 69, 2004: 44). Further, his writing does
not reduce everything to the level of signs or simulations, as is frequently
assumed. Symbolic exchange continues to 'haunt' simulation. Further,
Baudrillard stubbornly maintains a dual or *duel* vision, insisting upon
an irreconcilable antagonism *within* the simulacrum (1990a: 154–6,
2005d: 185–9). To summarise, there are signs that are ordered by laws
and codes and there are symbols or 'semiurgic material' that cannot be
codified because they are ambivalent, they are 'impossible' to exchange
economically because they are not subject to a law of value (1981: 123–9,
1993a: 195–242). There are signs that enable the accumulation of
meaning and knowledge and there are 'pure' signs that enchant and
seduce, signs that reverse, destabilise and annihilate meaning (1990a: 60–6,
1990b: 166–79). But theory is not a question of categorising signs as
either semiotic or symbolic, of simply positioning phenomena within the
first, the second, the third or the fourth order. These distinctions do,
certainly, operate as orientation devices, and Baudrillard will himself
engage in such categorising on occasion (1993a: 50–86, 1993b: 5–6; 1992:
299–300). What is crucial in Baudrillard's theories is the ironic
interplay *within* orders: the reversals, the instability, the ultimate unde-
cidability of these relations. No order is ever fixed or stable; nor are
they surpassed or transcended. Each order remains and is joined by
another, creating ever more paradoxical relations: 'You're talking
about the three orders? I don't believe it holds up' (Baudrillard, 1987b:
73, interviewed by Lotringer).

To map the transformations in the meaning of images over centuries of Western history is, of course, a vastly ambitious project and Baudrillard does not attempt it. He admits that what he offers is less than a sketch. Each phase in Baudrillard's scheme is accompanied by a 'law of value' or 'principle of equivalence': the underlying principle by which social value is established, exchanged and enforced. Baudrillard, wisely, avoids giving dates for the transformations between orders, but there is undoubtedly a historical dimension to his scheme. So, foolishly perhaps, I will venture some historical dates for the purposes of exposition, but it must be borne in mind that the orders cannot be separated out into historical blocks.

Baudrillard's scheme begins with the Renaissance, very approximately from the late fifteenth century with the dissolution of the feudal system. This is termed the 'first order of simulacra'. The second order is identified with the age of industrialisation, from about 1750 in Western Europe, while the third order is defined by Baudrillard as the 'present age': the post-industrial or consumer society. No 'end' dates can be given for the orders for the simple reason that they do not come to an end. Instead, each order is supplemented by another as its energy or 'principle' is weakened or undermined and this, Baudrillard insists, is quite different from an 'end' (1994b: 11, 2005d: 67–73).[1]

The symbolic order, crucial to Baudrillard's earlier analyses, does not appear in this scheme because it had no law of value. However, it is mistaken to understand the symbolic order as always already lost – as a fantasy or imaginary structure, as suggested by Lyotard (1993: 102–8) and Hegarty (2004: 54). Baudrillard states quite clearly 'this order has existed, and it was a brutal hierarchy' (1993a: 50). As Chapter 3 indicated, Baudrillard argues that ancient Egyptian society brought about a fundamental severing of symbolic exchange relations by introducing the concept of the immortal soul. This would occur, gradually, around 4000 to 2000 BCE. As I have stressed, it is vitally important to distinguish the *symbolic order* as time and place from *symbolic exchange* as act, gesture and social relation.[2] Clearly the symbolic *order*, cultures where symbolic exchange was the organising principle of social life, predates the Renaissance by many centuries, but forms of symbolic *exchange* persist throughout the periods covered by the three orders. Symbolic *exchange* as form or principle is 'indestructible', not the symbolic order as way of life, which is now 'lost' (2003a: 18).

To introduce each order in turn, Baudrillard terms the first order of simulacra the Counterfeit. It operates through the 'natural law of value' or use-value as the principle of equivalence. The second order of simulacra is the order of Production, based on the 'market law of value' or 'economic exchange-value'. The third order of simulacra is governed by the Code or 'structural law of value', an era of 'sign-exchange-value' as principle of equivalence.[3] Each of these orders, then, is defined by its modelling of the world through a principle of 'general equivalence', enabling comparisons, classifications and ordered exchange between elements in the system. Symbolic exchanges, by contrast, have no principle of equivalence and no law of value; the meaning of things exchanged cannot be abstracted from the exchange process and the participants in the exchange. Further, symbolic exchange is never completed because it sets up a chain of obligations that must, in time, be acknowledged and reciprocated. Baudrillard contends that we are now moving towards a fourth order, a fractal or viral order where 'value radiates out in all directions . . . without reference . . . there is no longer any equivalence, no law of value' (1993b: 5). The 'fourth order' is discussed in Chapter 6.

A THEORY OF POWER

Baudrillard's emphasis is on the object – the sign – not on subjects or 'historical actors' such as classes or capitalist corporations. Of course, the orders only come about and are maintained *through social practice*. However, the orders have impersonal and unconscious constraining effects on actors. Further, according to Baudrillard's appropriation of structuralist and poststructuralist theory, codes – initially languages and then the abbreviated codes of consumption – actually provide the conditions within which the very notions of agent, self or identity take shape and become meaningful. In other words the coherence and unity of the self – the thinking, knowing subject – is a property of language, an effect of discourse or a simulation.

Baudrillard is clear that 'simulacra do not consist only of the play of signs, they involve social relations and social power' (1993a: 52). Class power is actuated through signs, through the social logic of distinction that signs mark and reproduce (1981: 29–62, 1998a: 49–68). The fundamental purpose of each order is to enhance control over the world, over nature and over human beings. Unlike in Marxist theory, no class, group or individual specifically is 'behind' this drive for control. Following Foucault (1970) and Nietzsche (1968, 1994), Baudrillard understands power as a property of the system rather than an attribute of the individual. For Nietzsche 'knowledge functions as a tool of power' (1968: 266) and similarly, for Baudrillard, each order of simulacra produces knowledge, ideas and perceptions that maintain and reproduce the power relations of that order. Knowledge is never neutral and power is not located at a single point within the system but is dispersed throughout it, investing all of its relations, exchanges and processes. Power operates within a system or order of discourse with the power to represent, to construct knowledge; in this sense *power is knowledge*. Yet Baudrillard departs sharply from Foucault's Nietzsche-inspired analysis of power (Baudrillard, 1987b: 64). First, Baudrillard explores the constraints imposed by the system of consumption, a move Foucault did not make, and, second, he argues that the diffuse network of power relations analysed by Foucault (1977) is abolished in the third order of simulacra by a more effective means of control – the code. Baudrillard's critique of Foucault's theory of power is discussed below in the section on the third order.

THE FIRST ORDER OF SIMULACRA: THE COUNTERFEIT

During the sixteenth and seventeenth centuries the emergent bourgeois class dismantled the fixed ranks and restricted exchanges of the feudal order through the introduction of democratic parliamentary and legal institutions. The bourgeoisie introduced 'overt competition at the level of signs' (Baudrillard, 1993a: 50). The meaning and exchanging of signs was no longer restricted by the status or rank of birth and freer exchange enabled the emergence of the 'game of signs' of fashion and conspicuous consumption (1990a: 91–2, 1993a: 87–100).

Fashion and competitive consumption could not emerge in the symbolic order because 'signs are protected by a prohibition which ensures their total clarity and confers an unequivocal status on each' (1993a: 50). Yet the symbolic order is in no sense the absolutely *real*, a realm of unmediated, certain or direct access to truth. The symbolic order, as Baudrillard depicts it, consists of a play of exchanges, of challenges, of appearances: masks, dances, feasts, rituals. Signs, as the medium of meaning, are of course present but they are relatively fixed, 'certain', ascribed, bound. Crucially, signs in the symbolic order are not referential and not arbitrary:

> The arbitrariness of the sign begins when instead of bonding two persons in an inescapable reciprocity, the signifier starts to refer to a disenchanted universe of the signified, the common denominator of the real world, towards which no-one any longer has the least obligation.
>
> (Baudrillard, 1993a: 50)

Arbitrary signs are 'counterfeit' in that they are 'only a simulacrum of symbolic obligation' (ibid.). They have the 'appearance' of being 'bound to the world' but are abstract, referential (re)presentations of it. In positing the world on the one hand, and the representational exchange of signs on the other, world and sign are separated, qualitatively different things: the *sign* and the *referent*. The linkage between sign and referent is one of convention, where the sign actively represents the supposedly 'passive' referent or object. In other words, the severing of symbolic exchanges results in a qualitative transformation of both sides of the newly born binary opposition 'world' and 'signs'. This qualitative difference is not meaningful in symbolic exchange, or, we may speculate, in the symbolic order.

A wide range of new phenomena and new social practices become possible in the first or counterfeit order of simulacra. This was the age of baroque, of theatrical illusion and the flourishing of new movements in art and architecture. Baudrillard emphasises the use of stucco and the artistic device of *trompe l'oeil* as particularly characteristic of this period. Stucco, a term dating from the Italian Renaissance, is a kind of plaster used to coat architectural surfaces to produce smooth mouldings and designs. *Trompe l'oeil* painting, meaning literally 'deceiving the eye', presents the illusion of the three dimensions in two, and by removing the frame the image can appear 'real'.[4] Each order of simulacra remodels the world to render it more intelligible, controllable, manageable. The Counterfeit achieves this only 'at the level of substance and form, not yet of relations and structures' (1993a: 53). Stucco, then, was used as a kind of 'universal substance' that could model any shape or take any form – a principle of general equivalence, albeit of a very limited kind.

THE SECOND ORDER OF SIMULACRA

The second order of simulacra raises the level of control by attempting to restrict the play of appearances and impose a higher order of equivalence. This is achieved through production as both economic/industrial practice and linguistic, referential practice, 'the principle of operativity' (Baudrillard, 1993a: 54). While the first order functions through a general equivalent at the external level of form, the second order finds a general equivalent within class or market relations: the exchange of commodities in terms of economic exchange-value. Industrially produced or 'serial' signs exist without symbolic obligations. Further, as the ultimate 'origin' or reference of such objects is simply not an issue for mass produced objects, 'The extinction of the original reference alone facilitates the general law of equivalences, that is to say, the very possibility of production' (1993a: 53).

Signs characteristic of the second order are 'crude, dull, industrial, repetitive, echoless, functional and efficient' (1993a: 57) where signs of the first order were 'magical, diabolical, illusory . . . enchanting'. The second order of simulacra is highly unstable, indeed 'ephemeral', because it almost immediately shades into the third order:

> Serial production gives way to generation through models . . . all forms change from the moment that they are no longer mechanically reproduced, but conceived according to their very reproducibility . . . from a generative core called a model.
>
> (Baudrillard, 1993a: 56)

THE THIRD ORDER OF SIMULACRA: HYPERREALITY

Everything changes with the device of simulation.

(Baudrillard, 1983: 21)

[H]yperreality . . . puts an end to the real as referential by exalting it as model.

(Baudrillard, 1983: 85)

The status of the sign is transformed again with the third order of simulacra: *representation* tends to be replaced by *simulation*. Simulation is distinct from representation because signifiers lose their attachment to signifieds (the mental 'construction' of meaning inside our heads) as meaning is generated by relations between signifiers ('models') rather than in our reflective or 'inner' dialectical thought processes. Further signs (or rather pre-modelled signifiers) are disarticulated from referents because models *do not have referents*. Even if we assert that 'referentiality' is only ever an illusion generated by the apparatus of language (as Baudrillard does; see 1981: 143–63), the situation is transformed by the proliferation of signifiers lacking even an illusory referentiality (2005d: 67–73).

For example, the meaning of the term 'Gucci' is determined by relations among other signifiers such as 'Prada', 'Timberland', 'Marks and Spencer' and the like. Any 'referent', such as a sweatshop factory complex in the Third World, is bypassed by the play of signifiers: 'sexy', 'chic', 'rugged', 'good value' etc. These constructions are models without direct or stable reference. Further, many signifiers, particularly virtual or computer-generated images, render the notion of the referent entirely meaningless. Most of us are familiar with the virtual signifier 'Lara Croft', but when this simulation was simulated by the celebrity signifier Angelina Jolie, the latter, already improbably proportioned, was digitally enhanced to resemble more closely the former. It is meaningless to search for the 'real' world referent of either 'Lara Croft' or 'Angelina Jolie': both are brands, sets of modelled signifiers designed to circulate through the corporate media/entertainment loop. Representation does not cease or become impossible, indeed it even remains dominant, but, Baudrillard contends, simulation becomes increasingly prevalent.

Without the stable equivalence of sign–referent and signifier–signified, meaning becomes highly unstable, and binary distinctions implode, reverse or become radically uncertain in their meaning(s). The binary oppositions that structured the second order, and enabled the very opposition between the real and its representation upon which the notion of the 'real' depends, become increasingly volatile and uncertain. Baudrillard develops brief and somewhat repetitive examples with the oppositions of true/false, beautiful/ugly, art/anti-art, therapy/anti-therapy. The meanings attaching to the first or privileged term are changing and unstable – just what constitutes truth, beauty, art? In the era of simulation the second or negative pole of the opposition is deployed to energise or revivify the oppositions by feeding into the first term, rather than opposing it. For example, the fashion industry draws upon what was formerly considered ugly to generate new or alternative notions of beauty. In the past decade we have seen extreme thinness, 'heroin chic' and clothes that look worn, ripped or dirty. These strategies supplement the tried and tested, the routine and hackneyed, and actually protect the meaningfulness of the very principle of fashion and the possibility of capturing and promoting 'the beautiful', so maintaining its 'reality' and allowing more and more fashion to be produced and consumed.

In another favoured example, Baudrillard insists that psychiatry, and the therapy industry generally, received an injection of new life from the anti-psychiatry lobby of the 1960s and 1970s. Rather than diminishing psychiatry as a branch of knowledge, the critiques produced by the anti-psychiatry movement associated with R. D. Laing and others were incorporated and actually expanded and nourished the discipline of psychiatry. The critiques acted like an inoculation, making the discipline stronger, resistant to further critique and somehow more . . . *real*. The terms of binary oppositions come to have a 'tactical' role in the third order. Neither term is really distinctive; instead they operate together to maintain or simulate 'reality'. Yet this tactical operation actually increases the instability of meanings: in time the energy of the oppositions or distinction is weakened to the point where their supposed referents can no longer be retrieved. In other words, beauty and ugliness, art and anti-art, true and false become indefinable – this is the moment of *implosion.* By attempting to secure the 'real' and reality, signs are pushed into hyperreality. Once the binary oppositions weaken, losing their distinctiveness, *the object takes its revenge.* The object eludes attempts at codification and becomes what Baudrillard terms 'transpolitical' (1990b: 25–70).

ASPECTS OF THE THIRD ORDER: DNA, DIGITALITY AND THE TEST

> [T]here are no longer any questions to which there are no answers.
>
> (Baudrillard, 1993a: 64)

> [P]olls, tests, the referendum, media are devices which no longer belong to the dimension of representation, but to one of simulation. They no longer have a referent in view, but a model.
>
> (Baudrillard, 1983: 20)

In developing the notion of the third order Baudrillard draws upon a number of scientific concepts, a strategy characteristic of his later work. DNA is referred to extensively because it embodies, for Baudrillard, the moment when the code is 'discovered' *within.* The capitalist production of the second order enabled equivalence, or coding, at the level of economic relations, but the DNA code is inscribed inside our bodies, 'hardwired' into our cells, and therefore inescapable. The DNA map determines who we are, it is *the map that precedes the territory.* Human destiny is no longer meaningful because the genetic code has written life in advance. Baudrillard insists that DNA is, like capital, a metaphysical principle, and he theorises it as a cultural form rather than a fact of nature.[5] DNA, for Baudrillard, is the ultimate 'homogeneous substance' or principle of general equivalence; it is the ultimate in plural difference because it is a single universal scale on which all life can be plotted, measured and compared.

The third order allows a 'perfected' degree of control through 'prediction, simulation, programmed anticipation and indeterminate mutation' (1993a: 60). By eliminating the 'real' or referentiality any 'real' contradiction or tension in the social order is effectively displaced, Baudrillard contends, but he does not assert that the social order is free from discontent, violence and hatred. These exist in abundance, simmering below the surface (of signs) and frequently erupting in paradoxical non-dialectical or post-ideological form (1990b: 34–50, 1998a: 174–9). The era of class-based ideological opposition, the binary dialectic of bourgeoisie and proletariat, is fast receding. Empirical accounts may of course still discover 'evidence' of such binary conflicts but this does not invalidate or falsify Baudrillard's theory because he acknowledges that the second order still exists. However, its 'energy' has dissipated as the system attempts to secure itself through a new principle of general equivalence. Signs of freedom and equality are everywhere and prevent discontent being expressed in dialectical or 'progressive' form because any feeling or perception of discontent is immediately transcribed by the code into sign-form: the needs and wants of the consumer system. The structural law of value enables the limitless reproducibility of signs from pre-existing models.

Baudrillard's second major exemplar of the third order is digitality. The shift from analogue to digital technologies fits very neatly within Baudrillard's scheme. Analogue technologies, from the Greek *analogon* meaning 'proportionate', have existed for many centuries. Analogue provides a measure of variations in a property through proportionate variations in a medium. Barometers and thermometers are examples: in the latter temperature is measured using a graduated tube of mercury or alcohol, that expands or contracts according to the rise and fall of temperature.

Analogue technologies, then, are based on the principles of similarity, proportion and resemblance. Digital technologies, by contrast, operate through coded differences rather than proportion or similarity. Information is translated into a binary code and must then be decoded before it can be deciphered by human beings: the code is fundamentally inhuman. For Baudrillard, binary digital codes invest all aspects of social life: communication, work, education but also intimacy, sexuality and play. Digitality 'haunts all the messages and signs of our society' (1993a: 61–2) because in the phase of sign value all activities can be modelled as the transmission of codes. Particularly important for Baudrillard is the binary form of the test: the question and answer or stimulus/response.

> The test is everywhere the fundamental social form of control, which works by infinitely dividing practices and responses . . . the cycles of meaning become infinitely shorter in the cycles of the question/ answer . . . the total neutralisation of signifieds by the code . . . tests and referenda are . . . perfect forms of simulation: the question induces the answer, it is *designated* in advance.
>
> (Baudrillard, 1993a: 62, emphasis added
> in English translation)

The test operates in two directions. Mediated objects and information 'already result from a selection, an edited sequence of camera angles,

they have already tested "reality" and have only asked those questions to which it has responded' (1993a: 63). 'Reality', then, which is a
product of second order representations and consists of binary oppositions, is further reduced to stable, equivalent oppositions, rather than
unstable, ambivalent ones. Second, Baudrillard asserts, 'thus tested
"reality" tests you' (ibid.). That is, we are tested to decode meaning
in terms of the code. The code itself, as meta-principle, is not decoded
because it sets the terms for possible decoding.

A common variant of the test is the opinion poll. Opinion polls,
Baudrillard argues, are not 'real' or unreal but exist beyond this binary
opposition – *they are hyperreal*. The hyperreal is a state 'beyond' dialectics, not in the sense of passing through dialectics, but a state where the
dialectic and its distinctive binary oppositions collapse and implode.
With opinion polls, meaning, as far as it exists at all, is present from
the beginning of the operation; it is contained in the question. The
question is an ultimatum because you are expected to accept the terms
of the question; indeed, you must accept them simply to respond, to have
your say. You are, of course, at liberty to answer 'no' or 'strongly disagree',
but in doing so you accede to *the form* of the test, representing yourself through a preset binary or Likert scale of simplified, reductive
choices (1998a: 168). Significantly, any dissent or critique of the way the
questions and answers are set up utterly fails to challenge the form
of the test; either you refuse to answer at all and are eliminated from
the field of enquiry or your criticisms are absorbed by the apparatus
of the test through the category 'Don't know'. Opinion polls do not
'capture' meaning or opinion, they simulate it, they do not replace a
lived, meaningful reality with an image of it, they simulate something
that is not, and never was, there. Polled public opinion is 'both the medium
and message' (1993a: 66) because 'medium and message can only be
separated in the second order' (1993a: 84 n. 4).

Indeterminacy and implosion affect all spheres, according to
Baudrillard, particularly those institutions that are central to the
second order and its notion of 'reality': history, economics, science,
culture and politics. Baudrillard insists that 'the political sphere loses
its specificity as soon as it enters the media's polling game' (1993a: 66).
The two-party systems that dominate party politics in most democratic
countries mirror the binary code such that politics 'dies from the
over-regulated play of its distinct oppositions . . . duopoly is the completed form of monopoly' (ibid.). The structural law enables a regulated
play of oppositions, a simulation of choice, of difference: one or the
other political party, gay or straight, state or market, public or private,
budget or luxury. One pole questions the other, it supplements the other,

it *completes* the other at the level of content. But the form of the binary opposition is not questioned, it is placed outside the play of signs and simulations: 'the closure of a system in the vertigo of doubling' (1993a: 70).

There is a fundamental shift in the nature of the sign and its capacity to represent that defines the shift from the second order of 'reality' to the third order of 'hyperreality'. The second order's principle of equivalence, market capital, was a powerful controlling force. However, it was prone to conflicts and contradictions, making it vulnerable to Marxist critique. As models precede 'reality', they precede conflicts, contradictions, debate, contestation. The 'real' was 'that of which it is possible to provide an equivalent reproduction', the hyperreal is 'that which is always already reproduced' from a model (1993a: 73).

THE PRECESSION OF SIMULACRA

Nothing has come to the end of its history, or will henceforth any more, for nothing escapes this precession of simulacra.
(Baudrillard, 1983: 86)

Baudrillard's influential essay 'The Precession of Simulacra', first published in 1978, extends and clarifies this line of argument. The notion of the model is expanded through a reading of Borges's (1975: 131) fable 'Of Exactitude in Science', about a vast map commissioned by the ruler of an ancient empire. The map was constructed on a scale of 1:1 – an exact copy of the territory of the empire. Yet, as the empire falls into decline, as all empires do, the map rots away too, reduced to shreds flapping in the sands of the desert. Baudrillard presents this as an exemplary fable of the *second* order. The third order involves a significant transformation: simulation is *not* a mapping of territories. The cartographic exercise involves two separate phenomena: a *territory* preceding the *map* and clearly distinguishable from it, of which the map is a two-dimensional representation. Yet in the third order 'the map precedes the territory – a precession of simulacra. So now it is the "real" territory that slowly rots away with vestiges here and there, this is the desert of the real' (Baudrillard, 1994a: 1).

The clear difference between map and territory, between real and model, dissolves or implodes. The 'reality' now increasingly replaced by the hyperreal was, in itself, no more than a construction of the second order. The 'real' was the result of the 'structural effect of the disjunction' between signifier and signified (1993a: 133) dependent on the Saussurian bar that established the opposition between 'real' and 'imaginary'. It is our ability to represent – to recount, to reconstruct in writing, speech, and other media – that persuades us that there is a 'real' of which our representations are a copy or approximation. In this sense 'reality' is the 'imaginary of representation' (1994a: 2). With the third order, however, our techniques of representation are transformed, the 'imaginary co-extensivity of real and representation is lost' (1994a: 2). Simulation does not 're-represent' because it eliminates the distance or space between the 'real' and its representation. Simulation generates meaning from models that pre-exist experience or perception of the 'real'.

THE MASSES: END OF THE SOCIAL/END OF THE POLITICAL

> [T]he only genuine problem today is the silence of the mass.
> (Baudrillard, 1983: 23)

What becomes of society in the third order? Baudrillard was, after all, a professional sociologist for twenty years. In an influential essay of 1978 entitled *In the Shadow of the Silent Majorities or The End of the Social*, Baudrillard develops the notion of the mass and the masses, arguing that the social has imploded into the mass (*la masse*). The terms 'mass' and 'masses' have, by and large, been dropped from the vocabulary of sociology and media and communications studies because they seem to imply a patronising and derogatory attitude to the consumers and audiences of media content. Baudrillard reappropriates these terms, as with his use of the term 'savage' to describe 'non-Western' cultures and 'seduction' to describe feminine behaviour. The term 'mass' ridicules the niceties of liberal humanist thought. The latter, Baudrillard insists, deploy a range of 'sensitive' and 'politically correct' terminology that, ultimately, forcibly transcribes all 'otherness' on a single scale of (European, capitalist) values and so hides a deep contempt for those 'others' it claims to liberate and empower (1993b: 124–38). Baudrillard reappropriates these terms much as black people reappropriate the term 'nigger' and homosexuals the terms 'queer' and 'poof'. And since Baudrillard claims that he is 'mass' and that he is 'feminine', it is problematic to disallow him this reappropriation. He refers to the mass, or the masses in the plural, multiple and collective (1983: 46). There is very little elitism in Baudrillard's position: 'we form a mass, living most of the time in panic or haphazardly, above and beyond any meaning' (1983: 11).

The masses, then, are 'you, me and everyone' (1983: 46, trans. modified). The term 'masses' does not imply that people are stupid, docile and undifferentiated 'receivers' of media content, because by acting as 'mass' the system is actively defied and disrupted. The masses' strategies of defiance include the power of silence, of non-response, the power of inertia and neutralisation, and the strategy of hyperconformity, of an ecstatic fascination and total self-absorption that 'gives' back more than the system requires or expects: the potlatching counter-gift. The functioning of the system, then, Baudrillard maintains, can be destabilised by an unswerving conformity to its expectations.

The term mass (*la masse*) connotes matter, majority and earth, as in the earthing of an electrical current. This rich field of meaning does not simply enable a series of puns, it also allows direct and original argument. Baudrillard contends that the mass or matter of the mass/majority 'earths' or neutralises the energy of the social and political system:

> the masses have no history to write, neither past nor future, they have no virtual energies to release, nor any desire to fulfil: their strength is actual, in the present, and sufficient unto itself. It consists in their silence, in their capacity to absorb and neutralise, already superior to any power acting upon them. [The masses are] . . . an unacceptable and unintelligible figure of implosion.
>
> (Baudrillard, 1983: 3)[6]

This is a revealing passage. The masses possess the symbolic strategy of silence, of annulment and of actual, immediate exchange. Although the masses are clearly part of the system, not its outside or 'barred' other, they are a defiant, reversive, implosive effect *of the system*. The system of the sign-code, of consumer capitalism, of the global world order expands exponentially but has, in the process, destabilised itself, becoming vulnerable to internally generated reversive effects (1990b: 1–70). For example, capitalist media corporations generate 'celebrities' for our consumption, but public fascination with celebrity exceeds any rationality of planned consumption. Celebrities are hounded, sometimes to their deaths. We delight in watching their ritualised humiliation on 'survival' 'reality' TV shows.[7] In the UK more young people voted for the 'instant' celebrities of 'reality' TV than in the general election of 2005. It could be argued that the democratic political system benefits from such popular distractions: for example, allowing it to pursue undemocratic wars relatively unnoticed. Yet voter apathy has reached such a pitch that the political classes are now clearly concerned for the principles of representation and legitimacy and voting in elections has been made easier, or more like voting for a celebrity, with the introduction of postal and on-line voting. So the increasing silence of the masses disturbs the system. By contrast, class-based political movements seem ineffectual and easily assimilable. For example, the newspaper of the British Communist Party is stocked alongside the tabloids in supermarkets, reduced to one coded consumer choice among the range of choices: bare breasts, free DVD or Marxist politics? Single issue social movements, such as the Green Party and gay rights movement, are superficially (or semiotically) assimilated into mainstream party politics; for example, enabling the revitalisation and 'rebranding' of the British Conservative Party under David Cameron. This for Baudrillard is the 'disappearance' of politics. The disappearance is not total or definitive; it is not the end of history but the hyperreal *illusion* of the end. Indeed, '*History will not come to an end*' (1994b: 27, original emphasis) because its signs are infinitely recyclable. Events with a symbolic dimension, unanticipated and uncoded, were in short supply, for a time, after the fall of the Berlin Wall in 1989 but Baudrillard never precluded a return of symbolic social or political events in the future. Indeed, he anticipated such events (1994b: 28–33, 120) and termed 9/11 'the absolute event' (2003b: 4).

The political sphere emerged, according to Baudrillard, during the Renaissance with the collapse of ecclesiastic power. Politics, initially, was 'only a pure game of signs' consisting of strategies unburdened with notions of 'truth'. Only in the eighteenth century, after the French Revolution, did politics become concerned with representation, specifically with the representation of the social based on the ' "fundamental signified" – the will of the people' (1983: 17). Here 'the social' as distinct, circumscribed field or unit of analysis is born. The social, then, had a beginning, and a relatively recent one at that, and now it may be coming to an end, occupying only a brief phase of human history. Baudrillard's position contrasts sharply with functionalist, Marxist and critical theory, which tends to assume the unproblematic or transparent nature of the category of the social. For these approaches the social becomes a point of 'absolute reference, of omnipresence and diffraction in all the interstices of physical and mental space' (1983: 18). The social is everything and everything is social. At this point the specificity and meaning of the term is lost and, according to Baudrillard, the energy of the social is reversed: the result is 'THE MASS'.

THE SOCIAL AND SOCIOLOGY

The system constructs the 'social' from the remainders of broken and barred symbolic exchange, but it has, according to Baudrillard, produced, accumulated, amassed *too much social*. As a result the social, the idea of the social, implodes into the 'mass', the 'black hole which engulfs the social' (1983: 4). As with symbolic exchange, 'mass' is not a concept because it is 'without attribute, predicate, quality, reference . . . it has no sociological "reality". It has nothing to do with any real population' (1983: 4–5). In developing this new position Baudrillard steps up his attack on sociology, he claims to 'reverse' sociological understanding, which remains 'realist':

> Sociology can only depict the expansion of the social and its vicissitudes. It survives only on the positive and definite hypothesis of the social. The reabsorption, the implosion of the social escapes it. The hypothesis of the death of the social is also that of its own death.
> (Baudrillard, 1983: 4)

'Mass' is not, of course, a 'good' sociological concept. Sociology uses what its practitioners believe to be more 'subtle' categories and definitions, based, for example, on social class and income levels. Baudrillard's rejection of such categories is interesting, in part because he had used them himself to good effect, earlier in his career (1981: 29–62). The rejection of categories of class expresses a continuing and increasingly dramatic shift in Baudrillard's methodology. Apparently 'acritical' notions such as mass are turned against academe, deployed against the grain, against propriety, against banality. Eccentric and improper styles of thought and writing are vital, for Baudrillard, because the system is so adept at absorbing critique, at neutralising resistance. The capitalist system actively encourages critique while neutralising it by transforming it into sign or information form, Baudrillard insists (1975, 2005d: 132–3). For example, Marxism has long been taught in UK secondary schools. In 2006 the Blair government introduced A-level critical thinking to accompany its earlier 'innovation' A-level citizenship. Far from being threatened by critique, the system insists upon more and more of it. Critical or revolutionary thought does not remain so for long. The system expands to incorporate it, then sells it as sign, abstracted and awarded back to those seeking to critique it: the would-be critics always indebted to the system.

Methodologically, Baudrillard attempts to stay ahead of the system, to accelerate his concepts at a faster rate than the acceleration of the system, not to describe or represent the system. Instead he draws out 'empirical' fragments and uses them to push his ideas further and faster than the system can expand to assimilate them.

If the concepts of sociology are terms of the code 'preserving a certain code of analysis', then clearly Baudrillard requires alternatives.

One of his strategies was to ransack the humanities for odd, abandoned or paradoxical notions: kula, potlatch, mass, seduction, evil. Later Baudrillard appropriated scientific notions such as the virus, 'strange attractors' and fractals. These alternative concepts do not theorise 'on the plane of the real' (1993a: 36), they do not attempt to explain or understand things as they are because they *are* as the code arranges them. Baudrillard's methodology is to defy, provoke, hijack or derail the terms of the code by reopening the space of symbolic exchange: symbolic exchange between the system and its objects, between his writing and his readers, between theory and the world.

MULTIPLE HYPOTHESES OF THE END OF THE SOCIAL

What is the social? Or, more accurately, what was the social? The social, for Baudrillard, is formed from 'abstract instances' cobbled together from the ruins of the symbolic order. But the very drive to abstraction and formalisation into separate spheres and dynamics 'devours' the symbolic relations on which the social depends. This is a paradoxical situation:

> if the social is both destroyed by what produces it (the media, information) and re-absorbed by what it produces (the masses) it follows that its definition is empty, and that this term which serves as universal alibi for every discourse, no longer analyses anything, no longer designates anything.
>
> (Baudrillard, 1983: 66)

For Baudrillard the notion of social relations is not a universal: 'There were *societies without the social*, just as there were societies without history. Networks of symbolic ties were precisely neither "relational" nor "social"' (1983: 67, original emphasis). To speak of social relations, then, 'already presupposes a serious abstraction' (ibid.), a breaking into discrete elements based on a comparative equivalent – the 'good' of society, or usefulness to society. Baudrillard insists that, 'Ultimately, things have never functioned socially, but symbolically, magically . . . there are only stakes, defiances . . . something which does not proceed via a social relation' (1983: 69).

Baudrillard presents three irreconcilable, yet simultaneously possible, hypotheses of the social. First, '*The social has basically never existed* . . . there has never been any "social relation" [and] . . . nothing has ever functioned socially' (1983: 70–1). The social and social relations have always been a simulation, but the problem we face today is one of 'brutal de-simulation' (ibid.) where simulation models break down. Second, Baudrillard speculates, perhaps '*The social has really existed, it exists more and more* [but] the social itself is only residue' (1983: 72). Here the social is presented as broken fragments or debris of the symbolic order and all social 'value' is the accumulation of unexchanged residues: 'value in the economic order, phantasm in the psychic order, signification in the linguistic order . . . and the social in the social order' (1983: 90 n. 9). Following Foucault (1977), Baudrillard suggests that, initially, only the remainders or 'left-overs', the sick and lunatics, were taken charge of by the social, followed by children, the homeless, the jobless, with a final expansion to incorporate women, then minority 'races' and 'sexualities', until 'Everybody is completely excluded and taken in charge, completely disintegrated and socialised' (1983: 74). This is an exclusion *by inclusion*, an occupation of mental terrain.

Baudrillard's third hypothesis is that '*The social has well and truly existed, but does not exist anymore*' (1983: 82). These hypotheses, clearly, are irreconcilable, as Baudrillard states: 'The social has not always been a delusion, as in the first hypothesis, nor a remainder, as in the second . . . [but exists in] the narrow gap of second order simulacra' (ibid.). The social, according to this view, 'dies' in the third order, replaced by 'the sociality of contact', a world of networks and connectivity where individuals are merely 'terminals of information'. It is vital to emphasise that Baudrillard thinks not that people are only terminals of information, but that the system figures them as such. The sociality of the third order is one of contact, connectivity and interactivity – not of determinate relations or meaningful exchanges.

Baudrillard's notions of simulation, deterrence and hyperreality are still, in part at least, critical notions. That is to say that the system, and its key institutions of control – politics, finance, education, media and advertising corporations – still understand the world in terms of the second order, of representation and referentiality. For Baudrillard these institutions have precipitated a partial shift into a third order where representation and referentiality do not function. Indeed, these institutions actually push the system further and further into hyperreality by multiplying signifiers that are supposedly attached to stable signifieds but, in their very multiplicity, actually loosen the relationship between signifier and signified. There is a law of diminishing returns at work; the harder the system works to persuade us that we live in reality, by multiplying signs of reality, the less we are convinced that these signs refer to anything real:

Instead of transforming the mass into energy, information produces even more mass. Instead of informing, as it claims, instead

of giving form and structure, information neutralises even further
the 'social field'. Immense energy is expended . . . in maintaining this
simulation of the social and in preventing it from totally imploding.
(Baudrillard, 1983: 25–6)

RESISTANCE OR DEFIANCE?

The social, Baudrillard argues, can no longer be represented, it can only
be simulated. The silence of the silent majorities 'isn't a silence which
does not speak, it is a silence which refuses to be spoken for in its name
. . . far from being a form of alienation, it is an absolute weapon'
(1983: 22). The masses, for Baudrillard, are not subjects (of history, of
nation-states or of desire) *but objects*. The masses are incited to speak,
to participate and interact, they are polled and consulted, they are flattered
by the media and by politicians – endlessly being told that they are 'sophisticated', aware, not easily duped. Everything is offered, and all that is
required in return is that they *be* social, that they are cultured, educated
and responsible. But they are not: this is the 'retaliation' or 'revenge'
of the object (ibid.). Like the object of scientific study, the masses elude
any 'objective' form of enquiry because they 'send back the same conforming signals, the same coded responses, with the same exasperating,
endless conformity' (1983: 33). Asked a question, they will conform and
reply to it, but this produces only a 'circular truth'; not a truth about
the world but a 'truth' about a question.

Influenced by Alfred Jarry's pataphysics, defined by Jarry (1996: 22)
as 'the science of imaginary solutions', Baudrillard describes the masses
as 'a pataphysics of the social' (1983: 34). Sociology, as 'cumbersome
metaphysics of the social' (ibid.), cannot comprehend the masses.
Sociology, like any science, is metaphysical because it is based upon
certain founding beliefs or a faith that practitioners must hold in order
for their discipline to function: 'The scientist cannot believe that
matter, or living beings, do not respond "objectively" to the questions
he puts, or that they respond to them too objectively for his questions
to be sound' (1983: 34). This is the problematic of hyper-conformity
Baudrillard draws from Jarry (1996, 1999). Resistance, then, can take
many forms: silence and 'withdrawing into the private' are, Baudrillard
asserts, part of a long-standing resistance to 'the social', compulsory
education, policing, medicine, social security and information. Hyper-
conformity, it seems, is a more contemporary strategy of resistance,
one that is closely linked to the mass-mediated, digital age. The masses
'accept everything and re-direct everything *en bloc* into the spectacular,
without requiring any other code, without requiring any meaning,

ultimately without resistance, but making everything slide into an indeterminate sphere' (1983: 43–4).

Baudrillard does not neglect to theorise resistance, as both Kellner (1989: 216) and Callinicos (1989: 80–7, 144–8) claim. Instead he theorises in a non- or post-Marxist manner, which, in itself, is unforgivable to Marxists. Yet for Baudrillard effective resistance cannot be dialectical because synthesis or resolution is the very dynamic of the capitalist system as it constantly revolutionises itself through the sign code. In other words critique is rapidly absorbed by simulation: accused of racism, sexism, homophobia or exploitation of the 'Third' World, the system will immediately generate signs to the contrary. For Baudrillard the only strategy remaining is the annulment of the meaning of signs into indeterminacy. Further, the masses 'know there is no liberation, and that the system is only abolished by pushing it into hyperlogic' (1983: 46). While the supposed apathy and inertia of the people was useful to the system of power in the first and second orders, now the system needs to nurture active audiences and active participatory citizen-consumers. The masses refuse. They throw apathy and inertia back at the system, now 'doubled' into hyper-apathy, hyper-inertia. The masses are a force of reversal and annulment, an 'inverse simulation' held out to the system 'to be swallowed up in' (1983: 29–30):

> Defiance is not a dialectic . . . it is a process of *extermination* of the structural positions of each *term*, of the subject position of each of the antagonists, and in particular of the one who hurls the challenge. . . . Exchange value is no longer its logic. Its logic abandons positions of value and positions of meaning. The protagonist of defiance is always in the suicidal position, but it is a triumphant suicide: it is by the destruction of value, the destruction of meaning (one's own, their own) that the other is forced into a never equivalent, ever escalating response.
>
> (Baudrillard, 1983: 69–70)

In order to understand Baudrillard's thinking here we need to draw out the relationship between the remainder, residue or surplus and the notion of defiance. For Baudrillard utility was the dominant principle of the first order and, far from being surpassed, 'use and use-value constitute a fundamental ethics. But it exists only in a simulation of shortage and calculation' (1983: 78). Utilitarianism is a 'cruel and disillusioning moral convention' (ibid.). Life is reduced to use-value; death is 'sequestered', separated and made irreversible. Defiance and suicide 'reverse' death, they re-engage the system's construction of life/death at the level of symbolic relations. Suicidal defiance 'would abolish life as use-value' (ibid.) by giving life symbolic stakes, giving it the force of destiny, which is intolerable to the system. Further, 'it is not that everything should be reversed; just the remainder should be' (1983: 78). This is a somewhat cryptic remark, but, for Baudrillard,

> The social exists on the double basis of the production of remainders and on their eradication. If all wealth were sacrificed, people would lose a sense of the real. If all wealth became disposable, people would lose a sense of the useful and the useless. The social exists to take care of the useless consumption of remainders so that individuals can be assigned to a useful management of their lives.
>
> (Baudrillard, 1983: 78)

It is this assignation of useful (self) management that must be defied, and it is only defied effectively, according to Baudrillard, by challenging the system's separation of life and death into binary oppositions. The system of equivalences – sign-value, exchange-value and use-value – must be shattered. The system safeguards equivalence through 'controlled squandering' (1983: 79), which, we can assume, applies to the ceremonial system of potlatch as well as to modern consumer societies. Modern societies no longer perform sacrifices as such but they do develop many means of waste, in war, in consumption, in road accidents and in Baudrillard's examples: space exploration, missile systems, supersonic air travel. However, Baudrillard suggests, the sudden and disproportionate 'pouring back' of surplus into the system threatens its ruin. These vague, underdeveloped but interesting speculations seem to have been shelved for a time before re-emerging in Baudrillard's theorisation of terrorism.

5

The Body, Sexuality and Seduction

[T]he only drive that is really liberated is the drive to buy.
(Baudrillard, 1998a: 134)

PORNO/INTRO

I'm staying at a friend's house. He is away. I suspect he has porn videos so I search for them. He has. Several of the DVDs have an R18 (R = restricted) certificate. I have never seen an R18 film. Excited, I choose the one that appears to have the highest production values. There are many scenes to choose from but no 'film' as such. I choose a girl-on-girl scene. I am very excited. Previously I had only seen images of women pretending to be sexually attracted to each other: female pop singers desperate for media exposure kissing each other lightly while somehow remaining several feet apart, TV soap actresses claiming to 'break taboos' by kissing half-heartedly on screen – a hackneyed collision of political correctness and media-saturation. But now I was going to see the real thing!

A young dark-skinned woman is bending forwards over the side of an antique American car. She is naked from the waist down with her back to the camera. An athletic fair-skinned woman strides up to her, kneels behind her and, with her hands, spreads the woman's buttocks further apart. The camera angle switches to a close-up of the black woman's anus and labia and the white woman's tongue swipes across her exposed skin. And then . . . nothing. Nothing happens. The black woman does not respond with pleasure or arousal. The white woman does not respond with pleasure or arousal. Their faces are fixed in a grimace, and their bodies as if in *rigor mortis*, the only movement is that of a tongue over an anus. As if in admission of failure the camera pans out to other scenes of 'copulation' taking place in a garage. None of it looks real, despite – or perhaps because of – the prevalence of exposed genitalia. Were these women making love, having sex, screwing, fucking? I remain uncertain, unconvinced. The scenes were somehow less real than glossy pop music promos or tea-time soap operas. There was little evidence of desire or pleasure, or even arousal, and certainly not of 'liberation'. I decide to watch John Boorman's *Excalibur* (1981) instead and, as I switch the discs over, a vague recollection of Baudrillard's book *Seduction* comes to me. Yes, he was right all along! Strip away the illusions, the rules, the rituals, the veils and you get not 'reality' but *nothing*.

Baudrillard's interest in theorising the body dates back to his earliest work. He produced a sociological analysis of the status of the body in consumer society long before 'the sociology of the body' was being established as a major topic within the discipline. Baudrillard describes the body, in its toning, training, treatment and supposed 'liberation', as the 'finest' object of the object system. The body, then, is central to an understanding of consumer society and the form of gender relations and of sexuality that it promotes. For Baudrillard the body is understood as 'cultural fact' (1998a: 129), not as a biological or natural 'fact'.[1] In other words, the ways in which we understand our bodies, or our embodiment, depends upon the culture in which we live. In a capitalist society, Baudrillard points out, the body is understood as being the private property of the individual. That is, the 'cultural representation' of the body in capitalist societies is of the body as a form of *capital* owned by the individual. Yet it is also *a fetish*. According to Baudrillard, the body, in capitalist media-saturated societies, is our private fetish. That is, bodies seem to take on a magical dimension, as in the 'perfect body' or the body 'to die for'. The body is not repressed, in any straightforward sense, by the capitalist system; it is constructed or fashioned to the requirements of the capitalist system. The body becomes central to the system's project of the integration of subjects through their managed *self-investment*, both economic and psychical, in their body.

'SACRIFICIAL PRACTICES'

In *The Consumer Society* (1998a) Baudrillard argues that we produce, maintain, modify and enhance our bodies *as signs*. Bodies are sculpted and honed to signify 'health', 'fitness', 'sexiness', 'youthfulness'. These things are qualities or attributes of signs, not of a supposed 'reality' of the body. A body may *signify* fitness without being medically healthy – as in the case of professional body-builders, who frequently collapse from dehydration before contests. Further, pre-pubescent girls often dress in a way that signifies 'sexiness' before sexual maturation, and clearly 'youthfulness' is often signified by the bodies of the rich and famous, when we know them to be aged. More generally, competent members of the consumer society are required to 'signify' fashionability, to look fashionable and constantly to update 'their look'. The female body, particularly the youthful female body, Baudrillard contends, is subjected to this process of controlled or administered 'liberation'. In the third order of simulacra, roughly coincident with the consumer society, the skin of the female body is less an 'irruption of nudity' than a 'prestige garment' and 'fashion reference' (1998a: 130). As the body is 'sealed in signs', 'doubled in signification', 'there is no nudity other than that which is reduplicated in signs' (1993a: 105).

But Baudrillard's analysis goes far beyond a critique of sign-consumption. The body in consumer society, Baudrillard claims, is an 'object of salvation' and is subjected to 'sacrificial practices' (1998a: 129). That is, we make sacrifices to our bodies: time, money and energy are expended on our bodies. This is not merely profane work but a *moral duty*, a 'resacralisation': a transformation of the sacred, not a rejection of the sacred.

A spirit of moral terrorism presides over the body, all the more so now that it is supposedly 'liberated'. The body must be put on a diet, it must be exercised, it is enjoined to drink at least eight glasses of water and eat five portions of fresh fruit or vegetables each day. If we fail to perform such 'bodily devotions' we are punished, directly, by our bodies: we will look older, we will get sick, we will grow fat. If we look unattractive or die early we have only ourselves to blame, or so the story goes. The body and its sexual desires are not, any longer, repressed because the body itself is the 'maleficent, repressive agency' (1998a: 130). We do not repress our bodies, our bodies repress us! Thus the 'myth of liberation' obscures what is actually, Baudrillard insists, an increase in exploitation and control. Our 'voluntary' labour directed at self-management and maximization of our bodies is 'a more profoundly alien-ated labour than the exploitation of the body as labour power' (1998a:

132). The 'sexuality' that is 'liberated' is sexuality as coded exchange of signs, of 'calculated sexual signification' rather than of 'intimacy and sensuality' (1998a: 133). Consumerism, advertising and fashion, Baudrillard argues, deny the body as flesh in their evocation of *the body as sign*: the scrubbed, toned, perfected body is the body as sign. The semiotic reduction of the body to signs is a 'deterrence'. That is, the subversive, anti-economic, erotic charge of *bodies in exchange* is 'disavowed', removed or managed through the commercial exchange of bodies in terms of abstracted sign-value – of 'beauty' or 'fitness' – and these are things that can be bought and sold, manipulated and enhanced. Further, our symbolic relation to ourselves, to our 'otherness', is altered because our flaws and imperfections can be surgically removed, they can be cosmetically or digitally enhanced, 'airbrushed', perfected (2002b: 51–6).

Baudrillard emphasises the twisting together of puritan morality and modern hedonism (1998a: 129–50) in the society of consumption. Where in the past (the second order?) expressions of bodies' desires had suggested a 'critique of the sacred . . . a battling for humanity against God', today, by contrast, 'The cult of the body no longer stands in contradiction to the cult of the soul: it is the successor to that cult and heir to its ideological function' (1998a: 136). The naked, desiring body in its 'raw' sexuality had once seemed challenging, subversive and dangerous: intolerable to the authorities of the church, the state, education, the family. Great writers of the period – D. H. Lawrence, Anaïs Nin, Georges Bataille – shocked polite society with tales of erotic adventure, of the pleasures of the flesh, which could not be limited or denied by morality. Baudrillard seems to regard the version of 'sexuality' or eroticism promoted by such writers as genuinely subversive, but only for a particular, and now surpassed, phase of 'bourgeois-puritan' morality:

> it is only under repression that the body had strong sexual potential: it then appeared as a captivating demand. Abandoned to the signs of fashion, the body is sexually disenchanted, it becomes a mannequin – it is in fashion that sex is lost as difference but generalised as reference.
>
> (Baudrillard, 1993a: 97)

There is no subversion or challenge in the representation of sexuality as 'generalised reference'. For example, in the pop music videos of Madonna, Christina Aguilera or Snoop Dogg, there is nothing subversive and few except the artists themselves would, today, maintain otherwise. Yet there is more explicit sex in the Snoop Dogg video 'Doggy-style' than in the entire oeuvre of Bataille or Lawrence.

How have representations of sex become so banal, so unthreatening, so uncritical? Because the body and sexuality are liberated as signs and only as signs. Through the sign-system, Baudrillard contends, 'sexuality itself is diverted from its explosive finality' (1998a: 144) and transformed into 'promotional eroticism' or '*operational sexuality*' (1993a: 117): 'We must first have split off sexuality as totality, in its symbolic total exchange function, in order to be able to contain it in sexual signs . . . and to assign these to the individual as private property' (1998a: 149). Baudrillard is quite clear that women have, throughout Western history, suffered a far greater 'servitude' regarding the body than have men. Yet the modern 'liberation' of women is also suspect because:

> emancipation occurs *without the basic ideological confusion between women and sexuality being removed* – the legacy of puritanism still bears down on us with all its force . . . women once *subjugated* as a sex, are today 'liberated' as a *sex . . . woman becomes more and more merged with her body.*
>
> (Baudrillard, 1998a: 137)

Women are given 'woman' as sign, as simulation. Simulation floats free, it is virtual or disconnected, while in their lived or 'concrete' experience women are still subjugated. Further, the signs and simulations of the consumer society avert or deter the genuine possibility of a transformation of gender relations. Baudrillard does not deny that progress, of a kind, has occurred. Women, as well as young people and ethnic minorities, are 'freer' (1998a: 138), but such gains are, according to Baudrillard, little more than a 'spin-off' from the 'strategic operation' of the code. What exactly does this mean? The body as a sign (or field of signs) is 'interiorised' as personal(ised) value, such that our perception of our bodies is mediated by signs: we are put into service by the task of maintaining our bodies as signs. A particular vision or ideal of beauty is imposed as both *right* and *duty* in the consumer society. The preference of the fashion and advertising industries for the very slim, what Baudrillard calls the 'scrawny and emaciated', is now of many years' standing and represents nothing less than the 'negation of the flesh' (1998a: 140). Through constant dieting and exercise we direct violence against our bodies in an attempt to improve its status position as sign. While the system claims to have liberated 'a naturally pre-existing harmonious relationship' between the self and the body, it in fact promotes the violence of 'daily, obsessive, disciplinary exercise'.

Baudrillard surely has a point here, and once again was ahead of the pack in making it. Some large employers now provide on-site gyms or fitness centres. Employees are encouraged to spend lunchtimes on running machines before showering and returning to work. Here the circuit of self-promotion and self-maximisation is never broken. Brands of cosmetics are available for both men and women that, supposedly, allow the skin to breathe while the body is exerted: we can work out, run or have sex all in full make-up without the risk of clogging our pores and impeding cell regeneration. We then return home, eat a high-vitamin, high-protein, low-carbohydrate meal before slapping on the night cream and retiring to bed early in order to look 'fresh' in the morning. Or we don't; but we know this is what we are supposed to do. We are shown the lifestyles and sexual partners we can aspire to if we do this, and our bodies demonstrate to us, by their deterioration, what happens when we do not.

SEXUALITY AS THE SEVERING OF SYMBOLIC EXCHANGE

> Sex is a burial-chamber of signs / The sign is sex made fleshless, emaciated.
>
> (Baudrillard, 1976: 154, my translation)

The biological discourse of sex and sexuality buries the erotic potential of bodies under signs; signs render sex fleshless, emaciated, skeletal (décharné). Signs, Baudrillard argues, mark the body, they divide it, producing it as surface through demarcations such as 'face' and 'body', erogenous and non-erogenous zones, parts that must be covered and parts that need not be covered. The marking process dismantles the body's 'radical ambivalence' and, in its place, generates the skin as surface of signs, with sexuality defined through a binary system (male/female, masculine/feminine, straight/gay). As fashion and dress lose their 'ceremonial character' in the nineteenth century, becoming increasingly utilitarian and functional, 'costume becomes dress, and the body becomes nature' (1993a: 96). Indeed, according to Baudrillard 'the body's nudity defines its assignation to the *sex function . . . to sex as function, that is to say, the reciprocal neutralisation of the body and sex*'.

In the symbolic exchanges of bodies there is an ambivalence that cuts across all potential marks and demarcations, that annuls the Saussurian bar. For Baudrillard, 'sexuality' is not at the foundation of human desires and practices, hard-wired into our biological nature; it is instead the end product of cultural signifying processes. 'Sexuality', then, is not a fact or a thing, it is the product of signifying practices that are uniquely modern and Western. Baudrillard seeks to lift the Saussurian bar; 'radical ambivalence' expresses the immanent cross-cutting of binary oppositions, it describes intensities that exist on both sides of the bar and that will not be separated out. In his earlier studies Baudrillard referred to 'intensities' and 'desires' that are buried by signs and flattened out into what we now call 'sexuality'. These terms are problematic though, because Baudrillard, unlike Lyotard (1993), wants to insist on a 'radical difference' between the play of desire that cannot be contained within the term 'sexuality' and the play of desire that is promoted by the consumer system and its construction of sexuality. As to what forms 'desire' takes within the symbolic order, Baudrillard says very little, but there are important differences:

> In archaic society . . . all [signs] have the function of immediately actualising symbolic exchange, gift exchange with the gods or within the group. Here negotiation is not negotiation of identity by the subject . . . on the contrary, it consumes the subject's identity . . . the entire body becoming, just like gods and women, material for symbolic exchange.
>
> (Baudrillard, 1993a: 107)

Baudrillard's position seems to be that in the absence or suspension of the biological reality principle bodies are both 'male' and 'female', as these terms are not distinguishable as oppositions. Bodies, as 'material for symbolic exchange', are transformed through ritual, flowing into each other, exchanging according to rules. In symbolic exchange 'sex' and 'desire' are ritual practices, acts and relations of exchange, not things, not drives, not the preferences or choices of the subject. 'Sex' occurs in the spaces of exchange between ritual bodies; it is not a property, essence or resource of those bodies beyond the practice of ritual exchange. The person enclosed in symbolic relations is in a state of 'radical ambivalence' in relation to themselves and to others. Both self and other to our 'selves' and self and other to others: we never coincide with ourselves or with others, Baudrillard insists, *we exchange with them.* We are both 'male' and 'female', child and adult, good and evil: in a state of ambivalence, we are literally 'strong' on both sides of the bar. Here there is no identity, no fixity, no value, as the bar enabling these 'things' is annulled. There are, however, rules, which are quite different and are discussed below (see Chapter 6).

Baudrillard follows Lacan in writing of the 'Phallus Exchange Standard' (1993a: 114–16). This is the law or principle that enables and regulates the sexual exchange of barred bodies.[2] It would be too strong a claim to suggest that Baudrillard reads Lacan against Lacan, but he pushes the Lacanian opposition to biology as explanatory principle, arguing that sexuality, desire and eroticism are constructed by scientific discourses and articulated to the political economy of capitalism. Each sign, each mark on the barred body, is a Phallus. The Phallus is not the penis, it is not the biological or 'real' organ. The Phallus is the imaginary, phantasmal or unconscious representation of the penis. Further, the woman's body specifically is rendered phallic by its markings so that 'man's desire will be received in its own image . . . the void between one and the other becomes negotiable in terms of signs and exchanged phallic values . . . a political economy of desire' (Baudrillard, 1993a: 103).

'Sexuality' is, then, a 'phallic simulation' (ibid.). In a phallic signifying economy kissing and gazing are no longer gift exchanges but signifying practices, simulations that refer to, suggest, connote 'desire', 'love' or 'lust' in coded forms that all competent consumers can recognise and display. Indeed, we might suggest that barred sexuality takes on the form theorised by Lacan; in the Lacanian universe the sexual relationship cannot take place, women and men are condemned to an infinite, unsatisfiable desire and love is but a phantasy compensation for this situation (Lacan, 1977: 289).

All sexuality is fetishistic because it focuses on partial objects: lips, eyes, bottoms, boots, stockings. We never confront the other in its fullness, its radical otherness.[3] The barred body of a man has hunky shoulders, toned arms and pecs, a grin. The barred body of a woman has breasts, long legs and long hair, a come-hither stare. But the situation is still not equivalent because men fetishise women to a far greater extent than women fetishise men. Baudrillard is quite clear that the supposed 'erotic privilege' of woman – that they represent the powers, attractions and dangers of sexuality for both men and women – is, in fact, a sign of their 'historical and social subjugation . . . a sexual overvaluation so as to stave off the crucial examination . . . of the order of power' (1993a: 104).

THE STRIPTEASE

Baudrillard is clear that there is *fascination* and a 'cold', coded form of seduction in the barred system of sexual sign-value. In a somewhat lingering account of striptease Baudrillard describes this 'dance' as 'gestural' – a term he had used to describe the symbolic order (1981: 102, 1996a). The striptease is ambivalent because it involves 'a woman's auto-erotic celebration of her own body' (1993a: 109) that both evokes and revokes the other, the male onlooker. The other is both summoned and excluded by the traditional striptease, he must look but must not touch – those are the rules of the game. The gestures of striptease are slow, they '*have time to pass you by*'. These gestures are not referential signs, there is no transcendence'; instead they are immanent to the rules of striptease, they do not communicate, they 'pass you by'. Moreover, there is no nudity in the artful striptease, or rather there is a ceremonial 'transubstantiation of profane (realist, naturalist) nudity into sacred nudity'. The gestures should never descend to mere acts of undressing and, crucially, the genitalia are never revealed. The striptease, for Baudrillard, is a symbolic form *within* the coded Phallic exchange economy: 'you cannot give her anything, because she gives herself everything, hence the complete transcendence that makes her fascinating' (1993a: 109). The striptease, then, follows the pattern of the potlatch in that it is a gift (of beauty or enchantment) that cannot be countered or returned with interest. Baudrillard's descriptions of the striptease are clearly those of a heterosexual man looking at women as objects, but his account is not a red-blooded ode to striptease: there is a pronounced element of pro-feminist critique. There is no political subversion, he argues, no challenge to the Phallocentric system, because the symbolic form *is not exchanged*. Indeed, the possibility of exchange is denied and hence the striptease is a form of power that women are allowed to possess, for a matter of moments only, the better to obscure their lack of political power:

> if women are not fetishists it is because they perform this labour of continual fetishisation on themselves . . . the fetishised woman's body itself comes to bar the point of absence from which it arose, it comes to bar this vertigo in all its erotic presence, a 'token of a triumph over the threat of castration and a protection against it'.
> (Freud, *Fetishism*, 1927, quoted by Baudrillard, 1993a: 110)

Baudrillard's achievement is to lift these speculations out of psychoanalytic theory and to apply them to lived experience in consumer society, developing a distinctive theoretical and methodological position to explore modernity. For example, Baudrillard critiques Freud's notion of narcissism, lifting it out of the sphere of biology and arguing that women are not born narcissists (self-lovers) but are required to produce themselves as narcissistic sexual subjects by the 'socially imposed rules' of the consumer system. Women must position themselves 'on the market of signs . . . on pain of not being desired'. Baudrillard terms this 'planned', 'synthetic', 'neo-narcissism' (1993a: 111), which has no basis in biology. If women have a moment of power in the potlatch-like form of the striptease, the consumer system asserts the ultimate power over women, again by breaking the possibility of symbolic exchanges. The consumer society gives women the gift of sexualised bodies, of fragmented and marked bodies that they must 'use' on men. In return they must be complicit in the 'staging' of their bodies. Symbolic violence operates on women: they must give and continue to give of themselves as sexualised objects simply to receive the validation of the consumer system. It would not be inaccurate to argue that Baudrillard produces a feminist critique of Freud.

It is important to emphasise, as an aspect of Baudrillard's critique of Freud, that it is not 'brute', 'base' reality that is barred: it is ambivalence and the cycle of exchange. Reality, in all its many and changing forms, is nothing but the product of a binary demarcation that constucts the opposition between unreality, illusion, fakery and falsity – and *reality*. We cannot separate out reality and unreality, truth and illusion, because each term in the pair constructs the other. Even if we could seize absolute reality, why would we want to? And there is an alternative:

> The only alternative is that everyone should break down this phallic fortress and open up the perverse structure which surrounds the sexual system . . . leave the white magic of phallic identification in order to recognise their own perilous ambivalence, so that the play of desire as symbolic exchange becomes possible once more.
>
> (Baudrillard, 1993a: 123 n. 12)

Of course, there are problems in Baudrillard's position. First, symbolic exchange is dependent upon the existence of the incest taboo because this alone enables the flow of women, services, gifts and objects through society (1993a: 113).[4] 'Primitive' symbolic gift exchange required that participants give away a part of themselves. It is not clear to what extent women could be participants because they tended to be *the gift* rather than *the giver*, though this was not exclusively the case (see Clutesi (1969) and Strathern (1988), although neither is conclusive on this point). In Baudrillard's reading the distinction between giver and gift is annulled by continual circulation. However, the issue in question is the consumer society and here subjects (women and men) are no longer required to 'relinquish' any part of themselves in giving. The subject is no longer divided or split, no longer consisting of self and other. Further, the body becomes a 'simulated' completion, a 'positivity' that lacks nothing; symbolic exchanges with the other are abolished. We are no longer obligated to the other, we no longer give to them in order to receive. We require the other merely to signify, to signal their place in the hierarchy of the code. Baudrillard terms this an 'incestuous situation' (1993a: 113), likening it to the loss of the incest taboo because the repression (the 'no' of the father in puritan morality) is replaced by a suffusive total immersion in the code. Through its 'liberation' sexuality is reduced to a use-value, to the satisfaction of the body's physical desires (1987b: 33). Sexuality, like economy, is separated out from total social relations, from ritual meanings. It is abstracted, individualised and modelled on economic metaphors; for example, in 'investment' in our looks leading to an enhanced position in the relationships 'market'. So sexuality becomes central to 'the economy of the subject', to its 'physiological and mental equilibrium'. Sexuality is 'imprisoned' within 'the great oppositions (male/female)' such that a 'political economy of the body' is erected on 'the ruins of the body's symbolic economy' (1993a: 116). Any 'celebration of sexuality', from the music of the Rolling Stones, to Ann Summers sex toys, to hard-core and 'gonzo' porn, seals the subject within 'the fundamental norm of political economy . . . *liberating the unconscious as use-value*' (1993a: 116–17).

In the third order sexuality becomes a play of signs and part-objects that are no longer clearly attached to desires, wants or needs; there is a more powerful 'reabsorption' of symbolic exchange and its potential than was possible in the second order. As transgression and perversion are mapped, codified and marketed, sexuality *as sign-form* is a 'mode of rationalisation', not a mode of rebellion or subversion. Ambivalence *within* bodies is externalised as the difference between male and female, such that the body is no longer 'cut through' (*soit refendue*) by desire in disruptive or transgressive form: 'the ambivalence of sex is reduced by bivalence (the two poles and their sexual roles)'. With the current blurring of gender differences, 'the ambivalence of sex is reduced by the ambiguity of the unisex' (1993a: 119).

BAUDRILLARD'S *SEDUCTION*

[I]ntentional seduction: it is a contradiction in terms.
(Baudrillard, 2001c: 62)

Seduction (1990a) is probably Baudrillard's most controversial work, or at least it was until the publication of *The Spirit of Terrorism* (2003b). Kellner (1989: 143) calls it 'an affront to feminism', and it fairs little better with other commentators: Lane (2000) politely ignores it, Genosko (1994, 1998, 1999) and Merrin (2005) have little to say about it, Butler (1999), I feel, misunderstands it. Only Gane (1991b, 2000) and Grace (2000) really engage with *Seduction*.

Moreover, *Seduction* is not really concerned with the status or future of academic feminism or the women's movement. Baudrillard's focus is on the development of his ideas, particularly the reworking of symbolic exchange. There are essays on ritual and ceremony, on games and their rules, on *trompe l'oeil*, on fate, on cloning and on the deconstruction of meaning generally. In this text Baudrillard is still, perhaps above all, concerned with the possibilities of defiant and subversive social and theoretical practice, and he certainly argues that most feminisms fail in this regard, although he does not allow them a fair hearing.[5]

In *Seduction* it seems that a *return* to 'the play of desire as symbolic exchange' and the recognition of our own 'perilous ambivalence' (1993a: 123 n. 12) is no longer Baudrillard's central concern. The notion of seduction involves a spiralling together of symbolic and simulatory that could, in part, be seen as a response to Lyotard's (1993: 103–8) critique of symbolic exchange. At this stage in his theory not only is the notion of symbolic exchange eclipsed but also the 'reality' or referentiality of signs. As was prefigured in *Symbolic Exchange and Death*, sexuality *as simulation* begins to exhaust itself, following an 'ecliptic' path of disappearance. The 'ecliptic of sex' (1990a: 1–49) charts the path taken by sex and the eclipse of the meaningfulness of sex in the course it has taken. Sexuality – as barred phallic exchange – is becoming exhausted; the 'proliferation' of the signs of sex results in 'hyperrealism' and a state of indeterminacy. Where is sex? It is everywhere – in advertising, media, entertainment, therapy, commerce, public relations – everywhere except in the relations between people. Sex is but the click of a mouse, the turning of a page, the opening of the eyes away, *so who cares any more?*

> Desire is sustained only by want. When desire is entirely on the side of demand, when it is operationalised without restrictions, it loses its imaginary and, therefore, its reality; it appears everywhere, but in a generalised simulation. It is the ghost of desire that haunts the defunct reality of sex.
>
> (Baudrillard, 1990a: 5)

Baudrillard argues that seduction, which is defined as the play of femininity, appearances and artifice, is the excluded 'other' of sexuality, desire, liberation and production – all of which are masculine or phallic. In other words, *Seduction* is an expansion and development of Baudrillard's themes in *Symbolic Exchange and Death* concerning the body *in* symbolic exchanges. The rituals and games of seduction are the body in symbolic exchange, the body as pure sign or surface acting outside the confines of the Phallic Exchange Standard and the laws of value. The continuities between *Symbolic Exchange and Death* and *Seduction* have not been explored adequately by critics: the former is seen as a serious work, the latter as little more than a silly provocation.

Yet there is a remarkable degree of consistency across the two texts and with earlier work, particularly *Mirror* and *Critique*.

Sexuality is not a thing, but a process of production 'of discourse, speech or desire' (1990a: 1), it is a distinctly modern and Western phenomenon and will 'only ever be a hypothesis' (2005c: 200).[6] Sexuality, as discourse, presents itself as 'the order of nature', as natural or even the most natural of things. Seduction, by contrast, 'never belongs to the order of nature, but that of artifice – never to the order of energy, but that of signs and rituals . . . and exaltation of the malicious use of signs' (1990a: 2). These claims are important and require unpacking. For Baudrillard the 'order of nature' is a cultural accomplishment, not a fact of life. Nature is order, and this 'order' is brought about by the barring of symbolic exchange such that the binary opposition nature/culture can be posited. Nature is supposedly not-culture and culture is, supposedly, not-nature; indeed, the only thing we can say with certainty about culture or nature is that they are *not* the other.[7] Seduction is not evil and seduction is not female, since seduction, as Baudrillard defines it, is irreducible to binary oppositions. It is not 'beyond' binary opposition in some state of dialectical transcendence, it is outside binary opposition as their threat of the immanent collapse. Seduction, Baudrillard admits, is 'confounded', 'confused' with femininity (1990a: 2), but the paraphernalia of 'seductive' femininity – the stockings, high heels, mascara – are, as Baudrillard argues (1993a: 107–12), only the male's imaginary construction.

Seduction, like symbolic exchange, is a relation or pact formed between participants or partners. Power relations, Baudrillard insists, are reversed or annulled: does the male 'seducer' seduce the woman or is he seduced by her? Further, are we seduced by others when they consciously display their 'strengths' – firm breasts, toned muscles, healthy bank account – or when they unwittingly reveal their 'weaknesses', their otherness to themselves? Such 'radical otherness' cannot be deployed strategically because we are not even aware of it, but it is what makes us truly singular and unique, a 'secret', an 'enigma', even to ourselves (1990a: 107). Baudrillard's notion of seduction is not an 'essentializing discourse', as Kellner claims (1989: 146), because seduction refers to bodies *in* exchange, in ambivalence, undecideable, uncoded, on both sides of the bar: 'Seduction is founded upon my intuition of something in the other that remains forever secret for him' (1993b: 166). Further, Kellner is quite wrong to suggest that Baudrillard advises women to 'use their charms' to 'advance their aims' (1989: 148), since seduction in its symbolic form occurs beyond the conscious volition of subjects, although seduction in its banal or 'cold' form can be, and is, used in this way in the consumer system, as Baudrillard argues (1990a: 157–78).

Like symbolic exchange, seduction also operates at the level of meaning, thinking and writing. Here seduction again involves a play of appearances or surfaces, of signs that do not and cannot be related back to signifieds. Seduction is a 'malicious' use of signs, not only because it is a deception, but because it threatens to reveal that signs are never firmly attached to signifieds, that signs do not 'capture' referents, that the world of signs is not one of meaning and truth, but one of nothingness. In other words, the seductions of words undermine the metaphysics of representation. The code, consumerism, political economy and the progressive political discourses that, Baudrillard argues, 'mirror' political economy all claim to put signs to *good* use: fixing meanings, positions, definitions. If 'simulation is hyper-good', seduction is diabolical.[8]

Seduction, then, encompasses both symbolic exchanges between bodies and symbolic exchanges among language, reader and world, and is 'diabolical' or 'malicious' in that, as a principle, it undermines the separations and oppositions that allow abstract value and meaning to emerge.

What makes *Seduction* such a controversial text is that Baudrillard himself, contravening his own rule, frequently refers to 'women' or 'the female' in an apparently biological sense. Indeed, as a number of feminist critics have pointed out, he actually condescends to tell women what they should and should not be doing: they should not be attempting to secure themselves as subjects in a phallocentric economy, they should be aware of the symbolic powers of annulment and reversal. In their political 'liberation', Baudrillard maintains, these powers will be lost (1990a: 6). In our coded, deritualised Western modernity 'man' (as biologically defined sex) is the possessor of subjectivity and 'woman' (as biologically defined sex) is, according to Baudrillard, an object. Woman is an object of desire, not a subject of desire, and for Baudrillard is consequently in a 'much higher position' (1990b: 122). Baudrillard is not seeking to justify Western sex and gender roles; clearly these oppositions are produced by bio-materialist scientific thought, which he attacks repeatedly. However, Baudrillard insists that there is something seductive and enigmatic in the object – female, male or unsexed – that slips beyond the binary relations. Seduction is not, for Baudrillard, a strategy of the subject – of the rakish, handsome man or bestockinged temptress. Seduction occurs *despite* the will, efforts and desires of the subject. Seduction is an effect of words, of things and objects that seem to come from elsewhere, unexpected and enchanting. It is the

Western discourse of sexuality, a simulation that is 'our new morality' (1990a: 37), that reduces seduction to sexual attraction.

It would be easy to conclude that Baudrillard's thinking on sex and gender relations is a major weakness in his work, a weakness that can be traced back to the 'fact' that women are repressed in traditional society (or the symbolic order). For all the distracting signs and simulations of modernity women are now 'liberated' or at least well on the way to liberation. While this assertion may have seemed like a simple 'fact' to many at the time Baudrillard published *Seduction*, and remained the core critique of Baudrillard throughout the 1980s and 1990s, this and related issues are, of course, highly topical at the moment. Is a woman with bleached hair, fake breasts and anorexia really more free or 'liberated' than a woman in a hijab or burka? The Western world's claim to the moral high ground on the position of women in society is about as convincing as its claim to the moral high ground on the use of military action; that is to say, not entirely groundless but very far from secure. Applying a binary opposition such as liberated versus repressed is totally inadequate; silicone and suspenders and burkas and veils are different strategies in the marking of women's bodies and the demarcation of their roles, both strategies that signify the value of women in a phallic economy.

Baudrillard's theorisation of the status of the body and sexuality in consumer society is powerful and engaging. His positions in *Consumer Society* and *Symbolic Exchange and Death* are certainly compatible with feminist critique and amount to a largely unexplored contribution to feminism (Grace, 2000, does explore this contribution). What is sometimes disappointing in these works is that Baudrillard seems to remain embroiled in a Freudian-Lacanian frame of reference. There is little suggestion of a reading of Freud against Freud where the body and sexuality are concerned and Freud's brief essay on fetishism (1977: 351–7) is cited, straightforwardly, as authority by Baudrillard (1993a: 110). Yet where Baudrillard does manage to break with psychoanalytic vocabulary, no small achievement in itself, this is done through a symbolic provocation to feminism that does not really succeed in opening up a play of symbolic exchange because its rhetoric sometimes slips into a feminism wrong/Baudrillard right binary opposition.

But I did not watch *Excalibur* for long. Arthur had barely performed his magical reverse-penetration by drawing the sword from the stone when, guiltily, I switched the discs back. I chose a different girl-on-girl scene. The girls were very beautiful, lying together on a bed. They started. How many times can you watch a scene telling yourself it does not work, before it manifestly *is* working? Then some men arrived. The scenes were fascinating, not as sex (and I am still not convinced that I saw any 'sex') but in the way TV 'reality' shows can be fascinating. Compelling but empty, passionless yet filthy, gruelling to watch and no doubt gruelling to be in – the cutting edge of the exploitation of the body as capital. I wanted it to end, but could not turn it off. Finally one of the men ejaculated. It was over. What a relief!

6

Into the Fourth Order

Science fiction? Hardly.

(Baudrillard, 1993b: 38)

Everything is subservient to the system, yet at the same time escapes its control.

(Baudrillard, 1993b: 135)

INTRODUCTION

From about 1980 Baudrillard's writing changed significantly. He no longer claimed to represent the direction the world is moving in, as he had throughout the 1970s. From this point his writing claimed only to challenge and to defy, to cipher and render enigmatic (1996c: 94–105). Because there is no 'real' world to represent and no stable subject position from which to claim to represent the real, writing theory becomes, for Baudrillard, *an act, a gesture and a symbolic relation*. Baudrillard's writing *gives* in order to challenge, to provoke or to force a response. And Baudrillard succeeded in forcing many responses – from outrage and incredulity to incomprehension – but he also established a following. Baudrillard's later theory sets up a symbolic relation between text and readers, and between writing and the world (not the 'real' world but the illusion of the world). His writing challenges 'banal illusion' and is an affirmation of 'vital illusion' (2000: 59–83). This chapter explores what Baudrillard meant by vital illusion, by a symbolic relation between writing and the world and the possibilities for a radical, post-critical theory that this relation suggests.

Baudrillard's assertions concerning the nature of simulation, specifically the loss of referentiality, make it impossible for him to claim to describe an external 'reality' out there called the fourth order. In fact the term 'fourth order' hardly ever appeared in Baudrillard's work and he certainly did not construct a comprehensive theory of the fourth order. Instead Baudrillard developed a number of interrelated themes and notions – transparency, evil, the perfect crime, impossible exchange and poetic transference – that characterise the fourth order in various ways. These are not critical concepts but *dramatis personae*: the masks and guises of the fourth order, but not its 'reality'. So in developing fatal or radical theory and methodology Baudrillard moves away from critique as a form of thought that supposedly operated on the world, and increasingly turns to thought experiments. Where critical concepts attempt to operate on 'reality' to transform it, or at least expose what is questionable in it, Baudrillard sought to resist the simulation that is 'reality'. He returns to Nietzsche, an early inspiration, and to fiction writers such as Nabokov and Ceronetti, to engage *with the world as fiction, illusion and thought*, rather than 'the world' as objective reference supposedly known through the categories of subjective perception (1990b: 111–15, 1996c: 94–115).

Baudrillard's notion of the 'disappearance' of the subject, central to his writing on the fourth order, is complex and requires some elucidation. First, Baudrillard himself 'disappears' as a unified writing or knowing subject. He disappears behind competing irreconcilable hypotheses and into fragmentary and aphoristic reflection. For Baudrillard 'aphorisms . . . best do justice to that cerebral electricity, those myriad microscopic ideas that ascend from the nerves to the brain and are constantly passing across it' (2006a: 8). Baudrillard's methodology concerning the fourth order is not an exercise in the writing of post-modern fragmentation, nor is it characterised by the 'waning of affect' said to typify the postmodern (Jameson, 1991: 10–12). The aphorism is a quintessentially modernist literary device and Baudrillard's notion of 'cerebral electricity' recalls Woolf and Joyce as much as Nietzsche. Further, Baudrillard claimed to be affected on a very personal level by his theoretical ideas. The separation between life and theory, which, according to his interview with Lotringer (published as *Forget Baudrillard* in 1987 and appended to *Forget Foucault*, 1987b), had held throughout his works of the 1960s and 1970s, was, it seems, suddenly shattered. Baudrillard would no longer assume the secure position of *knower*, of the leading theorist of consumption or of simulation. Confronting the implications of his thought he writes, 'Somewhere along the line I stopped living . . . I stopped working on simulation. I felt I was going totally nuts . . . all this came to have extremely direct consequences on my life' (1987b: 105).

These consequences are never made explicit but are hinted at throughout the *Cool Memories* series (I–V) and elsewhere. Baudrillard writes of dreams and affairs of the heart (1990b: 155, 158–9 respectively), and in his 'second life' or 'later destiny' leads a fatal existence because 'what happens a second time becomes fatal' (1990b: 187). The first volume of *Cool Memories* begins with 'The first day of the rest of your life' (1990c: 1), as Baudrillard apparently begins a second life, a life *after* subjectivity, *after* desire, *after* his greatest successes (intellectual and romantic), after being *the* theorist of simulation. Yet, he suggests, there is 'a charm and a particular freedom about letting just anything come along, with the grace – or ennui – of a later destiny' (1990c: 3). There is a new openness here: 'Baudrillard' becomes persona, mask or simulacrum, always in metamorphosis, rather than a label that refers to a stable identity (1997: 22). Nevertheless, he continued to theorise, with considerable success, a very wide range of phenomena that he associated with the 'fourth order of simulacra'.

AFTER THE ORGY

[T]he concepts of liberty and liberation are diametrically opposed, unconditional liberation being the surest way of keeping liberty at bay.

(Baudrillard, 1994b: 107)

The fourth order of simulacra points to the phase of images or signs that becomes increasingly characteristic after the 'explosion' of modernity. But it is not, for Baudrillard, the era of postmodernity; that is, it is not a new era or structure. As Gane (1991a, 2000) argues, Baudrillard seldom uses the term 'postmodernity' and on the rare occasions that he does it is used not as an analytic concept but as a disparaging label for certain features of contemporary cultural production (see also Baudrillard in Gane, 1993: 21–3). The fourth order as an 'implosive', collapsing moment *within* modernity renders the term 'postmodernity' redundant: modernity continues but its 'idea', 'concept' or meaning becomes uncertain. This does not mean that modernity has weakened or become obsolete; indeed, 'things continue to function long after their ideas have disappeared, and they do so in total indifference to their own content. The paradoxical fact is that they function even better under these circumstances' (1993b: 6). Modernity accelerates its production of the social, of rights, of goods and services, but it has no end, purpose or goal other than the production of more and more and more.

The fourth order comes about 'after the orgy': that is, after modernity's drive for liberation in every sphere – economic, political, sexual – has lost its sense of purpose and no longer quite convinces us. Of course the project of liberation, the pursuit of freedoms, human rights, equality and tolerance, has not failed entirely. Baudrillard concedes that there have been improvements in material terms, particularly for women and ethnic minorities. However, liberation is not the same thing as liberty. The movements for liberty, equality and social justice were vital, critical forces and Baudrillard supported them in the 1960s. But liberty has, according to Baudrillard, been replaced by 'liberation' – that is, by *signs* of liberty, by simulatory, coded forms of freedom. For example, any genuinely transformative potential in political or sexual liberation has long been coded into simulatory form *as signs to consume*. 'Liberation' is, for Baudrillard, a 'dissuasive' strategy of the system, and is 'internal' to the system. The system effected a simulatory 'liberation' of the repressed terms of the binary oppositions set in place by an earlier phase of simulacra to deter any more radical challenge to the system. So women can claim to be stronger and smarter than men, gays can claim to be cooler and more sophisticated than straights, children can make new demands of their parents, students of their teachers: the privileged term of the opposition switches (at least in simulation) but the opposition remains in place and the potential for symbolic engagement or exchange between the poles is further submerged.

The project of liberation was, according to Baudrillard, one of the liberation of the under-represented in the terms of the already represented. This was a spurious 'liberation' based on control through the extension of already existing simulation models, such as production and sexuality, dominated by the values of competition, performativity and operativity. To put things very crudely, women and female sexuality are liberated, but only on the model of male sexuality – that is, as aggressive, self-centred, unemotional and based on the 'performance principle'. Women can drink like men, fuck like men, die in battle like men, but what they are not allowed to be is radically different because radical 'otherness' is a potential challenge to the system. Similarly, black people can go to university, appear in TV and advertising as 'role-models' and become wealthy lawyers but in doing so they conform to the expectations of competitive capitalism; again what they are not allowed is to be radically 'other'. A range of prescribed, coded differences are allowed, indeed they are expected: women must still look feminine, they must still signify sex, and the refusal to do so means they are 'uptight' or 'frigid'. Similarly, ethnic minorities are expected to promote themselves by setting up restaurants selling spicy, exotic foods, or through music, sport or fashion. The system secures assimilation at the level of form by parading 'diversity' at the level of content.[1]

With the fourth order any specific principle of equivalence or 'logic of value' disappears because everything – communication, ideologies, cultures, sexualities, bodies, capital – can be exchanged indiscriminately *as sign* (1993b: 8). Indeterminacy and indifference may undermine notions of 'progress' but, of course, do little to harm marketisation and profit. Capitalist corporations are able to feed off uncertainty and anxiety, fear and terror, largely unchallenged and unregulated. Corporate elites do better than ever from the fourth order's 'orbital phase' of capital circulation (1993b: 26–35). Capitalism, Baudrillard argues, is protected from critique, from dialectical negation, because it severs links with 'real' processes of production and labour and goes into electronic orbit. While increasingly (although never entirely) invulnerable to the actions of unions and leftist critics, corporations are vulnerable to stock market crashes and sudden devaluations. Examples might include the bursting of the dot com bubble in the late 1990s and, of course, the attacks of 9/11, which temporarily closed the New York stock exchange. For Baudrillard these are *systemic anomalies*, they emerge within the system and circulate throughout, often at the speed of information (1993b: 40). Similarly, for Baudrillard, radical Islam is not an archaic resurgence but a modern, or hypermodern, phenomenon (1993b: 83–4). These are dimensions of the 'revenge of the object', of 'objective irony', that seem to become more and more deadly with the fourth order. Indeed, the more the system strives to globalise, neutralising or assimilating all otherness, the more setbacks it encounters. Objects take their revenge as 'extreme phenomena', which 'play a prophylactic role by opposing its chaos to any escalation of order and transparency to their extremes' (1993b: 68). Baudrillard seems to be concerned with three main phenomena: AIDS, cancer and terrorism. It is not clear to what extent his comments have wider applicability. Each of these phenomena is, for Baudrillard, 'transpolitical', 'viral' and anomalous, yet also prophylactic or protective, in that they shield us from something even worse: total, systemic transparency.

Transparency refers to the liberation and circulation of information, knowledge, sexuality, human rights, cultures and consumer goods without restriction, limit or rule, a 'superfusion', of 'total positivity'. But, Baudrillard insists, it is in this total operationality with its eradication of critique, negatives, evil, 'dirt' that the West becomes increasingly vulnerable to extreme phenomena – a vicious circle or 'feedback loop' that makes the effects of extreme phenomena far worse. In short any threat, any uncertainty, any anomaly is 'treated' with more information, yet more information feeds uncertainty, and may generate new anomalies.

THE INFLUENCE OF NIETZSCHE

To understand Baudrillard's position regarding the fourth order, in greater depth, we must examine the influence of Friedrich Nietzsche. In *The Gay Science* (1974) Nietzsche announces the death of God, meaning that the idea of a God as master of the universe and guarantor of order is no longer credible in a rationalistic culture. However, for Nietzsche, the death of God does not amount to a 'liberation' for the human subject such as is envisaged in atheist and humanist thought. Instead, Nietzsche suggests, we are left adrift, 'straying as though through an infinite nothing' (1974: 181): distance, direction and measure are lost. Indeed, the very notions of truth and reality are undermined because there is no stable foundation on which to ground them. Any 'foundation' is constructed within language and is ultimately arbitrary because it lacks any foundation beyond its immediate context.' In short, without transcendent entities there are no transcendent truths: metaphysics is revealed as groundless. Baudrillard certainly does not follow Nietzsche in a disciplined fashion but there is clearly a profound influence (for Baudrillard's comments on this see 2004: 1, 35). Nietzsche's 'How the "Real World" at last became a myth' in *Twilight of the Idols* (1990b: 50–1) is cited by Baudrillard on several occasions and is vital to his later theory. The world, for Nietzsche, has become myth or fable. The illusion of 'reality', of an ordered and stable opposition between real and apparent, true and false, is shattered. Rather than lifting us out of a world of superstition into a world of solid realities, the death of God is also the death of fixed distinctions between real and apparent, true and false, right and wrong, good and evil, the very structuring principles of Platonic, Christian and scientific thought. Science is predicated on the orderly distinction between true and false, real and illusion, just as is religion. Freed from superstition, science cannot grasp the 'real' world as it 'is' because the real world has, for Nietzsche, become fable; 'reality' was part of the superstition. One of Nietzsche's clearest statements of this position is: 'That mountain there! That cloud there! What is "real" in that? Subtract the phantasm and every human *contribution* from it, my sober friends! If you *can*!' (1974: 121). In other words, anything we call 'reality' is already a human or social construction, a term in our language code. It follows that all knowledge is fable, not 'fake' but mythic, only ever a narration. After the death of God and the collapse of binary oppositions only the flow of immanence remains, the unfolding of fate, the roll of the dice.

Nietzsche's demolition of the real/apparent binary opposition, on which the belief in God was dependent (God as real, the apparent world as illusion), involves a radical repositioning of the subject. No longer can the 'knowing' subject be thought of as standing outside the world, in the neutral position of observer. The subject is written into the world, or rather the subject is written *by* the world, by myth, by fable. According to Pierre Klossowski's interpretation of Nietzsche in *Un si funeste desir*, 'The refabulization of the world equally signifies that the world leaves historical time to return to the time of myth, that is to say eternity' (Klossowski, 1961, quoted in and translated by James, 2000: 90). The world as myth or fable is eternal in that it has no end, no purpose and no foundation beyond itself. It is a world of the moment, and only of the moment. Klossowski, Baudrillard recounts, was a great influence on him (2004: 39). And for Klossowski the notion of the self or identity is replaced by a play of masks or personae, suggestive of the rituals described by Mauss (1990). Yet Baudrillard develops a distinctive position: we are torn between two irreconcilable principles. To live as nothing but a succession of masks is unbearable to the individual's sense of self as posited by rational, coded discourse. We have lost the mythic forms that made the ritual play of masks meaningful and we can never be rid of the banal illusions of subjectivity: identity, choice, free will and self-determination. Indeed, we cling to them as protection from the cruelty of fate. This is the unique anguish of contemporary life. Its impact on the self and interpersonal relations is explored in Chapter 8.

THE OBJECT: RITUAL, RULE AND FATE

Today, the position of the subject has become simply untenable. No one today can be assumed as the subject of power, knowledge or history . . . the only possible position is that of the object.

(Baudrillard, 1990b: 113)

Nearly all of Baudrillard's published work is concerned with the object. The *System of Objects* (1996a) explored the role of the object system as a language enabling people to express themselves, to articulate desires and relate to each other. The important notion of the 'revenge of the object', first appearing in *Mirror*, expresses the revenge of the object of analysis on the subject(s) performing the analysis. In *Fatal Strategies* (1990b) Baudrillard expands these ideas into a sweeping attack on the epistemology of scientific rationalism, seeking to abandon the role of the subject and to take the position or 'side' of the object.

What does it mean to take the side of the object? Baudrillard does not suggest that we begin speaking up for the rights of inanimate objects. In taking the 'position' of the object Baudrillard seeks that in the object that defies the subject, that which is incomprehensible or radically other to the subject and that 'pushes it [the subject] back upon its own impossible position' (1990b: 113). Baudrillard attempts to put back into play the subject/object binary opposition that bars symbolic relations and enables the illusion of an active, knowing subject and a passive, 'known' object.

According to Baudrillard we all live in ambivalence as *both* subject *and* object, both self and other: 'when I speak of the object and its profound duplicity, I speak of all of us and our political and social order . . . I'm speaking also of people and their inhuman strategies' (1990b: 182, 184). The play of appearances and disappearances is other than, and irreducible to, the subject/object relation. This he defines as seduction, the 'linkage' or 'unfolding' of 'pure signs' without referential meaning. Seduction and simulation are hard to distinguish: 'in seduction and in simulation, there are no subjects anywhere' (Baudrillard in Stearns and Chaloupka, 1992: 298). The relationship between them, as between symbolic exchange and signs, is unstable, uncertain and 'in transit'. They can be distinguished only as distinct moments or positions on a double spiral. The symbolic and seductive do not claim 'the real', they dissolve, annul or foil its emergence. Simulation, by contrast, does claim to be 'real', to secure or capture the real, but in doing so replaces the real with the hyperreal, and, in the fourth order, with the virtual.

The strategies of the object are experienced as ironic because they subvert the supposed mastery or sovereignty of the subject, ironic because indifferent to the wishes of the subject, yet also seductive and fascinating in the forging of connections that are felt to be more meaningful than causal connections. The order of the object is of 'what has already been fulfilled, and from which, for this very reason it is impossible to escape' (1990b: 182). There is, for Baudrillard, a 'precession' of the object antagonistic to the precession of simulacra, a 'reversibility of the causal order – the reversion of cause on effect, the precession and triumph of effect over cause', which is more fundamental that the precession of cause over effect, and of model or code in simulation. In fact the latter are used as strategies, roughly speaking of the second and then third orders, respectively, to ward off the 'primordial, fatal, and original' precession of the effect (1990b: 162).

What Baudrillard calls 'The Ceremony of the World' (1990b: 166–79) concerns ritual or ceremonial forms that are of the order of fate or 'fatality', not chance or accident, not meaning or non-meaning. There is no referential meaning to a ceremony; instead there is a rule. The rule is given at the beginning and remains unchanged throughout. The rule dictates a strictly limited number of possible outcomes. Ritual signs are fixed, 'necessary' or symbolic, there is no cause and effect, no choice, no desire but instead an unfolding, the play of destiny. In ritual, Baudrillard asserts, subjectivity is abolished, because notions of choice, desire and belief are rendered meaningless. There are only acts, communion and metamorphosis. Something of the 'voluntary servitude' of ritual is carried over into the modern forms of gaming and gambling:

> Each of us secretly prefers an arbitrary and cruel order, one that leaves us no choice, to the horrors of a liberal one where we don't even know what we want, where we are forced to recognise that we don't know what we want.
>
> (Baudrillard, 1990b: 169)

The ceremonial or ritual form is so crucial for Baudrillard because it offers an alternative to the 'banal' universe of identity, causality, probability and meaning: in ritual 'signs attain the highest level of intensity, fascination and *jouissance*' (1990b: 168). So in postulating a fourth order Baudrillard revisits the themes of ritual, initiation and exchange explored in *Symbolic Exchange*, though now in a metaphysical mode rather than an anthropological one. Ceremonial, particularly initiation, enables escape from the realm of biological 'reality'. We are able to escape our biological birth and experience a 'second, initiatory birth' rather than 'remain strapped in our Oedipal history' (1990b: 138).

In order to 'circumvent' causality we need only impose a set of rules. Rules that must be followed, arbitrary 'pure' signs, take us into the domain of necessity and fate. Gamblers, Baudrillard asserts, believe not in chance or probability, but in luck and fate. Further, 'We are all gamblers. What we desire most intensely is that the inexorable procession of rational connections cease for a while' (1990b: 153; see also 2001c: 87–8). In the symbolic or fatal universe there is no randomness, chance, accident or probability:

this is a world where there is no such thing as chance. Nothing is dead, nothing is inert, nothing is disconnected, uncorrelated or aleatory. Everything, on the contrary, is fatally, admirably connected – not at all according to rational relations . . . but according to an incessant cycle of metamorphosis, according to the seductive rapports of form and appearance. Seen as a substance in need of energy, the world lives in the inert terror of the random, it is shattered by chance. Seen as the order of appearances and their senseless unravelling, seen as pure event, the world is, on the contrary, ruled by absolute necessity.

(Baudrillard, 1990b: 150)

Chance and accident are, then, residual or 'waste' categories produced by rational, causal explanation. Anything that cannot be explained in terms of cause and effect is 'dumped' into the category of accident. So the more rationality dominates the more accidental, chaotic and random 'waste' is produced. However, in the third order, as binary oppositions reverse and implode, the belief that the fundamental nature of the universe is chaotic or accidental gains ground at the expense of belief in a rationally ordered or divinely ordained cosmos. Yet, according to Baudrillard, both of these views are mistaken:

Reason seeks to break the incessant cycle of appearances. Chance – the possibility of indeterminate elements, their respective indifference, and, in a word, their freedom – results from this dismantling. . . . The fatal is absolutely opposed to the accidental (as well as to the rational, of course).

(Baudrillard, 1990b: 152, 158)

These comments require some clarification. Baudrillard, inspired by Nietzsche, is suggesting that human beings have attempted to discover meaning behind appearances, the real behind the apparent. Religion claims access to such truths, as later does science – both seek to 'break the incessant cycle of appearances'. Only in the breaking of this cycle are 'reality' and scientific determinism possible, but this breaking is also the condition of possibility of indeterminism, chance and randomness. The accidental is a category of the rational, disorder is a category of order. To argue that the fundamental nature of the universe is chaos is still to claim that there is something beyond or behind appearances. Baudrillard does not subscribe to chaos theory because it seeks to impose a higher level of order 'behind' or beyond the level of human perceptions (1990b: 154). Baudrillard's themes of fate, illusion and seduction, as principles of radical otherness, are opposed to both rational determinism and chaotic indeterminism.

The destiny of the object is to take revenge on the subject by eluding categories of knowledge and meaning generated by the subject. As the subject's codes – social, political, sexual, genetic – implode (1993b: 36) the object radiates as 'pure' sign and 'pure event', as catastrophe: 'catastrophe is the abolition of causes. It submerges cause beneath effect. It hurls causal connection into the abyss, restoring for things their pure appearance or disappearance' or the 'spontaneous connection of appearances' (1990b: 156). For Baudrillard fatality – the supremacy of the object – and its ironic effects are 'senseless' but not random (1990b: 154). Instead fatality is a matter of fate, destiny 'an extraordinary necessity' (1990b: 155). Baudrillard defines fate as 'the precession of the effects over their very causes . . . Reasons come after' (1990b: 161).

INTEGRAL REALITY AND THE MURDER OF THE SIGN

'Integral', or virtual, reality is distinct from simulation because in it the real is completely replaced and eliminated. Simulation replaced uncoded symbolic relations with coded semiotic relations; its medium was the sign and its capacity to refer to a referent. If simulation hyper-realises the real, virtual reality jettisons the real. The total elimination of symbolic relations and also of the sign's referentiality would constitute what Baudrillard called 'the perfect crime'; that is,

> a world where everything that exists only as idea, dream, fantasy, utopia will be eradicated, because it will immediately be realised, operationalised . . . real events will not even have time to take place. Everything will be preceded by its virtual realisation.
> (Baudrillard, 2000: 66–7)

The real dies with simulation because 'the real is merely a particular case of that simulation' (1996c: 10).[2] For Baudrillard the murder of the sign 'Paves the way for Integral Reality . . . What becomes of the arbitrary nature of the sign when the referent ceases to be the referent? Now, without the arbitrary nature of the sign, there is no differential function, no language, no symbolic dimension' (2005d: 67–8). Both referential language and symbolic, poetic and anagrammatic language were dependent upon the sign. Without the sign there can be nothing but a virtual copy of the world, a perfected substitute for the world, a 'de-signification' or 'brutal de-simulation'. Reality is 'technically materialised without reference to any principle or final purpose whatever' (2005d: 18), resulting in a world of 'radical fetishism . . . the sign's becoming pure object once again' (2005d: 72). To clarify, the world is not restored to a status of myth or illusion, in virtuality it simply *is* in all its banality: 'things are no longer anything but what they are, and, as they are, they are unbearable' (2005d: 26). The process of the separation and abstraction of symbolic relations into signs founded 'objective reality', and this same process reaches its end or 'final solution' with integral reality. Integral or virtual reality is the total substitution of the virtual for the real, a perfect doubling or mirroring. Virtual reality expels all 'otherness, alterity or negativity' (2005d: 67), which is why it is so relentlessly banal.

Baudrillard develops a number of examples. Music is reduced to a digital code by computers such that all impurities, such as feedback and distortion, are removed. These latter can even be reintroduced digitally, at a later date, for greater 'authenticity'. But, Baudrillard asks, 'is this still music?' (2005d: 28). The 'quality' of music is, increasingly, measured by its degree of technical fidelity rather than existing in the measureless realm of the imagination. Digital coding purges music of negativity just as digital image processing purges the image of its negative (2005d: 91–104). A second example is the notion of 'real time'. Linear time replaced the cyclical time of symbolic exchange, but is in turn replaced by so-called 'real-time', which is not real at all but is virtual, is *the time of the medium*:

> With this notion of 'real time', all dimensions have contracted to a single focal point, to a fractal form of time. The differential of time having disappeared, it is the integral function that wins out: the immediate total presence of a thing to itself. All that is absent from itself, all that differs from itself, is not truly real.
>
> (Baudrillard, 2005d: 31)

The virtual supplants the real; in the fourth order 'the real is only a vestige' (2001c: 42). But fortunately, Baudrillard asserts, the perfect crime is impossible. The world, everything and everyone in it, is enigmatic, non-identical and radically other. While modes of 'symbolic resolution', resistance to or defiance of the system, available to the subject are increasingly neutralised by assimilation, the principle of reversibility, fundamental to symbolic relations, now reappears in object(ive) form as 'the maleficent reversal of the system itself'. This notion of internal reversibility Baudrillard also termed 'the principle of evil' (1990b: 181–91).

FATAL THEORY AND RADICAL THOUGHT

> Thought must, at all costs, keep itself from reality.
>
> (Baudrillard, 2005d: 72)

Baudrillard's position on the object, on fate and on ritual or ceremony as rule-governed forms has direct applications for the practice of (radical) theory in the fourth order. According to Baudrillard,

> Theory is just like ceremony . . . both ceremony and theory are violent; both are produced to prevent things and concepts from touching indiscriminately, to create discrimination, and to remake emptiness, to re-distinguish what has been confused . . . there is perhaps but one fatal strategy and only one: theory. And doubtless the only difference between a banal theory and a fatal one is that in one strategy the subject still believes himself more cunning than the object, whereas in the other the object is considered more cunning, cynical, talented than the subject.
>
> (Baudrillard, 1990b: 178, 181)

The Perfect Crime (1996c) develops these themes, with increased emphasis on the play of illusion. Baudrillard depicts the simulacrum, or the radical illusoriness of the world, as, in a sense, 'objective' or 'material':

> The objective illusion is the physical fact that in this universe no things co-exist in real time – not sexes, stars, this glass, this table, or myself and all that surrounds me. By the fact of dispersal and the relative speed of light, all things exist only in a recorded version, in an unutterable disorder of time-scales, at an inescapable distance from each other . . . never truly present to each other, nor . . . 'real' for each other.
>
> (Baudrillard, 1996c: 52)

This 'inescapable distance' prevents identity and is the condition for the 'dual form', or for radical otherness. Yet this distance is 'under threat' from the massive expansion of technology. Total self-presence and immediate verification would constitute the 'perfect crime' but this is always thwarted by illusion, appearance, absence, singularity, evil, nothing: symbolic forms. The supposed 'objectivity' of science is not fake, but 'simulated':

> The distinction between the subject and the object, a fiction that can be maintained in the zone of perception that is on a human scale, breaks down at the level of extreme and macroscopic phenomena. These restore the fundamental inseparability of the two, or in other words, the radical illusion of the world.
>
> (Baudrillard, 1996c: 54)

Similarly, in the human and social sciences, Baudrillard contends, a radical uncertainty reigns. And not because of the problem of complexity, which can always be managed; it is of a systemic, fundamental kind where 'the object slips away, becomes elusive, paradoxical and ambiguous, and infects the subject himself and his analytical procedures with that ambiguity' (ibid.). Since 'we cannot grasp both the genesis and the singularity of the event, the appearance of things and their meaning' (1996c: 56), we are faced with a stark alternative: 'either we master their meaning, and appearances elude us, or the meaning eludes us and appearances are saved' (ibid.).

Radical thought, as Baudrillard styles it, is not scientific, but nor is it critical. Both scientific and critical thought purport to operate on 'reality', but for Baudrillard, following Nietzsche, belief in 'reality' is an 'otherworldly spiritual consolation . . . one of the elementary forms of the religious life . . . the last refuge of the moral zealots' (1996c: 94). Baudrillard insists that 'No one believes fundamentally in the real, nor in the self-evidence of their real lives' (ibid.). Scientific and critical thought posit a 'comforting' and 'necessary' relationship between thought and reality. Baudrillard's radical thought, in contrast, claims a fundamental 'incompatibility between thought and the real' (1996c: 96). As they are not naturally connected, thought is singular.

Radical thought occurs 'at the violent intersection of meaning and non-meaning, of truth and non-truth', it 'wagers on the illusion of the world' (1996c: 97–8). Any attempt by thought to remain faithful to the world or to the 'real' is doomed because 'It arises from a total misunderstanding about language, which is illusion in its very movement, since it is the bearer of that continuity of the void, that continuity of the Nothing . . . at the very heart of what it says, since it is, in its very materiality, the deconstruction of what it signifies' (1996c: 98). Baudrillard's position here is in accord with that expressed, some twenty years earlier, in *Symbolic Exchange*; language should not be confused with its meaning alone, it is also material – the material illusion. That is, language is a medium, a form, a singularity: no language can be faithfully translated into another and no language faithfully translates ideas or thoughts. The physical form of language – sounds, silences, marks, spaces – 'deconstructs' the content of signified meanings. As with the anagrammatic dispersal, noble ideas and figures – gods and heroes alike – are 'sacrificed', becoming no more than a series of sound effects, sensuous forms of breath and song: 'Words move quicker than meaning, but if they go too quickly, we have madness' (1996c: 99).

Scientific and critical thought tends to treat language as a neutral medium of representation, or at least attempts to find a language that is adequate to representation, a tool that can 'extract' truths. The task of extraction is an exacting one, requiring much discipline and toil.

Baudrillard plays with a reversal of this image of thought, suggesting that 'reality asks nothing other than to submit itself to hypotheses. And it confirms them all. That, indeed, is its ruse and its vengeance' (1996c: 99). By contrast, radical thought

> must advance behind a mask and constitute itself as a decoy, without regard for its own truth. It must pride itself on not being an instrument of analysis, not being a critical tool. For it is the world which must analyse itself. It is the world itself which must reveal itself not as truth, but as illusion.
>
> (Baudrillard, 1996c: 99)

Writing should not aim to 'capture' the object, but should make the object more enigmatic by seducing it, by allowing it to 'disappear for itself' through a 'poetic resolution' (1996c: 100). In other words, as the object is abstracted, limited, coded, preceded by simulated models of itself, forced under the glaring lights of scientific rationality, it is allowed, by radical thought, to disappear from its coded position. Thought is allowed to be meaningless, poetic, 'useless': 'Cipher, do not decipher' (1996c: 104).

In any case the object takes its revenge both on those who believe in its reality – scientists, technicians, critical realists – and on those, like Baudrillard, who do not, by 'wreak[ing] vengeance on those who deny it by paradoxically proving them right' (ibid.). Baudrillard refers to his own hypothesis of simulation, which he put forward in the late 1970s, as 'the most cynical, most provocative hypothesis'. Yet reality, or the social world, he argues, refused to prove him wrong. Indeed, social reality seems to become more simulatory, more unreal, by the day. One example, if any more are needed, might be TV news channels, such as BBC News 24. The programmes begin with, and repeat at nauseatingly frequent intervals, the most portentous and strident clashing sounds accompanied by pulses of light (or 'information') beaming across the globe, strafing it and enclosing it within a matrix. These are interspersed with stock images of 'people': shanty towns in China, the business classes in the USA, cultured people in Europe, flashpoints in the Middle East, smiling children in Africa, the 'global world' reduced to a series of signs for your consumption. And then the reassuring images of 'our' professional news team: the energetic young career girl in designer specs, the mature and tenacious foreign correspondent in linen suit; all attentive, all on message, nodding sagely as they receive the latest updates, working for us, to deliver to us . . . the truth! And the BBC is, of course, a beacon of restraint in comparison to the fully commercial channels.

Yet descriptive and critical thought are so redundant, so banal, because 'The simulated disorder of things has moved faster than we have'. Hence radical thought must be 'exceptional, anticipatory and at the margin' (1996c: 101). Baudrillard denies that radical thought is depressive; it is meaning and critique that are 'unhappy' and disillusioned. Banal thought may aim to be optimistic but it is also 'maddeningly tedious and demoralizingly platitudinous'. For Baudrillard 'the definition of a radical thinking [is]: a happy form and an intelligence without hope' (1996c: 103). Radical thought plays with the beautiful materiality of language and generates ideas, rather than platitudes, and 'as for ideas, everyone has them. More than they need' (ibid.).

Fatal theory or radical thought are unexchangeable; they have no equivalence in use-value or exchange-value, but play with 'a reciprocal alteration between matter and thought' (2001c: 24). What might this mean for sociology?

> We analysed a deterministic society deterministically. Today we have to analyse a non-deterministic society non-deterministically – a fractal random, exponential society, the society of the critical mass and extreme phenomena, a society entirely dominated by relations of uncertainty.
>
> (Baudrillard, 2001c: 18)

In a non-deterministic society we do not know the rules that operate, or even if there are any rules: 'Nothing is simply contradictory or irrational in this state; everything is paradoxical' (ibid.). Baudrillard does not hesitate to apply Heisenberg's principle of indeterminacy (known as the 'uncertainty principle'; see Heisenberg, 1958) to social and political events, claiming:

> It applies also to the impossibility of evaluating both the reality and the meaning of an event as it appears in the information media, the impossibility of distinguishing causes and effects . . . of distinguishing the terrorist from the hostage (in Stockholm syndrome), the virus and the cell (in viral pathology).
>
> (Baudrillard, 2001c: 19)

If these examples seem rather limited or underdeveloped, they are. The 'Euclidean dimension' of cause and effect 'is still functioning' (2001c: 18), just as the first, second and third orders continue to function. The result is not chaos or apocalypse, but 'definitive uncertainty', and, Baudrillard insists, even the possibility of 'happy consequences'.

IMPOSSIBLE EXCHANGE, POETIC TRANSFERENCE AND 'HAPPY CONSEQUENCES'

The notion of impossible exchange expresses and extends Baudrillard's assertions concerning definitive or 'radical uncertainty':

> The uncertainty of the world lies in the fact that it has no equivalent anywhere; it cannot be exchanged for anything. The uncertainty of thought lies in the fact that it cannot be exchanged either for truth or for reality.
>
> (Baudrillard, 2001c: 3)

There is no possibility of a complete representation of the world, no 'mirror' of the world: 'Being without possible verification, the world is a fundamental illusion' (ibid.). Any concept or representation is still a part of the world, not a neutral or objective tool capable of 'capturing' it. Radical uncertainty affects all systems – economics, politics, law, morality, aesthetics – 'they have no meaning outside themselves' (2001c: 4). Moreover, 'The sphere of the real is itself no longer exhangeable for the sphere of the sign . . . the real no longer has any force as sign, and signs no longer have any force of meaning' (2001c: 5). Any system of meaning depends upon meaningful binary oppositions or values, but these are unstable and volatile and are exceptions, rather than the rule. When orderly exchange between terms breaks down a system does not grind to a halt; instead the residues 'proliferate wildly', throwing the system in question 'out of kilter' and into radical uncertainty (2001c: 6).

In his characterisation of impossible exchange Baudrillard draws upon many of the same tropes he used to give expression to symbolic exchange. The two are closely related; both 'haunt' the system, both exist 'Here and now' (1993a: 1, 2001c: 6, 7). Yet impossible exchange is more encompassing in its quasi-metaphysical or cosmological scope, whereas symbolic exchange was rooted in social practices, principally gift-exchange.

Baudrillard introduces two new terms to link these ideas. The exchange of values and signs according to a principle of equivalence is 'the exchange of Something'. This is contrasted with 'the exchange of Nothing . . . Death, illusion, absence, the negative, evil, the accursed share are everywhere running beneath the surface of all exchanges. It is even this continuity of the Nothing which grounds the possibility of the Great Game of Exchange' (2001c: 7). The 'Nothing', like symbolic exchange and seduction, is 'not a state of things. It is the product of the dramatic illusion of appearances.' Borrowing from contemporary physics, Baudrillard suggests that Nothing, 'dark matter' or anti-matter is the condition for 'Something', just as, in the social sphere, otherness is the condition for subjectivity or identity. The 'cycle of the Nothing' seems to be Baudrillard's version of the eternal return, and, as with Nietzsche, the thought of the Nothing, if embraced, soothes anguish, pain, unhappiness, regret:

> if the world emerged at a single stroke, it cannot have any deter-minate meaning or end. We are protected from its end by this non-meaning which assumes a force of poetical illusion. The world, admittedly, then becomes wholly enigmatic, but this uncertainty, like that of appearances, is a happy uncertainty. Illusion, being *par excellence* the art of appearing, of emerging out of nothing, protects us from *being*. As the art of disappearance, it protects us from death. The world is protected from its end by its diabolical indeterminacy.
>
> (Baudrillard, 2001c: 10)

This is, again, close to Baudrillard's position in *Symbolic Exchange*, where initiatory death/rebirth prevent the emergence of 'real', biological death as the end-point of life. We can, Baudrillard asserts, live in a happy uncertainty of appearance and disappearance, of becoming and metamorphosis. This is not a version of the 'postmodernist' freedom to make and remake ourselves through the dazzling array of choices offered by the consumer system. Baudrillard's 'happy uncertainty' involves, as a necessary precondition, the abandonment of self, of indi-vidualism and of performativity. As the world is going nowhere, pro-gressing towards nothing, all that remains is the moment, 'wholly enigmatic' and always capable of surprising or seducing us. The power of illusion is not a 'resource' that we can call upon to reinvent ourselves; instead it protects us from the banal illusions of a self, a body, being, identity, will and desire as possessions, things we must drag around with us. These themes are explored in greater detail in Chapter 8.

Baudrillard extends this notion of happy consequences through his notions of 'situational transference' or 'poetic reversal of situation (2001c: 111). These new terms, both etymologically and thematically, are intimately linked to symbolic exchange. In the third order, governed by the Code, symbolic exchange could, at any time, 'effract' or burst through the system of signs, annulling or sacrificing their meaning. But, in the fourth order, the situation has changed. The virtual, tech-nical systems of the fourth order actually 'pave the way' (ibid.) for sym-bolic reversal. The virtual replaces the real; it replaces the referential sign and the systems of value and equivalence. Computers and artificial intelligence 'relieve' us of the need to think in a performative, operational way, since they can do this better than we can. Rather than lamenting this situation, Baudrillard contends, we are actually left with the space for poetic thought that is quite 'useless':

> we should instead rejoice in this totalisation of the world which, by purging everything of its functions and technical goals, makes room for the singularity of thought, the singularity of the event, the singularity of language, the singularity of the object and the image.
>
> (Baudrillard, 2001c: 121)

But Baudrillard's argument is not altogether convincing. It is not clear whether Baudrillard meant this seriously or was being ironic. His comment that 'sexuality, freed from reproduction, becomes free to deploy itself in the erotic' (ibid.) is particularly odd given his position on sexuality expressed in *Consumer Society* and *Seduction* (see Chapter 5 for a detailed discussion). A more convincing example is photography, which, Baudrillard argues, is able to capture moments where 'the world shows itself to be radically non-objective' (2001c: 139). 'Reality', which is based on 'forced signification', disappears, or is conjured away for a moment, such that radical illusion of the world is expressed in its 'silent self-evidence' (2001c: 141). Photography became a important means of expression for the later Baudrillard. Many of his photographic works and essays on photography are collected in *Photographies 1985–1998* (Baudrillard, 1999).

Baudrillard's version of Nietzsche's death of God and eternal recurrence is clearly marked by his reading of Mauss, so it contrasts with the versions offered by Klossowski (1997) and Deleuze (1983). The following expresses something of the specificity of Baudrillard's position:

> Another explanation for our fall from grace is that the world is given to us. Now, what is given we have to be able to give back. In the past we could give thanks for the gift, or respond to it by sacrifice. Now we have no one to give thanks to. And if we can no longer give anything in exchange for the world, it is unacceptable. So we are going to have to liquidate the given world. To destroy it by substituting an artificial one, built by scratch, a world which we do not have to account to anyone.
>
> (Baudrillard, 2001c: 14)

Symbolic debt is crucial here, the counter-gift or potlatch form are impossible exchanges – exchanges without equivalence or equilibrium. We do not want to be indebted to God, who increased our debt by sacrificing his son for us, so we construct an artificial world of signs that is ours. Yet we are now indebted to ourselves, to our reason, our science and our consumer capitalist economy. We can only settle this debt, once and for all, by destroying the system, and by destroying ourselves through the construction of virtual reality as the total replacement for humanity and the social world. And, according to Baudrillard, these suicidal tendencies are very much in evidence. Through cloning and artificial intelligence we terminate the human race by replacing ourselves with copies (2001c: 26–39), and we also dream of smashing the system. Hence Baudrillard's reading of the 9/11 attacks: 'they did it, but *we* wished for it' (2003b: 5). So, to recap, all systems of meaning attempt to escape or 'conjure away' radical uncertainty and impossible exchange by finding a principle of equivalence, guaranteeing exchange. But all such systems have failed to banish radical uncertainty: religion has failed, science has failed, liberation has failed. But, Baudrillard insists, virtual reality offers a fully functional 'artificial double' for the world, a 'final solution'.[3]

EVIL

> [Y]ou cannot liberate good without liberating evil.
>
> (Baudrillard, 2005d: 142)

> I am playing devil's advocate here.
>
> (Baudrillard, 2005d: 155)

Evil is a major term in Baudrillard's later work. His earlier theory makes no mention of it, which is unusual in Baudrillard because very often terms develop slowly over the course of many years and, like the rules of a game, are present from the beginning. What does Baudrillard mean by Evil – a term he frequently capitalised?

One of the fundamental binary oppositions is that of Good and Evil. In monotheist religion Good and Evil tend to be separated out and placed in opposition. While serious theological thought and varied poetic traditions retain a sense of the ambivalence of Good and Evil – for example, in the figure of Satan the fallen angel – the moral and political pieties of humanist modernity tended to treat Good and Evil as binary oppositions. As the binary poles of the second order give way to the plural, tactical signs of the third and fourth orders the negative pole is 'liberated', supplying new energy to the positive pole. But Evil is hard to rebrand, so the term tends to be abandoned: to label anything or anyone 'evil' would be too discriminatory, too dramatic and too negative (1993b: 81–8). Baudrillard asks:

where did Evil go? And the answer is: everywhere – because the anamorphosis of modern forms of Evil knows no bounds. In a society which seeks – by prophylactic measures, by annihilating its own natural referents, by whitewashing violence, by exterminating all germs and all of the accursed share, by performing cosmetic surgery on the negative – to concern itself solely with quantified management and with the discourse of the Good, in a society where it is no longer possible to speak Evil, Evil has metamorphosed into all the viral and terroristic forms that obsess us.

(Baudrillard, 1993b: 81)

According to Baudrillard this signals the 'end' of power in the liberal democracies of the West. Power relations still exist, of course, indeed more and more power, or signs of power, is produced. But 'real' power, power over life and death, power to distinguish Good and Evil, cannot be exercised because no one will take responsibility for its exercise. No one, least of all politicians, is willing to embody power. Those with 'power' claim to be bound by forces beyond their control: an electorate, global economic forces, budget limitations, even time constraints. For Baudrillard,

power exists solely by virtue of its symbolic ability to designate the Other, the Enemy, what is at stake, what threatens us, what is Evil. Today this ability has been lost, and, correspondingly, there exists no opposition able or willing to designate power as Evil.

(Baudrillard, 1993b: 82)

Both the political power of the state and the opposing power of critical or progressive politics are undermined by the unwillingness to designate Evil. In this weightless, depressurised state the West is increasingly vulnerable to those who are *able to speak Evil*, who do assert the power over life and death, such as Islamist terrorists. The 'symbolic ability' to designate Evil is not an essence or a timeless force but becomes the 'ultimate weapon' against cultures that have rejected it because it receives the 'glamour' and 'energy' of rejection. Baudrillard's arguments concerning terrorism are discussed in detail in Chapter 7.

Evil, as Baudrillard theorises it, contrasts with the moral opposition of good and evil. We have failed to move 'beyond good and evil', as Nietzsche had hoped, because good and evil have become indistinguishable as so few people are willing to designate them (2005d: 155). For Baudrillard this indistinction itself expresses the principle of Evil, a principle of confusion, uncertainty and reversal:

The principle of Evil is not a moral principle but a principle of instability and vertigo, a principle of complexity and foreignness, a principle of seduction, a principle of incompatibility, antagonism and irreducibility. . . . It is a vital principle of disjunction.
(Baudrillard, 1993b: 107)

In other words, the principle of Evil 'protects us from the real and its disastrous consequences' (1990b: 185). The third order produces or simulates positive values. It separates out good and evil by producing and multiplying the signs of good or positivity: human rights, liberation, equality, consumerism. Baudrillard attacks this process as follows: 'The uninterrupted production of positivity has a terrifying consequence. Whereas negativity engenders crisis and critique, hyperbolic positivity for its part engenders catastrophe' (1993b: 106). Baudrillard seems to echo Nietzsche's contention in *Thus Spake Zarathustra* that 'whatever harm the wicked do, the harm the good do is the most harmful harm' (1961: 26). The influence of Bataille is also clear: 'Anything that purges the accursed share in itself signs its own death warrant. This is the theorem of the accursed share' (Baudrillard, 1993b: 106):

> The totality constituted by Good and Evil together transcends us, but we should accept it totally. There can be no intelligence of things so long as this fundamental rule is ignored. The illusion that the two can be distinguished in order to promote one or the other is absurd. (This applies to the proponents of evil for evil's sake as much as to anyone else, for they will end up doing good.)
> (Baudrillard, 1993b: 109–10)

Baudrillard's late works *Impossible Exchange* (2001c) and *The Intelligence of Evil* (2005d) attempt to 'think Evil' as 'inseparable' from Good, yet also 'irreconcilable' with it (2001c: 90). Criticising theology and moral philosophy for making Evil 'unreal', absent or 'always in the pay of Good', Baudrillard asserts that 'Evil has its own destiny, arising only out of itself, eternally enigmatic (2001c: 91). And today, increasingly, this 'eternal principle . . . shows through the universal hegemony of the Good' (ibid.). Good and Evil exist in an 'asymmetrical . . . antagonistic balance' (2001c: 92). Good is never able to become hegemonic because 'Good destroys itself: the optimizing of systems takes them to the verge of dissolution' (2001c: 94):

> Good and Evil are reversible. Not only are they not opposed, they can change into each other, and the distinction between them is ultimately meaningless . . . Good is just the part of Evil showing

above the water . . . they are secretly formed of a single substance
. . . [we] do not have a choice between Good and Evil, since they
are merely the transfusion or transfiguration of each other.
(Baudrillard, 2001c: 94–5)

Because Good and Evil are asymmetric the relationship between them
is not one of difference: 'Evil is more than different' (2001c: 96). The
moral distinction between Good and Evil is a construction from the
perspective of Good, which posits Evil as its opposite. Evil, though, does
not oppose itself to Good, except in the histrionic derangement of Sade,
which Baudrillard scorns as a 'desperate superstition' (2001c: 97). For
Baudrillard, both those who account themselves Good and those who
attempt deliberately to do Evil share a common prejudice in reducing
Evil to the experiencing or causing of 'misfortune'. Misfortune is 'the
transcription into the real of the spiritual instance of Evil' and fails to
confront the 'ambivalence' of the relation between Good and Evil.
Misfortune, defined by Baudrillard as 'poverty, violence, accident,
death' (2001c: 96), enables Good to equip itself with an illusory
identity. Evil, defined as 'semblance, illusion, uncertainty' (2001c: 98)
is radically different and is contrasted not with Good, but with reality;
Evil is the rule and reality is the 'exception'. The discourse of the
Good is unitary or integral; it expels otherness, illusion, enigma. So
'humanistic, pluralistic thought' offers only a *'trompe l'oeil* invocation
of the Other' (2001c: 100). For Baudrillard 'there is radical alterity only
in duality . . . the dual principle' (ibid.); indeed, symbolic engagement
or responsibility for the Other can occur only through the dual form,
because asymmetry 'gives rise to [the] reciprocal attraction' (2001c: 85,
101). This theme is further explored in Chapter 8.

In his final major theoretical work, *The Intelligence of Evil* (2005d),
Baudrillard pushes this notion of Evil much further. The ancient,
though by no means timeless, distinction between Good and Evil is
further reduced in modernity to an 'ideological distinction between
happiness and misfortune' (2005d: 139). Reduced to misfortune, Evil
is understood as accidental (or 'privative' in the canonical Christian
tradition; see Augustine, 1971) because human beings are understood
as naturally good. Indeed, both Christianity and secular humanism share
these basic assumptions: in the first perfection is given by God, lost
in sin and regained through Christ, while in humanism perfection is
given by nature, obscured by adverse social conditions and realised
by education and culture. For Baudrillard this way of thinking is
'our deepest imaginary conception and . . . our most serious confusion'
(ibid.).

Baudrillard's 'hypothesis of Evil' declares: 'man is not good by nature, not because he might be said to be bad, but because he is perfect as he is' (2005d: 140). To be human (Baudrillard writes 'Man' but on this occasion seems to mean human) is to be perfect, singular and 'incomparable'. Take away the idea of God, of nature, of evolution and progress, as Nietzsche did, and everything becomes perfectly singular because it cannot be referred to any conception of the universal. This includes Evil: 'Evil is perfect when left to itself' (ibid.). But Evil cannot be thought in isolation from Good: 'of Evil in its pure state it is impossible to speak' (2005d: 139, translation modified). Good and Evil are inseparable, dual forms. The 'Good' of humanitarian intervention enables the 'Evil' of extending Western capitalist hegemony; the 'Good' of regime change and the forcible imposition of happiness increases the amount of misfortune and misery. Baudrillard paraphrases Ceronetti in the following: 'it is not evil but good that is manifestly at the controls of the suicide engine' (2005d: 143, translation modified). The drive for universal happiness is a 'pathetic, sentimental vision' (2005d: 144). It is based on resentment and recrimination against ourselves and others, and it converts Evil into misfortune on an industrial level. In this nihilistic world of value, morality and 'progress' misfortune is the only victor: 'misfortune is easier to manage than happiness . . . we tend towards misfortune as the most sustainable solution – a kind of escape route from the terroristic happiness plot. The despair of having everything' (2005d: 145).

Misfortune, in its 'comfortable obviousness', wards off both unbearable happiness and 'the invisible continuity of evil'. Indeed, in modernity, there is a widespread 'wallowing in misfortune' (2005d: 151). An entire misfortune industry springs up: 'misfortune is exchanged on the Stock Exchange of values, whereas evil is inconvertible' (2005d: 152). Baudrillard ridicules such demands for compensation: for accidents, for depression, for rape, even for being born handicapped. This way of thinking could, of course, be cited by the left as 'evidence' of Baudrillard's dangerous extremism, his supposedly 'aristocratic disdain' (Kellner, 1989: 195) for ordinary people and their suffering. But, as ever, matters are not so clear-cut. According to Baudrillard the misfortune industry reduces the social to mere 'insurance and security', while also disseminating 'a very mediocre idea of oneself' (2005d: 152). Notions of destiny, tragedy and character are eliminated when misfortune is attributed to an objective cause. Character is replaced by existence: a diminished, disengaged state. Yet we are *of* the world, part of it, and for Baudrillard 'The intelligence of evil begins with the hypothesis that our ills come to us from an evil genius that is our own' (ibid.). In denying this we reduce ourselves, and worse, we reduce the status of the victims of misfortune, 'confining them to their condition of victim'. And, by inserting their experience within a universal scale of rights and compensation, a scale of abstract exchange (e.g. £10,000 for a lost limb), we deny the immeasurability of their suffering. Finally, and even more controversially, the misfortune industry denies our complicity, both our complicity in their suffering (enjoying it as a sign consumed on TV news, for example) and their complicity in their own suffering, their 'acting out in the fatal zone' (2005d: 153). That is, we deny them their originality, their singularity, their 'original will to commit, the act itself' (ibid.). But Baudrillard does not, for a moment, suggest that people are totally responsible for their own suffering:

> For the act we commit, it is right we should be dealt with – and indeed punished – accordingly. We are never innocent of that act in the sense of having nothing to do with it or being victims of it. But this does not mean we are answerable for ourselves, that we were invested with total power over ourselves, this is a subjective illusion.
>
> (Baudrillard, 2005d: 153)

Unfortunately the examples Baudrillard gives are underdeveloped. He cites Stockholm syndrome again (2005d: 154; see also 2001c: 19), where the hostage comes to share the cause of the hostage-takers. Baudrillard calls this a 'symbolic transference . . . part of the ironic essence of evil' (2005d: 154). But Stockholm syndrome is rare and certainly not new; because it was identified in 1973, we might consider this a third order phenomenon. Baudrillard also refers to the complicitous pact of seduction, but again this example adds nothing that is specific to the fourth order. But perhaps this is to fall into the trap of understanding the fourth order as a reality. In writing of the fourth order Baudrillard is involved in a wager, not an exposition, a challenge, not a description. Playing devil's advocate, Baudrillard wagers on ideas he finds stimulating, interesting, 'fun', not necessarily ideas that are convincing, coherent or 'true' (2005d: 155–8).

The intelligence of Evil seems to mean insight into 'duality and reversibility', which are, of course, symbolic forms. This is intelligence of evil not as 'objective reality', since evil has no objective reality, but evil as diversion, reversal and eternal return – for Baudrillard the 'reversible form of becoming' (2005d: 159). Evil, in this sense, cannot be willed; it is not a property of subjective intention or choice. Evil, for Baudrillard, is not a thing, it is not a force and it is not an unconscious principle as suggested by Freud's notion of the death-drive. Evil, like the symbolic, is a form, and like the object, it is a form that thinks us, 'in the sense that it is implied automatically in every one of our acts. For it is not possible for any act whatever or any kind of talk not to have two sides to it; not to have a reverse side, and hence a dual existence . . . contrary to any finality or objective determinism' (2005d: 160).

Evil as dual form, as the 'Nothing' that shadows the something, is 'irreducible', it is indissociably a part of life. Evil cannot be banished, corrected, treated – all we can do is 'come to an understanding with it' (2005d: 161). Evil, in this sense, is 'not the same thing as violence' (ibid.), which is directed towards a goal or purpose. Evil is ambivalent, it is reversible in its relation to the Good, it is impersonal, unwilled, it cannot be mastered or directed. Baudrillard develops these themes further in his work on terrorism, discussed in Chapter 7.

7

War, Terrorism and 9/11

> The revolution will never rediscover death unless it
> demands it immediately . . . only death can put an end
> to political economy.
>
> (Baudrillard, 1993a: 186–7)

> Direct political action was no longer possible. We were
> left to do the same thing the terrorists do: destabilise.
>
> (Baudrillard interviewed in Stearns and
> Chaloupka, 1992: 299)

INTRODUCTION: VIOLENCE

> [A]ffluence and violence go together; they have to be analysed
> together.
>
> (Baudrillard, 1998a: 175)

According to Baudrillard the affluent consumer society (and it *was* affluent in the late 1960s at the time of writing) is haunted by 'the
spectre of fragility' (1998a: 174); it is a vulnerable system because it
is a superficial one. The vulnerability of the consumer society, and, by
extension, of globalisation, is a recurrent theme in Baudrillard's work
(1993b: 81–8, 2002b: 57–61, 2003b: 87–105) and, as with many of his
key themes, it is present from the beginning.

Baudrillard begins his theorisation of violence in modernity by addressing the *apparent* contradiction that the consumer society is both 'pacified' and violent. This contradiction is only apparent, and does not constitute a resource for dialectical change, because violence is modelled, packaged and sold as commodity-sign to be consumed. Baudrillard certainly does not suggest that all violence is produced through mass mediation, that it is always specular or that it is 'just a representation'. In his early work Baudrillard even refers to 'real' violence, meaning violence that irrupts suddenly, seemingly from nowhere. Such violence is 'uncontrollable . . . aimless and objectless . . . unaccountable [a violence] which well-being secretes in its very achievement' (1998a: 174). Baudrillard's examples include the destruction of property and of people; he cites serial killers, spree killers and the Manson family killings of August 1969. But he also has in mind escapist behaviour through drug taking and the hippie 'drop-out' communities, and a range of psychological reactions such as depression, anxiety and chronic fatigue. Following Durkheim (1964: 353–73) on the condition of anomie – that it is difficult for individuals to adapt to new social conditions, even if these conditions are supposedly progressive or desirable – Baudrillard focuses on the new constraints imposed by the consumer society. The forms of violence and defiance that appear in the consumer system follow the form of the system. Where violence is 'wild, objectless, formless, this is because the constraints it is contesting are themselves also unformulated, unconscious, illegible: they are the very constraints of "freedom", of controlled accession to happiness, of the totalitarian ethic of affluence' (Baudrillard, 1998a: 176).

What is quite extraordinary in Baudrillard's writing on violence and terrorism is that his early position remained unchanged. Indeed, his initial arguments seem to have become more and more plausible with the passage of time and were applied, to strong effect, to new and unpredictable events of the twenty-first century, notably 9/11 (2003b) and the Abu Ghraib torture scandal (2005f), discussed below.

TERRORISM/MEDIA/MASSES

Against the perfection of the system, hatred is a last vital reaction.
(Baudrillard, 1996c: 147)

Those who live by the spectacle will die by the spectacle.
(Baudrillard, 2005e: 208)

In theorising terrorism Baudrillard continued to explore the complicity of the system in the forms of violence apparently directed against it.

Indeed, for Baudrillard terrorism and terror are, primarily, strategies of the system: of the state, the law, the market, the code. What is ordinarily called 'terrorism' – meaning organised violence and intimidation directed against the dominant system – is, for Baudrillard, the 'mirror' of the system's terroristic control over its population (1993b: 75–80, 1998a: 148). How can this be the case?

Baudrillard's writings on politics, resistance and terrorism are deeply influenced by situationism, particularly the movement's impresario Guy Debord (1932–94). The situationists departed from Marxism by attempting to resist capitalism through subversion, mockery and acts of *detournement* (derailing or hijacking) rather than through dialectical critique or protest. Aware that capitalism reproduced its dominance through the cultural, as well as economic, system the situationists targeted the mass media. They seized radio stations or set up their own 'pirate' stations, occupied TV studios, jamming or subverting their broadcasts, seeking to disrupt the orderly flow of information and advertising that constituted what Debord termed *The Society of the Spectacle* (1967).

During the 1960s and 1970s many 'terrorist' groups sprang up in Western Europe, inspired by the situationists, and Baudrillard discusses movements such as the Italian Red Brigade in *Fatal Strategies* (1990b: 34–50) and elsewhere. He emphasises the 'intimacy' and 'complicity' of terrorist groups and the mass media, as the situationists had before him, but Baudrillard adds a third term: the masses. Terrorist groups require the media to spread terror through the system, and the media revel in negative, horrifying, fear-generating stories because we, the masses, enjoy consuming terror: a symbiotic relationship. The Italian Red Brigade was, apparently, destroyed by the media when its subversions were labelled 'terrorist' after the bombing of the Piazza Fontana in 1969, which was thought to be carried out by Italian security forces specifically to achieve this effect (see Plant, 1992: 128–33). As Baudrillard has frequently noted, in a media-saturated world it becomes difficult, even impossible, to establish who did what and why: an excess of information is entropic (1994a: 79–86). All sides attempt to interpret or recuperate terrorist events for their own purposes: governments can extend state and police powers, media corporations profit from images of death and horror and the masses ('you, me and everyone'; 1983: 46) enjoy the spectacle.

The classic terrorist strategy is hostage taking, and, for Baudrillard, this involves a specifically symbolic challenge to the system, though one that ultimately fails to undermine it. According to Baudrillard the system thrives on continual expansion, proliferation and circulation of capital, objects, bodies and information (1993b: 1–13). Hostage taking is a radical act because it 'subtracts' capital from the system, creating, momentarily, a 'void' that the media rushes in to fill. Terrorist acts are ambivalent in that 'there is a simultaneous power of death and simulation . . . it brings together the spectacle and the challenge at their highest points' (1983: 113–14). Acts of terrorism enable terrorists to put their lives and the lives of others at stake, to challenge the system of slow, managed death with the threat of sudden, violent death. Where terrorists die by their own hands, or are killed by state security services, there is the potential for 'the purest form of symbolic challenge', the system is attacked at its symbolic foundations. Such deaths are 'a paradoxical configuration . . . the only original form of our time, and subversive because insoluble' (1983: 114–15). Death is wrested from social control, a fully symbolic challenge because the constant fear of death irrupts into life. Bomb blasts in busy high streets demolish the Saussurian bar that separates life and death: in blind terror we are only too aware that death inhabits life. In the carnage of terrorist violence life and capital are subtracted from the system, but so too is security – the general sense of orderliness and meaningfulness of the system is thrown into disarray.

Terrorist acts, Baudrillard asserts, cannot be understood as grounded in the objectives of the terrorists; that is, at the level of the 'content' of their demands. Such readings are reductive and serve only to reinforce meaning and order. For Baudrillard terrorist acts create a 'void' around themselves, a vacuum of non-meaning. The term 'void' expresses the collapsing or implosion of binary oppositions. Terrorist acts cannot be comprehended adequately through binary oppositions. The terrorist 'event' is constituted by the media and by the masses' consumption of it. Further, the distinction between victory and defeat is often unclear. If security forces wipe out the terrorist cell, is this a victory or has the state merely facilitated martyrdom and lost the moral high ground? What if hostages die in the process? What if it becomes impossible to distinguish hostages and terrorists, as in the case of Stockholm syndrome, where hostages develop attachments to captors and, apparently, do not want to be rescued (discussed by Baudrillard on a number of occasions; see 2001c: 19, 2005c: 198, 2005d: 154). Are the media exploiting terrorists, or are the terrorists exploiting the media? Are the masses watching in terror or are they enjoying a good spectacle?

The relationship between the distinctively contemporary triad of media, masses and terrorist is, then, exceptionally ambivalent. The hostage is 'Neither dead nor alive . . . it is not his destiny that awaits him, nor his

own death, but anonymous chance . . . something absolutely arbitrary':
'There is no distinction possible between the spectacular and the symbolic, no distinction possible between the "crime" and the "repression".
It is this uncontrollable eruption of reversibility that is the true victory
of terrorism' (Baudrillard, 1983: 115–16). Fundamentally, then, terrorism 'is not a question of real violence'. Real violence challenges
nothing, it is 'always on the side of power' (1990b: 119). Terrorism
possesses an implosive/symbolic energy and 'absorbs everything real',
its energy 'shines intensely for a moment before falling back into the
real' (1983: 121). For Baudrillard terrorism embodies the eclipse of
politics and representation (second order phenomena) and is post-
dialectical, ecstatic, 'transpolitical': 'more violent than the violent'.
Terrorism unleashes 'the scandal of accidental death' on a system that
is 'programmed for the prevention of accidental death' (1990b: 37).
Terrorism is, then, a displaced or placeless manifestation of death as a
symbolic relation, as a symbolic stake. Terrorism is singular and
uniquely challenging to the system because the system itself is terrorist:

> We are all hostages, and we are all terrorists . . . [Terrorism] only
> carries to its extreme conclusion the essential proposition of
> liberal and Christian humanism: all men are in solidarity; you, here,
> are in solidarity with and responsible for the wretched . . . a
> proposition of universal responsibility itself monstrous and ter-
> roristic in its essence.
>
> (1990b: 36)

We hold ourselves hostage to our coded identities, we are 'blackmailed
by identity', which amounts to 'symbolic murder' because, Baudrillard
asserts, we never coincide with our identities, we remain other to ourselves. To be forced to coincide with yourself and everyone else, always
to be who you are according to the definitions of the system, is to die
symbolically and live only as mass individual, customised, coded (but
not passive).

Yet terrorism, ultimately, fails. Baudrillard does not laud it as the
'future' of subversion or protest in a transpolitical or post-political world.
Terrorism fails because the hostage is 'unexchangeable', a 'pure' or 'fatal'
object that cannot be reinserted into the system:

> Violently withdrawing the hostage from the circuit of value, the
> terrorist also withdraws from the circuit of negotiation. The two
> are out of circulation . . . and what is established between them
> . . . is a dual figure . . . the only modern figure of a shared death.
>
> (1990b: 49)

Terrorism, then, is a failure, a failed challenge. It threatens the system by producing the 'inexchangeable' in a system that survives by ordered exchange, but it fails in its attempt to reintroduce exchange in terms of its choosing. It thereby reaffirms the system of value it had momentarily breached, and lapses into sign fodder for global TV companies.

THE EVIL DEMON OF IMAGES

Baudrillard's position on the 'effects' of mediated images or signs has been badly misinterpreted by his critics and so requires further elaboration. Kellner (1989: 146), for example, calls Baudrillard a 'sign-fetishist', suggesting that he uncritically celebrates or worships sign spectacles, but Kellner's critique misses the point. For Baudrillard, audience responses to media images are always ambivalent: fear, horror, arousal, excitement and enjoyment, pity, compassion, contempt and malice jostle for position. Our consumption of images cannot be broken down into neat binary oppositions and will not submit to the moral criteria of right and wrong, acceptable and unacceptable. Of course, film-makers such as Quentin Tarantino exploit this ambivalence ruthlessly by, for example, depicting beautiful women beating each other senseless, limbs being severed, blood spurting – all to a thumping soundtrack. When the heroine of Tarantino's *Kill Bill Vol. 1* (2003) murders a young Japanese women who is dressed as a schoolgirl, we rejoice that the heroine still lives and that the 'sexy schoolgirl' armed with ball and chain has not killed her. Yet we are confronted with a close-up of the dead girl's face, her snarl now erased, her skull fractured, her eyes dead and broken. But don't worry, there are plenty more men and women for our heroine to kill before the film is over! We enjoy images of violent spectacle, whether 'real' or fictional, and a sexual or pornographic dimension adds a *frisson*. Indeed, according to Baudrillard, the screen *as form* replaces the distinction between 'real' and 'fictional'. Of course Baudrillard did not contend that some people are just too stupid to 'tell the difference'. Nothing on a screen is 'real'; it is, by definition an image. 'Reality' is rendered hyperreal or simulatory as soon as it appears on a screen: it is cut up, segmented, framed, commodified – it is a sign (1981: 169–72, 1998a: 121–8). This does not imply that 'real' and 'fictional' can never be distinguished – of course they can – but they share a commonality at the level of form.

To clarify, the relationship between the image and the referent (the 'real') is not non-existent, but it is perverse and 'diabolical'. For Baudrillard, images

always appear to refer to a real world, to real objects and to reproduce something which is logically and chronologically anterior to
themselves. None of this is true. As simulacra, images precede the
real to the extent that they invert the causal and logical order of
the real and its reproduction.

(Baudrillard, 1987c: 13)

Images of violence, for example, no matter how cartoon-like or stylised,
'always appear to refer to a real world'. They seem to tell us something
about the world we live in: how violent and brutal it is when we strip
away the illusions and veils. Yes, sexy girls can kill; yes 'cool' men
in smart suits with good taste in music enjoy torture (to refer to
Tarantino's *Reservoir Dogs*, 1991). As Baudrillard argues, such images
are not isolated units of meaning, they form codes or models that 'precede' our experience of 'reality'. 'Reality' seems to be a more violent,
more unpleasant place, images 'contaminate reality . . . model it . . .
anticipate it to the point that reality no longer has time to be produced
as such' (1987c: 16). None of this, of course, implies that 'reality' was
a pure and harmonious place 'before' the contamination. 'Reality' is
simulacral, 'only ever a simulation', but technically produced images add
a new layer of simulation based on abstract, precessionary models
(1987c: 21). For Baudrillard this 'pretension to be real', to grasp the
real in its 'starkness' through images is 'naïve and paranoiac . . . [a]
puritanical and terrorist vision of signs' (1987c: 33). The image, for
Baudrillard, is 'fundamentally immoral'; it is an 'evil demon'.

So called 'reality' TV operates in a similar way. Baudrillard first wrote
about 'reality' TV in the late 1970s and argued that it exemplified 'the
mutation of the real into the hyperreal' (1994a: 30). Late essays, collected in *Telemorphose* (2001d), return to this theme: 'when everything
is on display (like in Big Brother, reality-shows etc.) we realise there
is nothing left to see' (2001d: 181). 'Reality' TV displays life through
models, 'the illusion of the real world' (ibid.). There is a 'loss of all
symbolic space' in 'the delirious exhibitionism of one's own nullity'
(2001d: 183). And, Baudrillard insists, there is a direct, logical connection between 'reality' TV and snuff movies, 'at the same time as they try
to make it (death) disappear technologically, death will reappear on
the screen as an extreme experience' (2001d: 193). 'Reality' TV is terrorism, a terroristic evocation of reality *as sign*, a violence directed
against us all in which we are all complicit. Baudrillard's writing is not
a fetishism of signs, as Kellner (1989: 146) suggests, it is a denunciation
of them. The scandal of Abu Ghraib some years later was confirma-
tion of the power of Baudrillard's provocative anticipations.

THE UNITED STATES, WAR AND POWER

Exchanging war for the signs of war.

(Baudrillard, 1994b: 62)

For Baudrillard, the USA had power, genuine power, in the mid-twentieth century, but this power has long been simulatory, it is now 'power as a special effect' (1988a: 107). The USA was 'Left brittle by the Vietnam War'; it fought an enemy and world opinion, neither of which it could understand. America kept a collective distance from this incomprehensible enemy by waging 'a television war', not a 'real' war. Indeed, according to Baudrillard, 'the Vietnam war never happened' (1987c: 17). It was instead an opportunity for the USA to 'test' its military and communications technology; both designed specifically to prevent engagement, military or otherwise, with the other.

For Baudrillard America is 'utopia achieved' (1988a: 75). This comment has been badly misunderstood by Callinicos (1989: 146–7) and others. It is not an endorsement but a recognition of the otherness of the USA to Europe, its inassimilability to European notions of history and progress. Baudrillard's writings on his travels in the USA, collected as *Amerique/America* (1988a), reveal his fascination with a country of great beauty, but he is scathing of its political system, particularly its treatment of the poor and dispossessed:

> this easy life knows no pity. . . . Reagan has never had the faintest inkling of the poor and their existence, not the slightest contact with them. He knows only the self-evidence of wealth, the tautology of power. . . . The have-nots will be condemned to oblivion, to abandonment, to disappearance pure and simple . . . utopia has arrived. If you aren't part of it, get lost.
>
> (Baudrillard, 1988a: 111–12)

Attacking Reagonomics (and Thatcherism) for abandoning progressive politics, for reducing the social order 'to include only economic exchange, technology, the sophisticated and innovative' (1988a: 112), Baudrillard again hints at the likelihood of a 'violent turn' in events. But it is not the poor and dispossessed who will strike back at the system, it is those who share in it, who have benefited from it, yet who seek to destroy it.

Reagan, like George W. Bush after him, seemed invulnerable to rational critique – 'How can it be that no mistake or political reversal damages his standing[?]' (1988a: 113) – because this is a simulatory power 'based on the advertising image' (ibid.). America is no longer a world power, it is a model and a near universal one, its business, fashion, culinary and entertainment styles recognisable – and apparently desired – the world over. Yet, for Baudrillard, the America of the 1980s existed in 'a fragile meta-stability', as 'power in a vacuum' (1988a: 116) because as a global superpower it had no serious competitors. It was becoming an 'over-protected organism', vulnerable to itself as the body is to cancer, from devastation from *within* (1988a: 117).

Baudrillard's three essays on non-war, collected as *The Gulf War Did Not Take Place* (1995) were once highly controversial and attracted outraged denunciation from Norris (1992) and others, arguing that the Gulf War did indeed take place because many bombs exploded and many people died. Merrin (1994) and Patton (in Baudrillard, 1995: 1–21) subsequently indicated the many weaknesses in Norris's knee-jerk response, principally his inability to comprehend Baudrillard's argument. In fact Baudrillard cites the number of casualties and the volume of explosives used (1995: 61, 71–2), arguing that what did take place was not a 'war', but something worse than a war.

Baudrillard's arguments are concerned with the nature of representation, and, specifically, the impact of communications media on the representation of war. Clearly wars have always been represented: the Bayeux tapestry represents the Battle of Hastings, it is not itself the Battle of Hastings. When attempting to imagine the Battle of Hastings I cannot help but recall the tapestry. Nevertheless, I would be quite willing to accept accounts produced by historians claiming, for example, that the battle was far more bloody than the tapestry suggests, or that certain other details are inaccurate. In this case there is a great deal of distance between the event and the representations, and for Baudrillard, this distance or space of representation produces a sense of the 'real'. The 'real' is representation; there is no 'real' that is not represented. We are convinced of the 'reality' of an event when we are convinced by representations that are supposedly caused by it. As Baudrillard and many other thinkers have argued, 'reality' is an effect of representation, not the cause of representation. Baudrillard probes the nature of representation in the contemporary world of satellite links, 24-hour rolling news and the Internet. In other words, the long-standing problem of representation is, according to Baudrillard, fundamentally transformed by the development of new communications technologies.

The first Gulf War (GW1) was the first major conflict to feature 'live' or 'real-time' battlefront footage. It was also notable for nose-camera video images of so-called 'smart' bombs: viewers were offered a 'bomb's eye' view of devastation served to their living rooms. It has frequently been argued, but first by Baudrillard, that the extensive use of such images enabled the construction of a 'clean', sanitised war of careful intelligence-led, surgical strikes eliminating Iraqi infrastructure with minimal loss of life. This, for Baudrillard, is a simulation of war, and a 'rotten simulation' at that (1995: 59). But no matter how offended we are by this rottenness we cannot retrieve the 'real' war from 'behind' the simulation because the very possibility of a 'real' war has disappeared and been replaced by simulation. The sub-Baudrillardian 'critiques' that attempt to uncover the reality behind the simulation fail in this task: the real is a simulation, and simulation is not unreal or 'fictive', but hyper-real (see Walsh, 1995: 1–20, and Ignatieff, 2000, for such attempts). Information and images of virtual war are not fake. Instead they are hyperreal, instantaneous, actual images from the ground, which the form of communications media abstracts, segments and renders into signs for our consumption.

The military efforts of the US and allied forces were, in themselves, based on technologies of simulation. Pilots are trained by computer simulations and military strategies are developed, refined and played out innumerable times through simulated war games. And, of course, war games simulations are a popular form of entertainment, with Gulf War simulation games appearing in 1990, before GW1, and in 2003, before GW2 (see Merrin, 2005: 108).

Further, on many occasions we, as consumers of news, experienced mediated simulations of mediated simulations. That is, the images of the war appearing on the news were themselves technical simulations or virtual models produced by the on-board computers of warplanes and strategic control centres. In such cases any 'real' referent, such as targets moving through the Kuwaiti desert, were replaced by techno-logical simulation models relayed by satellite technology. So the 'reality' reported, so proudly and so laboriously, by Western news organisations was, in fact, composed of simulations then further abstracted into con-sumable news images: two clear examples of what Baudrillard, in 1976, termed the 'precession of simulacra'.

But war, Baudrillard contends, is never merely 'real'. The 'real', as produced by representation itself, denies the symbolic level and any meaningful conflict has a symbolic dimension. Further, the 'real' level is joined by a hyperreal level – the war of images. On the symbolic level prestige or 'face' is at stake and humiliation is far worse than mere physical or 'real' defeat. Indeed, a 'real' defeat can involve the earning of the respect of the enemy, or even a favourable economic or political settlement. By contrast, in the first Gulf War the USA, according to Baudrillard, totally refused to acknowledge the enemy as worthy of respect, even a respect based on fear. Building on the model established for the Vietnam war, the American military machine attempted to bypass completely the symbolic dimension by remote, computerised elimination of the 'other'. Yet by failing to comprehend a symbolic dimension the USA becomes uniquely vulnerable to symbolic humiliation by its 'other'. Baudrillard makes this point repeatedly: the USA risks a massive symbolic humiliation by an enemy it cannot comprehend (1993b: 83–6, 138, 1995: 39, 54–5). These warnings now have an eerie ring of prophecy given the events of 9/11.

9/11

One of the most remarkable features of Baudrillard's (now notorious) essay *L'espirit du terrorisme/The Spirit of Terrorism* (2003b) is that his position on terrorism was not altered or revised at all following the events of 9/11. There was no hasty revision or back-pedalling; instead this momentous event seemed to confirm the strength of Baudrillard's original position. Baudrillard's *oeuvre* is not at all one of 'postmodern' fragmentation or provisional 'until further notice' pragmatism: it is one of dogged consistency. 9/11 suggested that events had actually moved in the direction Baudrillard anticipated: the West's terrible vulnerability to symbolic attack had finally been exploited to stunning, lethal effect.

For Baudrillard the events of 9/11 went far beyond a 'real' attack, it was an attack of mythic, symbolic and utterly humiliating proportions; not a real event, but a symbolic 'absolute event' (2003b: 4). The terrorists destroyed the notion of a 'Global World Order' based on universal, consensual, democratic values. Exploring these symbolic resonances, Baudrillard argues that the widespread moral condemnations following the attacks spring from a collective effort to mask our 'prodigious jubilation at seeing this global superpower destroyed . . . they *did it*, but we *wished for* it' (2003b: 4–5).

The symbolic dimensions of the event are complex and elusive. Baudrillard puts several interrelated themes into play, seeking to create 'a horizon of thought', not a closed explanatory account. The symbolic relation prevents or undermines ordered oppositions and separations: 'us' and 'them', self and other, life and death. The global system is terroristic and the violence directed against it had, in the past, followed the system's own simulation models. The results were 'real' or hyperreal violence that did not challenge the system at a fundamental level. But where terrorism had failed to shake the system in the past, the 9/11 attacks were different because it was 'the combination of two mechanisms – an operational structure and a symbolic pact – that made such excessiveness possible' (2003b: 22). The suicide attackers possessed, in addition to expertise in communication and aviation technology, 'the absolute weapon of death' (2003b: 8):

> It was the system itself which created the objective conditions for this brutal retaliation. By seizing all the cards for itself, it forced the Other to change the rules . . . Terrorism is the act that restores an irreducible singularity to the heart of a system of general exchange. All the singularities (species, individual and cultures) that have paid with their deaths for the installation of a global circulation governed by a single power are taking their revenge.
>
> (Baudrillard, 2003b: 9)

The events of 9/11 were not evidence of a 'clash of civilisations' (as argued by Huntington, 1998) but, according to Baudrillard, 'triumphant globalisation battling against itself' (2003b: 11). The process of globalisation had secreted its own antibodies that attack it internally, an 'automatic reversion of its own power' (ibid.) that resonates within each of us as part of our imagination revolts against a global consensus: 'we are all hostages, and we are all terrorists' (1990b: 36). The terrorists studied in America and Europe, they were not the excluded or disenfranchised, but became 'insiders', recognisable or readable as part of the code. The terrorists 'used the banality of American life as cover and camouflage. Sleeping in their suburbs, reading and studying with their families, before activating themselves suddenly like time bombs' (2003b: 19–20). It was a 'terrorism of the rich . . . they had become rich . . . without ceasing to wish to destroy us' (2003b: 23). Yet, according to Baudrillard, as a symbolic act the terrorists did not seek to eliminate the other, it was still 'a pact with an adversary' (2003b: 26):

> the action of the terrorists, from which death is inseparable (this is precisely what makes it a symbolic act), does not seek the impersonal elimination of the other. Everything lies in the challenge and the duel . . . dual, personal relation with the opposing power. It is that power which humiliated you, so it must be humiliated. And not merely exterminated. It has to be made to lose face.
>
> (Baudrillard, 2003b: 25–6)

The symbolic dimension of the attack is, then, multifaceted. The terrorists attacked the symbols of US global power, the twin towers of the World Trade Center. The architecture of the twin towers, Baudrillard had argued in 1976, was a perfect symbol of economic and cultural hegemony in their doubled, mirrored nature. The twinness symbolising that any otherness, critique or alternative is redundant, the towers reflected each other in a closed totalitarianism, like a binary code: not the US Trade Center but the *World* Trade Center (1993a: 69, 82, 186).[1] Attempting to destroy this potent symbol of US power is, then, a symbolic assault in the commonplace meaning of 'symbolic'. But further, the terrorists reintroduce 'sacrificial-suicidal' death into a system built on the severing of all symbolic relations including that of life and death. In their readiness to die the terrorists refuse the slow death of normalised, affluent, modern, educated existence in a terrible 'potlatch-like' act that the system cannot comprehend and that shakes its (binary) foundations. But this was not, of course, a conscious, wilful strategy of symbolic exchange. No one, including the terrorists, could predict that the twin towers would actually implode and collapse to the ground. It was as if, Baudrillard insists, the twin towers were committing suicide, repaying the 'symbolic debt' of the suicidal sacrifice of terrorists and the deaths of innocent passengers. The deaths of the hijackers were 'symbolic', Baudrillard insists, 'sacrificial': 'the irruption of a death that is far more than real' (2003b: 16–17). By reintroducing sacrificial death the terrorists

> shift the struggle into the symbolic sphere, where the rule is that of the challenge, reversion and outbidding. *So that death can be met only by equal or greater death.* Defy the system by a gift to which it cannot respond except by its own death and its own collapse.
>
> (2003b: 17, original emphasis)

Baudrillard's position on defiance had not changed since the publication of *Symbolic Exchange*. The 'spirit' of terrorism resides in the symbolic obligation to reciprocate, the spirit of the gift, the symbolic relation that has always 'haunted' the code and its simulations. In the absence of any subjective understanding of symbolic relations there can be no counter-gift, but this does not mean that the symbolic relation is annihilated, forgotten or surpassed. The fundamental rule of obligation holds and the object responds directly: the towers themselves commit suicide.

Hence for Baudrillard the symbolic level of objective irony and fatal strategies came into play; this was an objective as well as a subjective suicide. The 'incandescent images' of the towers' implosion were so powerful and evocative that they could not be neutralised by the mass mediation of the images. Despite being repeated *ad infinitum* the images of the collapsing towers retained their power to appal. So, according to Baudrillard, these images annul simulation models and, as if by chain reaction, cause each and every one of us to experience an illicit joy in the images of destruction. On the real level the event may be abhorred for its terrifying loss of life, but on the symbolic level there was a sense of a wish fulfilled.

For Baudrillard 9/11 did not signal the return of the real from the hyperreal: the level of the real remained peripheral.

> The collapse of the World Trade Center towers is unimaginable, but that is not enough to make it a real event. An excess of violence is not enough to open on to reality. For reality is a principle, and it is this principle that is lost.
>
> (Baudrillard, 2003b: 28)

In the images of devastation 'the real is superadded to the image like a bonus of terror, like an additional *frisson*: not only is it terrifying, but, what is more, it is real' (2003b: 29). The 'real', then, is a special effect, an effect of images. Utterly humiliated on the symbolic level, the American military-informational complex responded in the only way it knew how: by generating new images of its effectiveness and might. It waged new virtual wars in Afghanistan and Iraq, simulating the ordered binary oppositions of 'us' and 'them' and seeking to inflict its own humiliation on this elusive enemy.

THE PORNOGRAPHY OF WAR

> [T]he idea of war has to be rescued from time to time by spectacle set pieces, such as the Gulf War, or the war in Afghanistan. But the fourth world war is elsewhere. It haunts every world order, all hegemonic domination . . . for it is the world, the globe itself, which resists globalisation.
>
> (Baudrillard, 2003b: 12)

According to Baudrillard the images of Abu Ghraib depicted a 'worse' humiliation and degradation of human life than the destruction of the World Trade Center. The treatment of Iraqi prisoners was a 'symbolic and completely fatal humiliation' (2005e: 205), not only an 'atrocious' attack on the victims, but, for Baudrillard, a humiliation for American and Western power. This was a humiliation that the Western powers inflicted on themselves, a 'non-event of an obscene banality' that reveals that the West is at war with itself (2005e: 206).

Unable to wage a 'real' war against a 'real' enemy, the Western powers, embodied by American soldiers, were forced into 'a desperate simulacrum of power', constructing a 'parody of violence' (ibid.):

These scenes are the illustration of a power which, reaching its extreme point, no longer knows what to do with itself – a power henceforth without aim, without purpose, without a plausible enemy, and in total impunity. . . . The ignominy, the vileness is the ultimate symptom of a power that no longer knows what to do with itself.

(Ibid.)

According to Baudrillard the world-wide availability of images of Abu Ghraib inflicts a 'murderous' reversal on American power, which had grown to obscene and 'pornographic' levels. The obscenity of this global power is neatly summed up in the slogan 'Globalise or die', adopted widely by business schools and business corporations in the 1990s (see Friedman, 2000). Of course many people, across the world, have taken this injunction with a deadly literalness – opting to don a suicide jacket and die. The violent literalisation of metaphor is, for Baudrillard, a symbolic strategy for the reversal of power (1990a: 82–3, 1993a: 219–20), a violent turning of the tables where the apparently dominated asserts 'symbolic' mastery over those with a 'real' (or hyperreal) power. Baudrillard's argument is consistent with his earlier position on the symbolic power of femininity (1987b: 94–6, 1990b: 119–28), discussed in Chapter 5 of this volume, and of the masses (1983), discussed in Chapter 4. The extraordinary violence of the slogan 'Globalise or die' lies latent until violently literalised by the suicide bomber, and it is a slogan applied to 'the West and the rest'; it is a violence that the West inflicts on itself as well as on its 'others'.

The images of the Abu Ghraib abuses are not necessarily reliable or true, a 'real' exposure of the depths of the depravity of occupying armies. The images are beyond the true and false, they are 'virtual', yet also 'fatal' – a spiralling together of the semiotic and symbolic, the banal and the fatal that is characteristic of the fourth order (1998b: 47). The fatal or symbolic form irrupts through the virtual. Baudrillard's argument is not as abstract as people imagine; it is often rooted in empirical events, though it involves a very particular reading of the empirical through Baudrillard's notion of symbolic exchange. So, according to Baudrillard, with the abuses of Abu Ghraib the Americans sought to inflict a humiliation on their enemies greater and more extreme than 9/11. The American soldiers attempted to inflict a fate worse than death on an enemy that, apparently, does not fear death. A humiliation was constructed that was pornographic and sexually degrading, a humiliation that would strip bare, that would literally dis-illusion, a desire 'to tear off the veil of women or abuse men to make them appear more naked, more obscene' (2005d: 209). The images of Abu Ghraib resembled extreme pornography and snuff. Baudrillard cites the images 'of the young American woman turned torturer in the jails of Iraq, holding the naked or hooded Arab on a leash' as similar to 'some Western, women-only club' (2006a: 61). Further, as Baudrillard notes, the hooded figure with electrodes attached to his body recalled the shameful activities of the Ku Klux Klan, recalling America's ignoble past as well as ruining its carefully crafted image as a bringer of peace and democracy to the contemporary world. But Baudrillard did not single out America, or Americans, as uniquely blameworthy. Eschewing the stock position of European left-wing intellectuals, Baudrillard emphasises the complicity of all of us, including terrorists, in a system of hatred and indifference.

HATRED

> We've all 'got the hate'. It is more than we could manage not to.
> (Baudrillard, 2002c: 95)

> Until we feel security, you will be our targets.
> (Mohammed Sidique Khan, 'Martyrdom Video', 2005)

Consider the failure of the 21 July London bombers to blow themselves and others apart. The hatred presumably felt by the would-be bombers was, if we follow Baudrillard's position, a 'last vital reaction' against the tyranny of the system – vital in that it does, at least, express a rejection and communicates that rejection to the other (1996c: 147). It restores speech, albeit a stunned, horrified and uncomprehending speech. But if we argue that 'radical Islam' is another code, and a more restrictive and totalitarian one than capitalism, then the failed suicide bombers have defied, through failure, both the capitalist imperatives to succeed and maximize, and the terrorist imperative to die in sacrificial glory. Yet in doing so they remain firmly entrenched within codes. Indeed, Sidique Khan's absurd formula, quoted above, demonstrates the coded, totalitarian, Western and distinctively modern nature of the 'demands' made by 'Islamist extremists'. 'Islamic' cultural identity is insecure, as any identity-claim necessarily is, and it seeks to destroy the other rather than engage with it. They are not the other, they are the same. The terrorists, like me, like us all, have 'the hate'. A hatred of the Code, the system, that is part of the Code or system, a response to it that plays out within the terms it sets. This is not a 'vital reaction', not a restoration of speech between self and other, but the self at war with its self. And as with the beating of a butterfly's wings, what starts out as petty hatred might lead to atrocity, and, reciprocally, what starts out as a will to destroy might lead to failure and farce.

Failed suicide bombers appear absurd, redundant, residual – like hostages without exchange-value (1990b: 34–50). Even the Western media seem relatively uninterested in them. They have become nothing: not martyrs, not victims. Where Mohammed Atta, Shedzad Tanweer and Mohammed Sidique Khan can be deployed as sign-exchange-values, as signifiers of horror with considerable yield as entertainment capital, the failed bombers cannot even be put to work, made to perform as TV signs. Paradoxically, they have strayed outside the value system, discovering not martyrdom or sacrificial glory but radical indifference.

In Baudrillard's later work it is in turning to the other that we refuse the self-same: 'The Other is what allows me not to repeat myself forever' (1993b: 174). To defy the gift of self we embrace the otherness of the other, not their sameness, not their compulsory registration within a system of coded differences. It is also to embrace the otherness of the self-same, the foreignness or alterity within, since we are all, fundamentally, 'other'. We must not deny our otherness in our engagement with the other; we must not 'whitewash' ourselves in order to produce something that we imagine is acceptable to the other, that will not offend anyone. Such a strategy would be to kill otherness and die ourselves. There is, for Baudrillard, no self or other in the act of symbolic exchange; there is only ambivalence, or 'complete foreignness'. With the symbolic order 'lost' there remains only the dual form, the pact, the following of the other.

8

Subjectivity, Identity and Agency

> Baudrillard's project is vitiated by the absence of a theory of agency.
>
> (Kellner, 1989: 216)

INTRODUCTION: THE CODED SUBJECT

> The loss of (spontaneous, reciprocal, symbolic) human relations is the fundamental fact of our societies.
>
> (Baudrillard, 1998a: 161)

> Today, whether it be groups, nations or individuals, people are no longer fighting alienation but a kind of total dispossession.
>
> (Baudrillard, 1998b: 19)

It is perhaps surprising that a book on Baudrillard should include a chapter entitled 'Subjectivity, Identity and Agency'. The consensus among critics, on both left and right, is that Baudrillard has no theory of these phenomena and that this constitutes the major weakness of his work, marking it as characteristically 'postmodern' (Callinicos, 1989: 144–8; Kellner, 1989: 215–16; Norris, 1992).[1] But these critics are mistaken on both counts: Baudrillard does theorise agency and his is not, in any recognisable way, a 'postmodernist' theorisation.

In order to understand Baudrillard's approach to subjectivity, identity and agency we must, once again, take up the distinction between symbolic relations and simulatory abstractions. In modernity symbolic relations *between* people are severed, abstracted and reduced to semiotic, commodified relations plotted on a single, universal scale of identity/difference. Baudrillard did not, of course, contend that the individual is free, authentic or 'whole' in the symbolic order, or in the making of symbolic exchanges. Instead the severing of symbolic exchange relations sets the fundamental precondition for the historical emergence of the 'individual', which itself inaugurates the modern 'project' of identity.[2] The 'individual' – meaning separate, autonomous, indivisible unit – emerges as kin, clan and ritual ties are broken. The individual comes to be understood as a creature of needs and desires, the possessor of a rational conscious will and an autonomous psychical structure consisting primarily of the instinct for survival (1981: 63–87). But, as we know, for Baudrillard, this individual creature of needs is a term of the code, a simulation (see discussion in Chapter 1).

According to Baudrillard, the relationship between the social and the individual is transformed by the system of consumption. Social conduct remains remarkably orderly because the process of *individualisation* is also a process of *integration* – as the etymology suggests, parts or units become wholes, or rather the unit is conceived in such a way that it must be integrated within the whole and makes sense only within this integration. Individuals as constituted by the code, according to Baudrillard, are in no sense singular beings but are expressed through a range of personality 'types' that fit into a larger whole – through the play of identity/difference that is the system of consumption. Types of person, like 'types' of consumer, 'types' of race and 'types' of social class, are designated by alphabetical or numerical series. The police speak of IC1s and IC2s, marketing and public relations people speak of A1s and C3s, most social researchers are no better, positing 'pink', 'grey', 'red' and 'green' types of consumer. These are abstractions, not representations of actual people. They are not even ideal-types in the sense developed by Max Weber (1949) because they are not heuristic devices designed to aid the understanding of social relations, they are *simulations* that are designed to replace the mess of lived relations with an ordered, inert, version of the social. Social life is broken into elements, that which cannot be defined or located as an element (that which is 'ambivalent') is rejected and the remaining elements are reconstituted through the code into a 'simulation' of the social.[3]

PERSONALISATION

> It is upon the loss of difference that the cult of difference is founded.
>
> (Baudrillard, 1998a: 89)

> Things get a lot more exciting when you say 'Yes'.
>
> (Virgin Mobile advertisement, UK, 2006)

The concept of personalisation was central to Riesman's influential study *The Lonely Crowd* (1961). According to Riesman the major obligation of the modern citizen is no longer to produce goods, but to 'produce' a personality. Personality is the essential mode of integration and control in advanced modernity because it is the anchoring-point of the will, of choices and decisions made during the life course. Personalisation refers to ways in which society offers consumers differentiation, distinctiveness or uniqueness through product choices. In other words, consumer products do the work of 'personalisation' for us, we merely have to choose one brand or another, using the 'marginal or 'inessential' coded differences presented to us, in order to express our 'selves'. We are 'cool', 'trendy' or 'alternative' because the signs we consume are 'cool', 'trendy' or 'alternative'; the work of identity has been done for us, we are only required to say 'Yes', which is nevertheless an *active*, discriminating endorsement, never a dumb passivity.

Baudrillard extends Riesman's analysis by using the concept of personalisation as a basis for a critique of the 'metaphysics' of the subject. Just as Marcuse (1961) retained a distinction between true and false needs, Riesman (1961) operates with a distinction between true and false forms of personalisation. Baudrillard allows neither distinction and makes it clear that a new critical stance is needed because 'it cannot be denied that even superficial differences are real as soon as they become invested with value' (1996a: 153). Further:

> to differentiate oneself is precisely to affiliate to a model, to label oneself by reference to an abstract model, to a combinatorial pattern of fashion, and therefore to relinquish any real difference, any singularity, since these can only arise in concrete, conflictual relations with others and the world.
>
> (Baudrillard, 1998a: 88)

The individual, as it appeared in Enlightenment philosophy, a creature of passion and character, is 'swept out of our functional universe' (ibid.). This 'lost being' is then reconstituted in coded, differential and semiotic form by the consumer system, resulting in 'a synthetic individuality' (ibid.). People as constituted by the system are *not different or singular* in any meaningful way. They are *merely different from each other* according to a coded system of marginal differentials: a 'chav' is not cultured, a 'square' is not fashionable, a 'goth' is not mainstream. These differences, no matter how marked or dramatic they seem at the level of content, represent conformity at the level of form; that is, at the level of the code, an 'integration within a sliding scale of values' (1998a: 89), the scale of identity/difference.

Consumption, as a 'generalised code of differentiation' (1998a: 94), establishes a new and distinctive mode of exchange between individuals: 'the unconscious discipline of the code' is a system of 'competitive co-operation' (ibid.). Baudrillard insists that 'the status of the individual is changing totally':

> It is a move from an individual principle based on autonomy, character, the inherent value of the self to a principle of perpetual recycling by indexation to the code . . . of 'personalisation', which traverses each individual in his signified relation to others.
>
> (Baudrillard, 1998a: 170)

Consumerism is saturated with 'false spontaneity' and 'orchestrated emotions': the 'have a nice day culture'. It is certainly possible to move around *within* the code, there are freedoms *within* the code, and, of course, power relations and constraints. Indeed, we are enjoined to manoeuvre within it, to improve ourselves, to become more assertive, or more attractive in the career and relationship markets. Within the code everything is a market, an abstract system for the interactive exchange of goods, money, bodies and images: communications companies tell us that 'It's good to talk', that we should 'get closer' (Wrigley's chewing gum), celebrity chefs tell us how to cook, how to eat, government initiatives tell us how to parent, popular publications tell us how to flirt or perform cunnilingus. The code entreats us to 'be', to verify ourselves, to *be* through self-coding; indeed, to take responsibility for oneself is to be self-coding. These processes lead to new or deeper forms of alienation and to a 'terrorism of solicitude' (1998a: 167). The code presents a gift, but at the same time makes a request and demands a response. The response can only be made in the terms of the code; the code leaves 'practically no way of saying "no"' (1998a: 168). This is the symbolic violence of the code; it closes off the possibility of symbolic exchange by giving a gift that cannot be reciprocated or annulled – the gift of self.

AFTER ALIENATION AND ANOMIE: THE END
OF THE PACT WITH THE DEVIL

Baudrillard develops his discussion of 'contemporary alienation' through a reading of the German Expressionist film *The Student of Prague* (1926, directed by Henrik Galeen). In this film an impoverished but ambitious student, Balduin, sells his mirror image to the Devil and thereby enters the whirl of high society. However, his image, become flesh and blood, appears to him and begins to follow him, apparently seeking revenge for having been sold. In fear he hides from public view only to discover that his double has now replaced him in society. In despair the student resolves to kill his *doppelgänger* and when it appears in his room and passes between him and the mirror from which it emerged, he fires a pistol at it. The mirror shatters, the phantom vanishes, but the student himself collapses to the floor, dying. In killing his image he kills himself. Yet in losing his life he finds salvation as, with his dying glance, he sees himself *as* himself: restored within a broken shard of the looking glass.

Baudrillard's commentary focuses, initially, on the status of the commodity-form. In the film the mirror image is sold, separated from its rightful owner, and takes on a magical and ghoulish life of its own – just as in capitalism creative toil is separated from the worker by the capitalist class and takes on a life of its own as a commodity. Indeed, for Marx the commodity becomes, in capitalism, a fetish: an illusory and abstract 'thing' that is treated as if it has magical properties of its own, rather than being simply the sum of the labour of others (Marx, 1995: 42–50). But Baudrillard rejects the Marxist position that alienation could be overcome by the abolition of the private ownership of wealth (Marx, 1995: 383–6): 'the alienated human being is not merely a being diminished and impoverished but left intact in its essence: it is a being turned inside out, changed into something evil, into its own enemy, set against itself' (Baudrillard, 1998a: 190). The consumer age is, then, 'an age of radical alienation' because 'the individual is no longer ever confronted with his own split image' (1998a: 191). For Baudrillard the consumer society marks the end of the possibility of transcendence because human relations, culture and sexuality, not just economic products, are based on pre-coded options and 'consumable models' (ibid.).

The double is an important theme throughout Baudrillard's work, reappearing on many occasions (1993b: 156–60, 1994b: 101–9, 2001c: 67–73). There is no space for the double or, indeed, for any sense of otherness in the relations of the contemporary self to other selves.

All otherness, all senses of the double within, have been materialised or real-ised, and in mythology, Baudrillard notes, when one's double materialises death is imminent (1994b: 101–9). The double or other was vital because through the relationship to the double 'the subject's simultaneous estrangement from himself and intimacy with himself are played out' (1993b: 113). There was, then, something protective in the figure of the double, it prevented an absolute or transparent encounter of the subject with itself – an occasion that can only provoke madness. The double added a dimension, a metaphysical one in the case of the soul, yet even the simple mirror image, our appearance to our 'selves', protects us from total identification with our 'selves'. Our image in the mirror is laterally inverted so we are protected from the nightmare of encountering ourselves as others see us, or coming 'face to face' with ourselves (1993b: 121, 1996c: 52). Concerning the double,

> Ours is the only period ever to have sought to exorcise this phantasy . . . that is, to turn it into flesh and blood, to transform the operation of the double from a subtle interplay involving death and the Other into the bland eternity of the Same.
>
> (Baudrillard, 1993b: 114)

Cloning, for Baudrillard, is the ultimate nightmare of the elimination of all otherness, all seduction and illusion, because 'it allows us at last to dispense with the other and go directly from the one to the same . . . No more mother, no more father: just a matrix' (1993b: 114). Cloning abolishes the subject, replacing it with the genetic code: mapped, coded, transparent individuals feeding the system.[4] Is there an alternative?

OTHER THAN THE CODED SUBJECT: FAILING TO SHOP

> Once exchange value has been neutralised, use value disappears with it.
>
> (Baudrillard, 1981: 205)

> We have no will of our own.
>
> (Baudrillard, 1993b: 164)

The final chapter of *Critique*, entitled 'Concerning the fulfilment of desire in exchange value', has attracted little commentary or debate. However, it is immensely suggestive. It develops a critique of the metaphysics of the subject of needs and desires from the perspective of everyday lived experience in modernity:

Objects, and the needs they imply, exist precisely in order to resolve the anguish of not knowing what one wants. . . . There is no use value without exchange value. Once the latter is neutralised in the gift-process, or gratuity, prodigality, expenditure, then use value itself becomes unintelligible.

(Baudrillard, 1981: 205)

The influence of Bataille's general economy of excess is strong here.[5] The fundamental problem for human beings, according to Bataille (1988: 27–41) is not that we have too little energy or too little time ('free' or otherwise). Instead we have *too much* and we have to think of ways, as individuals and as a society, to *expend* this time, how to 'get rid of it', to consume it and so to reduce the anxiety it induces. The critical traditions of Marxism and Freudianism, by contrast, actually reinforce the prejudices of the Enlightenment by depicting as fundamental a 'drive for appropriation and satisfaction, performance and supremacy' (1981: 204). But, according to Baudrillard, there is always something in the subject and its experience that resists this 'fail-safe rationality' (ibid.).

Baudrillard presents two scenarios; he claims these as factual occurrences but they function within his text as thought experiments rather than case studies. The first concerns a 'politico-symbolic' raid on a large department store, of the type staged by the situationists in the late 1960s. Staff flee as agitators occupy the store. The raiders then invite the bewildered shoppers, by loudhailer, to help themselves and take whatever they desire. Yet the shoppers cannot decide how to respond. Either they take nothing at all or they take merely the most 'insignificant items', displaying an unexpected lack of interest concerning objects that, moments earlier, they presumably eyed with interest. There is widespread resistance to the supposed 'drive' for appropriation and the revolutionary gesture fails – but why? For Marxists and situationists alike, such apparent 'passivity' might be explained through the notion of 'false consciousness': the consumers are so duped by the commodity system and the laws and norms supporting it that they cannot oppose the system even when the opportunity to do so stares them in the face. But Baudrillard's account is quite different: the value system, as 'impoverished, unilateral and positive modality' (1981: 207), itself generates the desire to fail, to refuse the unilateral gift of a self locked within the consumption system. A gift of this magnitude creates a symbolic debt that can never be reciprocated or countered; the only remaining strategy is its annulment or refusal. The resistance to satisfaction, the refusal of fulfilment, Baudrillard argues, are radical acts of defiance, they are an expression of 'violence towards the principle of identity and equivalence' (ibid.). The refusal is an immanent revolt, it wells up from inside the code, from within the coded self. Yet it is not a critical gesture, it does not express an alternative set of values and has little content or shape. It is, then, a revolt as shapeless and post-ideological as the code itself.

The second scenario depicts successful athletes who, at the point of triumphing over clearly inferior opposition, 'choke' and somehow 'snatch defeat from the jaws of victory', as the saying goes. This example, like that of the department store shoppers, shows that success and victory – and the status and power these confer – are difficult to accept. We are often prepared to compete with others, to play the capitalist game of 'invidious distinction' (Veblen, 1979), to run in a race that we do not expect to win. Competition becomes a routine, a reflex, and it helps us to position ourselves in the system. But victory terminates the security of being in the race, of running with the pack. The fulfilment of the 'desire' to win is not, then, an unambivalent positive.

In order to understand the social and emotional processes involved in the shoppers' and athletes' refusals Baudrillard introduces what became an important and recurrent theme in his work, the *rule*:

> If there is no longer a set of rules to play by, the game is no longer interesting, for even cheating and stealing are ruled out . . . safe-guarding the rules turns out to be a more fundamental imper-ative than winning itself. Each participant implicitly obeys the structure of exchange, this collective and unconscious function.
>
> (Baudrillard, 1981: 210)

The 'passivity' of the shoppers is a form of defiance of the metaphysics of the code and its grounding in use value. It is a defiance more fundamental than that of the radicals who storm the department store because the latter have broken the rule of symbolic exchange by attempting to 'give' unilaterally to the shoppers the gifts of freedom, liberation and the goods of their choice. This gift is unacceptable: it is structured by the Marxian metaphysics of a pure use-value (no longer obscured by capitalist exchange-value) and worse still it attempts to impose the unilateral gift of *liberation* on the shoppers, and so attempts to exert power over them, which they refuse. For Baudrillard, 'if no counter-gift or reciprocal exchange is possible, we remain imprisoned in the struc-ture of power and abstraction' (1981: 210). The shoppers have invested emotionally, as well as financially, in the giving of payment in return for goods as a refusal of further obligation, as the removal of symbolic debt. People are not then unthinking slaves to the system; they do not suffer from 'false consciousness'. Instead they seek to maintain a

minimal symbolic space by discharging their debts and by refusing to
accumulate, maximize and succeed if this would compromise their symbolic space: these are the rules of the game.

PLEASE FOLLOW ME

> [A]n arbitrary, inexplicable game that does not have – above all
> does not have – the excuse of sex.
>
> (Baudrillard and Calle, 1988: 79)

In his short essay *Please Follow Me*, published with Sophie Calle's
photographic project *Suite Venitienne* (1988), Baudrillard makes some
fascinating observations on identity, subjectivity and agency, which
develop the theme of symbolic ritual or game with rules. Calle's
project consisted of her following someone she hardly knew from Paris
to Venice and back, photographing him and the places he visited. Yet
Calle, at least according to Baudrillard's commentary, had no intention
of getting to know this person, and certainly no sexual agenda. Instead
a subtle game or ritual is played out:

> The other's tracks are used in such a way as to distance you from
> yourself. You exist only in the trace of the other, but without his
> being aware of it. . . . You seduce yourself by being absent, by being
> no more than a mirror for the other. . . . You seduce yourself into
> the other's destiny, the double of his path, which, for him, has
> meaning, but when repeated, does not. . . . It's as if someone
> behind him knew that he was going nowhere – it is in some way
> robbing him of his objective: seducing him.
>
> (Baudrillard and Calle, 1988: 76–7)[6]

This passage tells us a great deal about Baudrillard's approach to
the self and other. The other enables us to become radically different
from ourselves, to annul our coded position and to gain a vital distance
from our selves. The simulation models of need, production and sexuality require us to be identical to ourselves, to coincide with or 'verify'
our selves. We are constituted as subjects, as subjects of the system
and also as subject to ourselves through the notion of identity. The
(radically) other is vital because it holds the possibility of the breaking of this subject-ion, this 'unheard of servitude', since: 'the Other is what
allows me not to repeat myself forever' (1993b: 174). There is a 'secret
complicity' between self and other, a symbolic relation that enables
an alternative existence; '*it is the shadowing in itself that is the other's
double life*' (Baudrillard and Calle, 1988: 78, original emphasis).

The second, fatal or double life is lived outside of meaning, know-ledge, will, self-awareness, self-reflection, self-monitoring. Only by defying all coded meaning and value can we experience the compli-city of seduction, a 'pact' or symbolic bond of 'reciprocal absence' (ibid.). This complicity is the sphere of destiny, becoming and meta-morphoses. Becoming and metamorphosis are crucial terms in the later Baudrillard because they imply a changing of forms without the continuity of underlying essence: a total transformation from one form to another, a becoming other. The target of Baudrillard's defiance is, once again, determinate, referential meaning anchored to a law of value.

In this symbolic ritual there is, Baudrillard suggests, also an annul-ment, or at least 'volatilisation', of power relations. Both players have power, neither is 'victim' of the other, neither is alienated by the other. The differences of position depend on their relative positions in the game and their positions can be reversed, as indeed they are when the man realised Calle was following him. Power is not undone or transcended but it is unfixed, put into play. Since it is volatile and reversible it cannot be taken for granted or accumulated. The man may attack Calle but actually does not. Real violence is not part of this game, symbolic violence is:

> It is to the unknown that one yields most impulsively; it is toward the unknown that one feels the most total, the most instinctive obligation. . . . A challenge involves the overwhelming necessity of meeting it. One cannot opt not to respond to a challenge, but one can very well not respond to a request.
>
> (Baudrillard and Calle, 1988: 80)

By responding to the challenge – to follow and be followed – we loosen the 'servitude of the will' and move 'into a dreamlike disengagement' (1988: 81). To partake of this game or ritual 'you renounce respons-ibility for something that does not "belong" to you anyway, which is really more easy to enjoy without constant direction from the will' (1988: 82). This is a renunciation of the fiction of autonomous individual existence, of subjection to identity:

> a wonderful reciprocity exists in the cancellation of each existence, in the cancellation of each subject's tenuous position as a subject. Following the other, one replaces him, exchanges lives, passions, wills, transforms oneself in the other's stead. It is perhaps the only way man can finally fulfil himself.
>
> (Baudrillard and Calle, 1988: 82)

The gendering here is certainly problematic. Is this a game for men only, for men to use women as a conduit to a selfish, self-defined fulfilment? This is certainly how *Please Follow Me* is interpreted by feminist critics such as Gallop (1987: 111–15) and Moore (1988: 165–92). For Moore, Baudrillard is merely a 'pimp'; an age-old figure of the male exploitation of women. But Moore's argument is not at all convincing.[7] To begin with, Baudrillard's early work is a powerful attack on the principles of use, need and desire. In seduction we escape our needs and desires, we do not realise them. Seduction, in Baudrillard's sense, is not about procuring sex: it is opposed to the discourse of sexuality and its bio-material foundations. Seduction is not an intentional or willed strategy but the reciprocal or reversible (but not 'equal') play of appearances and disappearances. Seduction is 'feminine', but it is not female, nor is it male. Baudrillard himself asserted this symbolic power of femininity, or rather he claimed to abolish himself through a becoming-feminine. Femininity is a role, a ritual mask, a form of consensual play with one's inevitable status as object. It is not anchored to a biological sex or to a culturally constructed notion of feminine gender: this has been badly misunderstood by Baudrillard's critics.

But two further issues remain. First, Baudrillard does indeed make prescriptions to 'women' (by which we can only assume he means biological 'women') that they should reacquaint themselves with the symbolic power of femininity, which, he argues, they are losing in the course of their supposed liberation (1990a: 6–7). Second, as several feminists have argued, he seems unwilling to be seduced by feminism (Gallop, 1987: 112–13; Moore, 1988: 182–3). On the first point Baudrillard seems to be pursuing his general position that liberation is simulatory and that it deters genuine liberty by seeming to offer it in semiotic, commodified packages. Sexual 'liberation' is merely one instance of this process. Interestingly, female writers such as Levy (2006) have recently made exactly this point on the submersion of genuine freedoms for women through the pseudo-liberation offered by 'raunch culture', where lap-dancing, live sex on 'reality' TV and the porn industry are presented as 'cool' career options for young, assertive and free-spirited women. Nevertheless, Baudrillard's occasional pronouncements on what women should think or do are irksome, and disappointing in that they seem to reintroduce notions of bio-materially fixed sex poles that are challenged elsewhere in Baudrillard's work. On the second point, Baudrillard was clearly unseduced by Marxist, structuralist and standpoint feminisms, but he seemed to be inspired by the ideas of other, more marginal but certainly 'powerful', female figures. These include Joan Riviere, a psychoanalyst, and Nico, an artist and musician associated with Andy Warhol and The Velvet Underground. Both are referenced, or rather celebrated, in *Seduction* (1990a: 10–11, 13), while Nico's haunting performance on The Velvet Underground's 'I'll Be Your Mirror' seems to have inspired a short essay of that name (1990a: 67–71; see also 1996c: 149). Finally, Baudrillard was sufficiently seduced by feminism to throw down a symbolic challenge to it, a challenge to which, so far, only Victoria Grace (2000) has responded.

THE DECLINATION OF WILLS

Baudrillard continued his exploration of will, agency and the 'Other' in later works, which are increasingly preoccupied with the notion of a double, dual or second life. In Baudrillard's thought the sources of defiance, subversion and also of destiny and radical thought lie outside the self as 'determinants from elsewhere' (1993b: 165): 'embrace the foreign form of any event, any object, any fortuitous being, because, in any case, you will never know who you are . . . [this is] a symbolic form of obligation, and enigmatic form of conjunction' (1993b: 165). This 'collusive mode' is, for Baudrillard, preferable to the dominant democratic mode of moral responsibility, which 'requires that the individual should transform himself into a slave to his identity, his will, his responsibilities, his desire . . . a truly unheard of servitude' (ibid.). The democratic mode involves 'an expulsion of the other' (ibid.) and a breaking of collusive, symbolic relations. Our otherness to ourselves as well as the otherness of others is denied or assimilated in coded form. For Baudrillard the politics of difference – gender and identity politics, multiculturalism, pluralism and 'diversity' – are, simultaneously, the politics of indifference, of disengagement and the breaking of symbolic obligations. An ethics of engagement with the other, even where violence may be encountered, enables a lifting out of the crippling anxiety, uncertainty and resentment of individuation, of self-imprisonment by the will. In engaging with the other, Baudrillard suggests, we can discover a faith and belief in the other more than we could entertain of our selves because we are too 'self-aware' (1993b: 166–7).

There is something like an ethics in Baudrillard's attacks on coded, personalised, responsible identities and his injunctions concerning the recognition of the other: 'How much more human to place one's fate, one's desire and one's will in the hands of someone else . . . [a] circulation of responsibility, a declination of wills, and a continual transferring of forms' (1993b: 165). Such circulation is highly suggestive of gift-exchange, and indeed Baudrillard refers to this as 'a symbolic form of obligation' (ibid.). Baudrillard, like Derrida before him, attacks the Enlightenment notion of the individual human agent as the source or foundation of social meanings (what Derrida termed logo-centrism). For Baudrillard, we depend upon others, always, for our sense of who we are, what we desire and what we can become. A sense of 'second agency' is vital to our well-being. For example, while we might doubt ourselves – disbelieve our own desires, pleasures and satisfactions – we do believe in the desires and pleasures of others, we believe in the pleasure they take in us such that they are our 'second agency' (1993b: 166–7). Baudrillard goes further in suggesting that a sense of alienation, the feeling that 'an age-old enemy [is] holding the alienated part of us captive', also provided the comfort of a second agency, the fantasy that we would be complete if it were not for X, Y or Z. We are nostalgic for the era of alienation because, in the consumer system, we are awarded all that we desire (virtually or in simulation, not in 'reality') and so are left alone confronting our selves – a greater and more terri-fying servitude than has ever been experienced before:

> it is better to be controlled by someone else than by yourself. Better to be repressed, exploited, persecuted and manipulated by some-one other than oneself . . . it is likewise always better to be made happy, or unhappy, by someone else rather than by oneself. It is always better to depend in life on something that does not depend on us. In this way I can avoid any kind of servitude. I am not obliged to submit to something that does not depend on me. I am free of my birth – and in the same sense I can be free of my death . . . there has never been any freedom apart from this one.
> (Baudrillard, 1993b: 167–8)

This is a difficult passage. It returns us to the themes explored in *Symbolic Exchange* of life and death, and of the pact with the other. Individual will, or rational agency, is declined – that is, it is politely, ritualistically refused – and it is circulated, like the gift. It is put into play, movement and metamorphosis. As 'We have no will of our own' (1993b: 164), so 'Placing oneself in the hands of the other with respect to will, belief, love or choice is not an abdication but a strategy', and an ethical one it seems, though 'far from innocent' (1993b: 168). Baudrillard's examples are by now familiar: political power is reversed by the masses, the power of adults is reversed by children and the power of the masculine by the feminine. In each case power is reversed because the group in the subordinate position allows the other to believe in its identity while it does not believe in it.[8] Masses, children and those with femininity (not necessarily biological women) are not subjects or agents – they are objects: 'The object is an insoluble enigma, because it is not itself and does not know itself' (1993b: 172). For Baudrillard, it seems, we must follow him, just as he volunteers to be the object of Calle's experiment: *please follow me*. We must throw off the subjection of our desires and place ourselves within 'the total artifice of rules' (1993b: 173). We must not consent to existence, individuality or will; they are banal illusions of a fictive autonomy 'conferred' on to us (1996c: 11). They are the residues of symbolic exchange relations; they emerge in a breaking of the symbolic pact, and from this rupture

> Two kinds of violence ensue: a violence of liberation, and an opposite violence in reaction against the excess of freedom, safety, protection and integration, and hence a loss of any dimension of fate, of destiny – a violence directed against the emergence of the Ego and the Self, the Subject and the Individual, which takes its toll in the form of self-hatred and repentance.
>
> (Baudrillard, 2001c: 46)

We are at war with ourselves. By seizing our selves, appropriating our selves as our 'property' or capital, we deny the radical otherness or vital distance in our relation to our selves and others: that which we cannot own, appropriate, direct or maximise. But, according to Baudrillard, radical otherness returns in 'our many neuroses and psychical disorders . . . [our] thwarted destinies . . . intense self-hatred' (2001c: 45). This Baudrillard terms the 'fractal subject . . . closed on himself and doomed to endless identity . . . the subject without other' (2001c: 47–8).

The early influences of Marcuse and Riesman, critical social theorists, are still discernible here, but Baudrillard is distinctive in his contention that, increasingly, we seek to avoid freedom and we actively embrace 'voluntary servitude'. If, in high modernity, people sought an escape from destiny (as set by biology, ethnicity, class, occupation), we now experience a reversal:

> This is how it is with all those who deliberately submit themselves to extreme conditions: solitary climbers or sailors, cavers and those who play jungle war games. All risk situations . . . are today recreated artificially in a form of nostalgia for extremes, survival and death. A technical simulation of pain and sacrifice.
>
> (Baudrillard, 2001c: 49)

Without God and Satan battling over our souls, without the Last Judgement to face, the contemporary 'fractal' subject, the self without other or otherness, is reduced to 'daily inflicting the ordeal of the last Judgement on themselves' (2001c: 50). But there is an alternative, 'the path of radical strangeness which breaks the vicious circle of identity; the path of radical illusion which breaks the vicious circle of reality' (ibid.). To be 'liberated' is to be made responsible for every aspect of your existence, for Baudrillard a deeply 'ambiguous' outcome.[9] Liberation frees us as individuals, but the 'individual' is not a naturally 'pre-existing' phenomenon that is somehow rediscovered. Liberation constructs us as individuals, and as very particular types of individuals at that: creatures of needs and desires who must control and direct those needs and desires responsibly in order to maximise their achievements in a competitive system.

We are *given* an array of choices. We are made to believe that if we make the wrong choice and fail, it is nobody's fault but our own. For example, if we choose the wrong university, or wrong course, and cannot find a job after graduation, it is our fault. At most we might, as individuals, question other individuals, blaming our tutor or careers advisor: 'My lecturers were rubbish, it isn't my fault I only got a third class degree.' Individuals come into conflict with other individuals but what is left unquestioned is the nature of labour markets under 'casino' capitalism or the phenomena of university managerialism and bureaucratisation. Awarded liberation (but not liberty), individuals are fulfilled but 'only virtually'; we resent others, and we resent ourselves, we get 'the hate' (1996c: 142–7, 2005a: 141–55). This theme was explored in Chapter 7.

Such virtual liberation, according to Baudrillard, leads to the greatest servitude, a condition of 'servility without master':

> Each stage of servitude is both more subtle and worse than the one which precedes it. Involuntary servitude, the servitude of the slave, is overt violence. Voluntary servitude is a violence consented to: a freedom to will, but not the will to be free. Last comes voluntary self-servitude or enslavement to one's own will: the individual possesses the faculty to will but is no longer free in respect of it. He is the automatic agent of that faculty. He is the serf to no master but himself.
>
> (Baudrillard, 2001c: 61)

So, today, in the parts of the world that consider themselves the most 'advanced', we are 'perfectly emancipated, perfectly servile'. We are slaves to our will, slaves to our promotional, coded identities. In this argument Baudrillard is not merely attacking the construction of subjectivities and identities by the code of consumption, but challenging the dominant Western tradition of moral philosophy and the metaphysical system of individual autonomy, choice and freedom. The following passage is particularly important:

> Adopting a decision immediately turns it into a prohibition: it becomes something not be transgressed. There is then no difference between it being your decision or someone else's. To decide 'sovereignly' you have to be able to determine how to proceed in relation to your own decision, to reconsider it freely, as though it were in fact someone else's.
>
> (Baudrillard, 2001c: 60)

There is no freedom, according to Baudrillard, in the world of the will, desire and choice. The 'banal' subjective illusion of the will confronts us with two alternatives. Either we cannot be said to be free because we have already made a decision to which we are bound or, alternatively, we achieve freedom by treating our past decision as if it was someone else's, so that we are 'free' to revise it. In the first instance we lose our freedom, in the second instance we lose our self: *we cannot practice free individual autonomy*. Freedom, if it exists at all, lies elsewhere, away from the binary oppositions of self/other, of autonomy/constraint.

DOUBLE LIVES

Baudrillard clarifies the notion of double lives through a discussion of the case of Jean Claude Romand (erroneously referred to as 'Romans' in *Impossible Exchange*, 2001c: 67–72; see also 2005d: 60–2). Romand was a promising medical student, but failed his first year exams. Instead of retaking them, the rational option, he hid his initial failure by setting up what Baudrillard calls 'a complete parallel life' (2001c: 67). Romand presented himself as a successful doctor and medical researcher – a career high-flier – to friends and family, despite not being qualified and holding no medical post. He married, had children and maintained the pretence throughout, funding their lifestyles through property dealing. Romand became 'a veritable simulation machine' (ibid.). Then, nearly twenty years after the original deception, and fearing exposure, Romand murdered his parents, wife and children in a fateful 'shoot-out with reality' (2001c: 69). The case was declared inexplicable by the media, yet according to Baudrillard the events can be understood in terms of the spiralling of symbolic and simulatory relations. Romand 'could not stand the idea of those who believed in him ceasing to do so' (2001c: 67). Killing them was a logical solution:

committing suicide – the apparently honourable way out – would not have 'spared them the shame of knowing' (ibid.). Romand was 'jealous' of the image others had of him; to be unmasked would be an unbearable humiliation. According to Baudrillard, the case became so notorious not because of Romand's violence, but because of 'the fantastic suspicion he cast on personal identity, and hence on the whole of the social order. For this he clearly deserves to be locked away indefinitely' (2001c: 69).

More specifically, for Baudrillard, the simulatory double life was not an effect 'caused' by the failure of the exam. There were many opportunities for resits, as Carrère's eloquent account describes (Carrère, 2001: 68–82). Romand's double life had 'no initial motive; its motive force arises out of the process itself' (Baudrillard, 2001c: 70). Like ritual, ceremony and gaming, the meaning is generated from within through the throwing off of identity and 'fail-safe rationality' (1981: 204) and the acceptance of the rules of the game, their unfolding come what may. Romand, according to Baudrillard, found a 'solution' to the impossible exchange of his life. Rather than maximizing his own life as an operational performance, as 'commanded to be what he wants and to want what he is', he invented a second life for this, a simulation. Romand gained distance from his coded life by treating it 'as though it were another's' (2001c: 70), and, in a sense, for Baudrillard, it was another's (2001c: 60). Rational decision-making, the exercise of our individual will in abstraction from all symbolic relations, does not amount to freedom, or to rational choice.

The coded self exists 'somewhere between sameness and otherness' (1998a: 192). The system establishes the sameness of the other and obscures the otherness of the same. Yet the otherness of the same haunts and follows us, as it does the student of Prague. In Baudrillard's earlier work we can break out of the code only through our death or suicide, our violent counter-gift to the gift of self made to us by the sign-system (1993a: 38–43). But in his middle and later work a new possibility emerges. We can become shadow or phantom and follow the otherness of the other, discover their seductiveness of which even they are not aware. This path leads away from both their coded position and our own. To decline will is not to decline agency, but to place oneself within a radically different space, one bound by rules and with no place for desire or choice once the space is entered. Yet, having chosen to enter such a space, we do act within it; a sense of agency no longer driven by the fiction of a unitary will. We act out a role as persona, gaining distance from ourselves and embracing fate, the unfolding of events.[10] Without the other the subject would disappear into a 'definitive narcissism . . . diffuse, floating, insubstantial' (2006b: 5).

There are, then, Baudrillard insists, less destructive ways of maintaining a vital distance from simulatory existence, and in 'resisting the easy solution' of identity. We might practice an 'exoticism' towards our selves, to be other as well as self, to refuse the Saussurian bar. Or we might follow the other, allowing them to divert us from our prescribed or willed paths. In any case, Baudrillard argues, we all do engage in such symbolic relations and rituals, though probably without theorising it in precisely this way: we are all 'the exotics of our own lives' and are never 'taken in' by the world of simulation, information and virtuality. Like great actors, we should not immerse ourselves too fully in our roles, we should observe a 'subtle differential', practise a form of 'snobbery' in relation to identity (2001c: 72–3). We are all much more than our identity, greater than the sum of our constituent sign-parts, and we will never be reduced to them. Baudrillard clearly had more faith in his fellow human beings than any of his critics have appreciated.

Conclusion

> When I write I don't feel that it is a political act. I feel it maybe as a symbolic act. Maybe it is a fatal strategy itself – a theoretical fatal strategy – and maybe it has some symbolic effects to accelerate.
>
> (Baudrillard, 1992: 300)

DISAPPEARANCE

> Death orders matters well, since the very fact of your absence makes the world distinctly less worthy of being lived in.
>
> (Baudrillard, 2006a: 10)

> [T]he whole trick is to know how to disappear before dying and instead of dying.
>
> (Baudrillard, 2006b: 4)

I find myself standing over Baudrillard's coffin. It is a beautiful spring morning in Paris. Having decided to attend his funeral only at the last minute, and struggling to find the correct entrance to the cimetière Montparnasse, I expected to take my place at the back of a long funeral procession. But in fact there are few mourners, so few that

I even thought I had arrived on the wrong day, or in the wrong place. There are no TV cameras, no media; this is not a hyperreal non-event, it is a symbolic ritual for family, friends and admirers.

The first thing I notice is a particularly large wreath from the French Ministry of Culture and Communication: an ironic object given Baudrillard's long-standing hatred of culture ('I spit on it'; 1987c: 81) and his oft-repeated argument that communication has been replaced by information. About two hundred mourners have gathered now and we follow the hearse, Baudrillard's second wife, Marine, and his two children along the avenue to the eight division of the cemetery. A number of leading French intellectuals, including Marc Guillaume, Sylvere Lotringer, Jacques Donzelot and Michel Maffesoli, give speeches in tribute to Baudrillard and his work. One notable anecdote emerges concerning the first time Baudrillard met Marine. Being familiar with his work, she asked Baudrillard if he would, at least, call himself a democrat? Baudrillard's only reply was 'You must not ask me such things.'

Finally, there is a symbolic exchange: after the coffin is lowered into the ground each of the mourners sprinkles earth over it:

> disappearance may be the desire to see what the world looks like in our absence (photography) or to see, beyond the end, beyond the subject, beyond all meaning, beyond the horizon of disappearance, if there is still an occurrence of the world, an unprogrammed appearance of things. A domain of pure appearance, of the world (and not of the real world, which is only ever the world of representation), which can emerge only from the disappearance of all the added values.
>
> (Baudrillard, 2006b: 4)

> Never believed in reality: I respect it too much to believe in it. Never had any imagining of death: it should remain a surprise.
>
> (Baudrillard, 2006a: 1)

Which of Baudrillard's ideas will live on? Which will disappear with him? Ironically, Baudrillard will be remembered as the theorist of simulation, a term he hardly used in the last twenty-five years of his life. His most important idea, symbolic exchange, is hardly known outside of specialist Baudrillard scholarship and will probably remain obscure, though I have given it central place in this study. Yet Baudrillard will be remembered for his many provocations, for his symbolic exchanges with other thinkers and ideas, and with his readers. He will be remembered for his wit in attacking the commonplace and unexamined, for challenging the accepted and taken-for-granted, for defying received wisdom. Some of his ideas became (hyper)realities, some of his predictions came to pass, still others remain dissonant and unsettling, they lie in wait, traps for an unsuspecting 'reality' to fall into.

SOCIOLOGY

Baudrillard himself claimed not to be an important figure in sociology and to have never, fundamentally, been a sociologist : 'If anything, I'm a metaphysician, perhaps a moralist, but certainly not a sociologist. The only "sociological" work I can claim is my effort to put an end to the social, to the concept of the social' (1987c: 84). Baudrillard was being rather disingenuous here; his early work from *System* through to *Symbolic Exchange* was clearly recognisable as sociological in places, though it was far more daring and inventive than mainstream academic sociology.[1] This raises the question: what, in the early twenty-first century, is sociology? Fewer students choose to take sociology degrees, university departments of sociology contract or are even closed. Many departments are characterised by what Weber termed 'methodolatry', by the pursuit of even more 'sophisticated' techniques of data collection and manipulation at the expense of ideas, of relevance, of influence, of imagination.[2] Sociology itself is disappearing!

Practitioners of the discipline frequently bemoan their lack of social and political influence but, as Baudrillard remarked, academic thought is increasingly empty and too often 'demoralisingly platitudinous' (1996c: 101), so what influence can it expect to have? Baudrillard's work contains nothing whatsoever of interest for sociology and sociologists of this kind. But for anyone who wishes to think, and think again, Baudrillard's work is invaluable.

THOUGHT

> The more daily life is eroded, routinized and interactivized, the more we must counter this trend with complex, initiatory sets of rules.
>
> (Baudrillard, 2005d: 215)

> Things live only on the basis of their disappearance, and if one wishes to interpret things with entire lucidity, one must do so as a function of their disappearance.
>
> (Baudrillard, 2006b: 6)

I have offered criticisms of Baudrillard's positions only as I feel they arise in the course of exposition. That is, I have not insisted, as many writers do, on inserting a wedge of stock criticisms at the end of each section. I share the view expressed by Gane (2000) and Merrin (2005) that Baudrillard's ideas have not yet been understood, and they should be understood before the process of meaningful critique can begin. I hope this work will enable more accurate and incisive criticism of Baudrillard's ideas than has been the case. A critique that does not engage with Baudrillard's ideas is no critique at all. That critical writing demands symbolic engagement is not generally acknowledged, but is, of course, central to Baudrillard's methodology.

For Baudrillard, radical thinking is a ceremonial form, it is a symbolic exchange ritual performed 'to remake emptiness, to re-distinguish what has been confused' (1990b: 178). Banal thinking, the dominant form, produces more and more and more, which means less and less and less: thought is reduced to information, and it circulates in the virtual sphere of the 'information economy'.

For Baudrillard, there is no binary distinction between thinking subject and thought object – they are inseparable, complicitous, duelling. The subject is an object and is part of the world, and the world is thought by the subject. Both scientific and critical thought posit a necessary connection between thought and the 'real' world, but, for Baudrillard, this is superstition and a banal illusion. Both thought and the world are singular, not naturally or truthfully connected but, nevertheless, fundamentally inseparable, constantly in play. Radical thought remakes our domesticated, coded language: 'Through writing, language, which is a domesticated species, becomes a wild one again' (2006a: 7). Language is never a neutral medium of representation, but it can 'tear living concepts to pieces' (1996b: 71, translation modified). And we all think, all of the time. We have more ideas than we will ever need or use.

For Baudrillard, radical thought is a 'decoy', not a truth, it advances behind a mask. It is not an instrument of analysis but a ruse by which the world analyses itself, revealing not the 'truth' or the 'real' but the fundamental and singular illusion of the world. Thought must seduce the world, but thought is only seductive with the complicity of the world. Anyone who seeks to verify their hypotheses, to capture the 'reality' of the world, will not be disappointed because the world will elude them by 'proving them right', by submitting to any hypothesis, no matter how banal. By submitting to all hypotheses, even Baudrillard's provocations and speculations, the world generates a radical uncertainty and remains ultimately elusive. And if many of Baudrillard's anticipations proved well founded and became 'true' – the disappearance of politics into simulation and then indifference, the deterring of sexual freedom by the simulation of 'liberation', the vulnerability of Western power to symbolic violence and humiliation – this signalled the time to move on to new provocations, new seductions, or else disappear.

> The generations steeped in the virtual will never have known the real. But that is not so serious if we accept that the real is merely a referential illusion. More serious is the case of those who, steeped in sex and images of sex will never have known pleasure. But this is nothing in relation to the possibility, for future generations, of never knowing death.
>
> (Baudrillard, 2006a: 55)

Notes

INTRODUCTION

1   Baudrillard's Marxist critics, Kellner (1989), Callinicos (1989) and Norris (1992), are the best known of these, but for a more recent example of a shocking misreading of Baudrillard's position on the Gulf wars see Wheen (2004: 144–5).

2   For Baudrillard's comprehensive rejection of Fukuyama's position, which even seems to have involved a face-to-face spat, see Baudrillard's tellingly entitled *Illusion of the End* (1994b) and his interview 'The Violence of Indifference' (2005a: 141–55).

1   THE OBJECT SYSTEM, THE SIGN SYSTEM AND THE CONSUMPTION SYSTEM

1   Baudrillard's use of the term symbolic order is quite different from Lacan's. For Baudrillard it refers, at this early stage in his thought, to 'traditional' or pre-industrial social practices and sensibilities. He contrasts the 'ambivalence' of the symbolic order with the 'equivalence' of the semiotic orders. This distinction is discussed in the present chapter, pp. 11–16.

2   At this stage Baudrillard seems to be supplementing and re-working Marxist concepts, rather than 'breaking' with them. His

assertion that '*the object is liberated only in its function, man equally is liberated only as a user of that object*' (1996a: 18, original emphasis), strongly recalls Marx's critique of the capitalist pseudo-liberation of the worker, who is free but only to work, a *formal* freedom rather than an *actual* freedom. There is a strong sense, then, in which Baudrillard, at this stage, attempts to be more sociological than Marx by insisting on the existence of a far wider network of 'ideological integration' than Marx envisaged. Quite simply, Baudrillard's approach is sociological in that he insists that society is changed fundamentally by consumption.

3   Baudrillard, at this stage, writes of desire in the psychoanalytic sense, as an impersonal force of the unconscious rather than as the desires or wants of particular individuals for particular things. In *The Mirror of Production* (1975: 102–3) Baudrillard argues that within the symbolic exchange order the producers and users of goods are not distinct and so share a common 'desire'.

4   Baudrillard, in common with many poststructuralist thinkers, follows Nietzsche in regarding individual psychological meanings as superficial and indeed illusory because they depend upon the discredited Cartesian notion of mind/body dualism. The psyche is not autonomous at all but is dependent on environment, material resources and, above all, the structures of language that constitute its very possibility of awareness. Baudrillard develops this critique in *Symbolic Exchange* and it is discussed in the present volume in Chapter 3.

5   Ambivalence is an important term in Baudrillard's early work and it is developed, in *Critique* and *Symbolic Exchange*, in contrast to the more usual psychoanalytic connotations it has in *System*. The important point is that ambivalent emotions cannot be tracked or coded by the consumer system. They can be reduced to the level of signification and thence to the buying and exchanging of commodities but the undercurrents remain: the ghosts of the symbolic relation haunt semiotic reality.

6   As a very simple example of the operations of the sign code: a return to the bottle of designer shampoo that does not actually thicken hair. We do not really 'consume' this individual object (plastic bottle with brightly coloured 'funky' label filled with indeterminate chemical gunk); instead we consume the *social relationship* established between ourselves (as desirable, fashionable etc.) and others in society who will recognise us as such. This process positions

us within the code, at the very least above those who do not use a designer shampoo. Signs exist only in relationships of coded connections to other signs: they operate in combinations or commutations, readily interchangeable precisely because they are arbitrary, abstract and plastic. A number of possible strategies of resistance to consumerism can be envisaged. We may decide not to follow fashion or to be so cool we are ahead of fashion; we may make our own clothes. But even if we manage to bypass the system of exchange-value (very unlikely) we cannot avoid being defined and located by the sign-exchange system. This is the fundamental level of control: individualisation, personalisation and integration.

7 A further example: the canteen at my university features enormous banners with the words 'Go Eat' and images of those attractive, relaxed young people that populate the world of advertising. 'Go Eat' is a truly redundant and absurd injunction in what is, by definition, an eating place. What is even more ridiculous is that very little food is actually available: there is little choice, the food is of poor quality and is more expensive than comparable high street outlets. The magnitude of the sign-images expands as the 'real' possibilities diminish.

2 THE 'BREAK' WITH MARXISM

1 Baudrillard insists that critical and revolutionary arguments founded on the notion of production are destined only to feed into the capitalist system, helping it to expand, resolve and neutralise 'critical negations' and so becoming immune to revolutionary transformation. Marxist theory is Baudrillard's main target but he also attacks other would-be revolutionaries and their theories, particularly Gilles Deleuze, Jean-François Lyotard and the *Tel Quel* group including Julia Kristeva. His main contention is that such 'revolutionary' discourse 'emanates from political economy and obeys its reality principle' (1975: 18).

2 Interestingly, in Baudrillard's early writings there is a pronounced anti-theoreticism, overlooked by many critics who contend that his work is too abstract. For example, Baudrillard denies that sociological explanations can be derived from abstract principles – or metaphysics. Further, as symbolic exchange refers to the immediacy and totality of 'actual practice' and Baudrillard insists that all abstraction and separation from this immediacy is critiqued, there

is a sense in which Baudrillard's notion of symbolic exchange is not metaphysical.

3　In support of his argument Baudrillard offers the following quotation from Marx: 'labour is a necessary condition, independent of all forms of society; it is an external nature-imposed necessity, without which there can be no material exchanges between man and nature and therefore no life' (Marx, 1995: 42).

4　There are problems in Baudrillard's appropriation of Bataille's notion of sacrificial economy. Most serious among these is that Bataille understood his approach as materialist, indeed as 'base' materialist, while Baudrillard draws on Bataille to construct an anti-materialist theory, elaborated in *Symbolic Exchange* (1993a: 233–8). The world of production is 'restricted economy' in Bataille's sense, a limited system that can only function by denying its relationship to what lies beyond its limits: excess, waste and death. The influence of Bataille is powerful at this stage in Baudrillard's thinking, although this declines after Baudrillard's critiques of Bataille made the following year (Baudrillard, 1987a) before resurfacing in *Transparency* (1993b: 106–10).

5　While Baudrillard argues that the separation of humanity and Nature is fully realised in the capitalist system of political economy he makes clear that this was a long and complex process with roots in 'the great Judaeo-Christian dissociation of the Soul and Nature. God created Man in his *image* and created Nature for man's *use*' (Baudrillard, 1975: 63).

6　This argument is clarified in Baudrillard's well known essay 'The Order of Simulacra' (in 1993a: 50–86), which is discussed in Chapter 4.

7　Once again, Baudrillard does not contend that within symbolic societies 'Nature' was respected and valued in ways that we have now forgotten (a familiar conservative 'hippie'/eco-warrior argument). Instead his position is that the Nature/Human separation or abstraction was not made and so had no meaning.

8　Marx's theories on this issue cannot be rescued by arguing, as Kellner (1989) does, that Marx did occasionally recognise 'natural' values other than utility, such as health, well-being and artistic expression. It does not even help much to say that for Marx all natural, undistorted values are social and relational because the social here is modelled on production as universal essence with all other social practices, everywhere, as reflections of that essence. But the point, for Baudrillard, is not to critique Marx but to defy capitalism.

3   SYMBOLIC EXCHANGE AND DEATH

1   In my opinion the first and second assertions are not controversial, although to hold opinions one and two simultaneously is certainly unfashionable. The culturalist view, promulgated widely by the discipline of cultural studies, might take issue with the first (ontological) postulate by arguing that all cultures are dealing with the same fundamentals – birth, death, reproduction, survival – albeit in diverging ways according to local context and conditions. This might be termed the culturalist method of avoiding the challenge of what Baudrillard calls 'radical otherness'. Such thinking also applies to the second (epistemological) assumption to suggest that Western rationalism is perfectly sufficient to understand other cultures because 'we are all human' at some level. Such views are surprisingly commonplace among anthropologists, especially those whose speciality is fieldwork rather than theory. This might be termed the humanist strategy of avoidance. Alternatively, deconstructive readings might turn to an examination of how Western writers construct texts or stories around other cultures to satisfy their own agendas. This might be termed the deconstructive strategy for avoiding confrontation with the 'radical otherness' of other cultures. There is also an insidious form of postmodernist conservatism that suggests that it is impossible to know anything about dead or rapidly dying cultures that only want to Westernise anyway. This could be termed the postmodernist avoidance strategy. The US government is keen to depict the potlatch as non-violent and non-destructive, and as containing nothing that is challenging to Western notions of economy. The potlatch, construed as 'neutral' cultural practice, can then assume its rightful place, as sign, among all other cultural practices within the universal system of value that is 'world heritage'! Baudrillard's project, during the mid-1970s, was an attempt at head-on confrontation with the radical otherness of 'other' cultures. It can of course be argued that such a confrontation is impossible, and Baudrillard himself seems to have adopted this position by the late 1970s. See *Seduction* (1990a) and *Ecstasy of Communication* (1988b), where the terms seduction and destiny largely replace the notion of symbolic exchange.

2   Lane (2000) is right to question the 'evidence' Baudrillard draws upon because anthropological texts are sometimes treated as if they are unproblematic empirical data. In other words, Baudrillard's method of playing sources 'against themselves' is not always pushed through. It is not clear that Baudrillard reads Leenhardt

against Leenhardt or Mauss against Mauss; often Baudrillard's relationship to these writers is one of debtor, rather than of hijacker or 'potlatcher'. However, Lane (2000) and Kellner (1989) are wrong to suggest that Baudrillard's approach fails to be deconstructive; instead they fail to follow Baudrillard's argument beyond its opening salvoes. Baudrillard's 'radical anthropology' has not received the detailed critical consideration that it deserves (the closest we have is Genosko, 1998: 12–47) and his contribution to post-colonial theory goes unacknowledged (see Lane, 2000).

3 This is important because, while Bataille has been criticized for a one-sided reading of Mauss that greatly over-stresses the violence of the gift (Habermas, 1987), this cannot be said of Baudrillard, whose reading of the gift is not confined to the violent and exceptional form of the potlatch on the North-West coast of America.

4 For Baudrillard there is no 'unconscious' in the Freudian sense of a reservoir of instincts separated from the conscious mind by social repression. Instead, there are only the broken 'obligations and reciprocities' of barred or severed symbolic relations. Indeed, modernity is built upon the remainders that emerge when wealth and meaning are no longer symbolically exchanged. The 'residues' become 'value in the economic order, phantasm in the psychic order, signification in the linguistic order' (Baudrillard, 1983: 90 n. 9). Western rationalism is built upon these remainders: the unexchanged remainders *are reality*, the '*objective* dimension' (1993a: 146, original emphasis).

5 Interestingly the notion of a 'life cycle' is still comprehensible to modern minds. In other words, medical science has not succeeded in imposing a strict binary opposition.

6 There is a problem here. How dangerous or destructive must an act be in order to amount to a symbolic attack on the system? The criterion must be this: does the act genuinely subvert the system's values, i.e. use-value, exchange-value and sign-value? Lifestyle 'downsizing' or 'eco-living' would not constitute a symbolic operation because these are recognised strategies within the consumer capitalist system: happy families who leave the rat-race behind and move to a farmhouse in Provence; and can afford to because they have done so well out of the rat-race! Such people also conform to the imperatives of use-value based on 'nature' through their 'rediscovery' of a 'natural' lifestyle. Similarly, 'extreme' sports such as bungee jumping or parachuting and travel to far-flung places to 'discover yourself' do involve risks to life and limb but they are also very good for the CV, having high sign-exchange-value.

7   For example, car crashes often draw crowds and increasingly emergency services erect screens to shield the victims from the hungry eyes of assembled onlookers, rapt in fascination.

4   SIMULATION AND THE END OF THE SOCIAL

1   It is mistaken to assume that any phenomenon or event could be thought of, exclusively, as first order, second order, third order or fourth order. However, it is equally mistaken to under-estimate these distinctions, to assume that all phenomena are necessarily first, second, third and fourth order. Baudrillard's orders of simulacra are inspired by, and closely related to, Foucault's genealogical studies. Genealogy, as Foucault adapts it from Nietzsche (1994), attempts to break with Enlightenment thought by replacing an ontology of Being and essence with an emphasis on becoming and flux, and replacing epistemologies of Truth as a property of the world with 'truth' as a property of a particular set of ideas or discourse. The discursive order sets the conditions for the very possibility of thinking in a certain way: 'truth' is produced rather than 'discovered'. To understand all phenomena as simultaneously first, second, third and fourth order as if these distinctions refer only to different aspects of the same 'thing' is to allow the transcendental subject of consciousness, the Kantian subject, to roam freely up, down and across the four orders, casting its eye over all and any phenomena as if they pre-exist the simulacra or discourse that generates them. Of course Baudrillard himself, as writing subject, is at times dangerously close to this position, but what is made clear is that the symbolic order and the first order of simulacra lacked a philosophy of consciousness, a perspective space of representation (Baudrillard, 1983: 15–19). Further, Baudrillard insists, there is a 'point of no return' within the third order. Once simulation is established as the dominant principle of simulacra in the third order 'everything changes'. The 'reality' of the second order, the reality of production and representation, of politics, art and culture, 'disappears'. With the shift from representation to simulation the 'earlier' orders exist as simulations, as simulatory remnants.

2   Lyotard's critique of Baudrillard fails to appreciate this distinction, even though it is apparent in those works cited by Lyotard, namely *Critique* and *Mirror*. There is a well established tradition of French intellectuals taking critical 'pot-shots' at each other without really engaging with each other's work. Baudrillard's repeated sideswipes

at Lyotard and Deleuze in *Shadow* and *Seduction* are wearisome but no more so than the slights others direct at him.

3   Sign-exchange-value does not merely concern the external appearance of signs. Baudrillard is making an argument not simply about advertising or consumer images but about social power relations. Sign value enables a fully integrated code based on the equivalence of the individual sign, whereby everything is translatable into a code and so refers to and is meaningful only in relation to other terms of the code – not just the terms of a language, as Saussure indicates, but also, according to Baudrillard, our understandings and perceptions of history, politics, communication, sexuality and, via the DNA code, our own bodies and lives (1993a: 6–9).

4   In *Seduction* Baudrillard seeks to recover the diabolical aspects of *trompe l'oeil*, which through their staging of illusion actually reveal the constructed and staged nature of reality (1990a: 60–6).

5   So does DNA exist or not? Is it the truth of the universe or not? If it does exist where is the space for Baudrillard's critique of it? If it does not, then how can Baudrillard use it as the principle or ideal-type of his third order of simulacra. Baudrillard's answer is 'The hypothesis of the genetic code DNA is also true and cannot be defeated. . . . Science explains things which have been defined and formalised in advance and which subsequently conform to these explanations, that is all "objectivity" is' (1993a: 61). For Baudrillard 'nature' is a product of the Imaginary, of human culture, language and imagination, the 'other' of culture in the binary opposition nature/culture.

6   Baudrillard does offer examples. On religion he argues that the masses have always rejected transcendence, preferring the images and icons of ritual practice. Similarly, the masses reject the educational and cultural content provided by the communications media and instead revel in spectacle and scandal. The masses behave in this way not because they are mystified, senseless or passive, but because they 'sense the hegemony of meaning' and effect 'an explicit and positive counter-strategy – the task of absorbing and annihilating culture, knowledge, power, the social (1983: 10–11).

7   In the case of reality TV, 'sexuality', 'aggression', 'competition' and 'survival' are used as the major signifiers of 'reality'. In short, if someone is fucking, screaming or fighting that supposedly constitutes 'reality' because it reveals intensity, 'emotion' and 'desire', the repressed 'truths' of the human condition freed from social convention. It might even be argued that 'celebrities' whose 'reality' has been seriously depleted by their 'conversion' into

commodity-signs undergo a ritual conversion from hyperreal status back to 'reality', from a mass of signifiers back to 'real' people capable of symbolic exchanges – or at least of simulated friendships. Careers as commodity-signs are revitalised by a brief injection of (second order) 'reality'.

5 THE BODY, SEXUALITY AND SEDUCTION

1 The extent of Baudrillard's anti-materialism can be overlooked so I will emphasise it: 'the body as instituted by modern mythology is no more material than the soul. Like the soul, it is an *idea* . . . the privileged substrate of objectivizations – *the guiding myth of an ethic of consumption*' (1998a: 136).

2 Baudrillard follows Freud and Lacan by assuming that we become subjects through subjection to the Phallic principle or Name-of-the-Father (Lacan, 1977: 67). Baudrillard's version is termed the Phallus Exchange Standard. At the unconscious and imaginary level the Phallus is the fundamental grounding signifier. It enables signification to operate by resolving the Oedipus Complex and producing the castrated or barred subjects required by society, although this process is never stable or complete. Lacan plays on both divine connotations as *In the Name of the Father* and the homophony of '*le nom*' (the name) and '*le non*' (the no) in French: the Name-of-the-Father is also the 'No' of the Father. The 'No' of the father is the 'No' of the Law, the 'No' of God, the 'No' of incest prohibition, the 'No' to the mother's body. The Name/No of the Father is the principle of authority, the figure who has castrated girls (because they have no penis) and who will castrate boys if they remain too attached to their mothers. Castration – or the threat of castration – is, for Lacan, the point of access, for both boys and girls, to the rational, ordered, civilised world. Confusingly, Lacan calls this world 'the symbolic', while Baudrillard calls it semiotic or 'real'.

3 Fetishism is a form of sexual perversion whereby men attempt to deny the radical sexual difference of women, that women have no penis and in its place there is only a 'void' (according to Freud). A fetish, such as a shoe or an item of underwear, becomes a substitute 'something' for this 'nothing'. The fetish enables the fetishist or 'pervert' to avoid confrontation with the material difference of a woman's body, while also enabling sexual arousal (see Freud, 1977: 351–7).

4 According to Baudrillard, the symbolic exchanges that depend on the existence of the incest taboo, unlike the principle of the first

and second orders, are not repressive. This is because symbolic exchange both requires and, in its practice, annuls or 'cancels the prohibition on which it is based' (1993a: 123 n. 18). Symbolic exchange is the annulment of value. In symbolic exchange the body is not object but 'anti-object', non-value, ambivalence without positive value or meaning: 'for the body, as material of symbolic exchange – there is no model, no code, no ideal type, no controlling phantasm, since there could not be a system of the body as anti-object' (1993a: 114). Sadly, Baudrillard offers no examples!

5   Feminists and other critics have responded in the same vein, rushing to condemn Baudrillard without allowing his ideas a fair hearing. It could be argued that some feminists have responded to Baudrillard's challenge with an appropriate 'counter-gift', an escalation of the refusal to weigh up ideas fairly. However, it could also be argued that Baudrillard has succeeded in pushing the stakes of academic argument into his own, alternative universe of symbolic exchange and seduction where his own rhetoric, and the rhetoric of his 'opponents', is drawn off into an annulment of referential, representational argument.

6   Here Baudrillard is influenced by Foucault's 'Incitement to Discourse' in his *History of Sexuality, Vol. 1* (Foucault, 1979: 17–35).

7   The sciences of nature and the study of culture flourish only because practitioners consent to work within a narrowly circumscribed 'field'. If the study of culture has not 'developed' as quickly as the sciences of nature this is because the 'field' of culture is less easily circumscribed.

8   When I met Baudrillard, in Leicester, UK, in 1998, I asked him if simulation was 'good or evil'. He replied, 'Neither. Simulation is hyper-good, non?'

6   INTO THE FOURTH ORDER

1   An issue Baudrillard did not explore fully was the possibility that some may judge what he chose to call a 'simulatory' freedom to be preferable to 'real' exclusion, inequality or prejudice. But for Baudrillard the point is that simulatory freedom is 'real' exclusion and, worse, it buries any possibility of 'real' freedom beneath a kaleidoscope of signs.

2   Despite Baudrillard's return to Nietzsche a surprising number of Marxist themes and tropes remain in his later work. The project of critical thought has, for Baudrillard, 'substantially ended'; just as

for Marx the critique of religion was, by the late nineteenth century, 'substantially ended' (see Marx, 1969: 13–15). For Baudrillard simulation signals the obsolescence of critical thought, just as, for Marx, the dominance of capitalist ownership rendered obsolete the critique of religious authority.

3   Baudrillard used the term 'final solution' frequently to suggest a parallel with the Nazi *Endlösung* or 'final solution' to the Jewish question: the death camps. The use of this term is certainly provocative and it expresses what for Baudrillard is the profound violence of the global (see also 2003b: 85–105).

7 WAR, TERRORISM AND 9/11

1   It might be objected that the twin towers of the World Trade Center were not an iconic symbol of US power before 9/11, but became so only *in* their destruction. Yet it is clear that the twin towers were a symbol of US hegemony for Baudrillard long before the attacks took place 'Why has the World Trade Center in New York got *two* towers . . . The fact that there are two identical towers *signifies* the end of all competition' (1993a: 69–70, original emphasis, see also 186).

8 SUBJECTIVITY, IDENTITY AND AGENCY

1   These critics only manage to demonstrate that Baudrillard does not have a Marxist understanding of the subject, and on this they are correct.

2   This is, of course, a complex and gradual process. Baudrillard is certainly influenced by the Durkheimian and Maussian critiques of individualism but the sociology of Max Weber also theorises this process, particularly in *The Protestant Ethic and the Spirit of Capitalism* (1992) and 'Science as a Vocation' (1970), which impact, clearly, on Baudrillard's thought (see 1993a: 163–4).

3   Social problems are treated *at the level of signs*: inner cities have 'make-overs' or 'face-lifts'; there are media campaigns against drug-taking or gun crime; 'problem' individuals are 'treated' by therapists so that they say the right things; the unemployed are put on courses so that their CVs *look* better. Equality *at the level of the sign* is promoted everywhere. Cosmetic surgery is performed on individuals and on the social so that they might appear healthy on the surface.

4   But the subject, for Baudrillard, is not an essence or truth that is destroyed by the 'evil' of cloning. The subject eliminated by

cloning is the subject as constituted by the second order of simulacra: the divided subject of Freudian psychoanalysis, the alienated
subject of Marxist sociology.

5   Excess that cannot be profitably invested, but must be squandered,
Bataille termed the 'accursed share'. Baudrillard engages with this
important notion at many points in his career. Initially he presents
his own idea of symbolic economy as coterminous with it, then he
begins to differentiate the terms (Baudrillard, 1975, 1993a), but
Baudrillard's theoretical trajectory remains deeply influenced by it
(1993b: 106–10).

6   Baudrillard's repeated use of the masculine pronoun requires
comment. Rather than this being a sign of sloppy sexism or a refusal
of politically correct circumlocutions, Baudrillard actually seems to
be reversing the expected gendering in a *becoming-feminine*, since
his postulated other in this pact is designated 'he'. However, this
should be taken to refer not to biological sex, but to ritual role,
persona or position.

7   And it seems many people were looking for such rhetoric in the
late 1980s and early 1990s – *please tell us Baudrillard is wrong* –
and a number of Marxists and feminists duly provided conveniently
packaged rejections of ideas that they hadn't actually bothered to
try to understand. The last gasp was provided by Sokal and
Bricmont (1998): not only is Baudrillard wrong but all variants of
French poststructuralism are wrong, hooray – we can all get on with
our realist science, our realist sociology and our realist feminism
again! Yet in an ironic turn of events Sokal and Bricmont, who claim
to be Marxists infuriated by poststructuralism's alleged political
quietism, have been championed by right-wing websites such as Defy
the Left Elites! Their *Intellectual Impostures* (1998) is recom-
mended alongside books condemning Islam as terroristic and
calling for a halt to the immigration of Muslims in the West. It seems
that reactionary and xenophobic readers want to believe that
Baudrillard, Deleuze and Irigaray have nothing worthwhile to say.

8   Again Baudrillard's argument slips from femininity to women in
suggesting that women risk losing their symbolic advantage in
gaining economic advantages. And he never asks whether this
trade-off might simply be a worthwhile one.

9   In his critique of identity/difference, Baudrillard attacks the pieties
of both the left and the right with equal vigour. Both left and right
seek to promote identity 'Without inner alterity . . . a dream that
is pathetically absurd' (2001c: 52). On the left we find the promotion of certain minorities, particularly sexual, ethnic and 'lifestyle'

minorities: 'I am gay', 'I am bisexual', 'I am a woman trapped in a man's body'. On the right we find the promotion of national and cultural identity, and the increasing demand that we demonstrate our loyalty, commitment and understanding of 'our' national or cultural identity: 'I am British and proud of it', 'I am American and I believe in . . . what ever it is that I am currently expected to believe in to satisfy citizenship tests.' For Baudrillard these are 'hopeless affirmations . . . since when you need to prove the obvious, it is by no means obvious' (2001c: 52).

10   Positioned by the system as interactive beings, there are, of course, a wealth of possible connections, new 'freedoms' and even 'second lives' available on-line. These allow interaction with people all over the world, very cheaply, and further erase our bodies and genders through the construction of virtual selves. Yet, according to Baudrillard, there is no actual exchange taking place in these activities. Baudrillard does not deny that there are pleasures and fascinations in on-line interactivity but asserts that these derive, in large part, from a delight in the technological medium, not in our interactants: there is no symbolic exchange. Pleasure derives from the fact that technology can do this for me – we interact with the medium, not the other.

CONCLUSION

1   Baudrillard's early work, particularly *Consumer Society*, contains recognisably Durkheimian themes; his discussion of waste as socially functional (1998a: 42–7) recalls Durkheim's famous discussion of crime (1982: 85–107) and there are a number of references to anomie (Baudrillard, 1998a: 174–85). However, I think it is an exaggeration to call Baudrillard a Durkheimian (as Gane, 1991b, and Merrin, 2005, do). There is simply not enough of Durkheim in Baudrillard's work to make this claim stick.

2   Baudrillard curses those many who would reduce sociology to realist programmes and empiricist 'data' at the expense of theory, imagination and challenge.

Bibliography

Adorno, T. and Horkheimer, M. (1971) *Dialectic of Enlightenment*. London: Verso.

Ansell-Pearson, K. (1997) *Viroid Life*. London: Routledge.

Augustine, St (1971) *The City of God*. Harmondsworth: Penguin.

Barthes, R. (1983) *The Fashion System*. Berkeley: University of California Press. First original language publication 1967.

Bataille, G. (1986) *Eroticism*. San Francisco: City Lights. First original language publication 1957.

Bataille, G. (1988) *The Accursed Share, Volume 1*. New York: Zone Books. First original language publication 1967.

Bataille, G. (1992) *On Nietzsche*. New York: Paragon.

Baudrillard, J. (1975) *The Mirror of Production*. New York: Telos Press. First original language publication 1973.

Baudrillard, J. (1976) *L'échange symbolique et la mort*. Paris: Galilee.

Baudrillard, J. (1981) *For a Critique of the Political Economy of the Sign*. New York: Telos Press. First original language publication 1972.

Baudrillard, J. (1983) *In the Shadow of the Silent Majorities or The End of the Social*. New York: Semiotext(e). First original language publication 1978.

Baudrillard, J. (1987a) 'When Bataille Attacked the Metaphysical Principle of Economy', *Canadian Journal of Political and Social Theory*, 11(3): 57–62. First original language publication 1976.

Baudrillard, J. (1987b) *Forget Foucault: Forget Baudrillard*. New York: Semiotext(e). First original language publication 1977.

Baudrillard, J. (1987c) *The Evil Demon of Images*. Sydney: Power Institute.

Baudrillard, J. (1988a) *America*. New York: Verso. First original language publication 1986.

Baudrillard, J. (1988b) *The Ecstasy of Communication*. New York: Semiotext(e). First original language publication 1987.

Baudrillard, J. (1990a) *Seduction*. New York: St Martin's Press. First original language publication 1979.

Baudrillard, J. (1990b) *Fatal Strategies*. New York: Semiotext(e). First original language publication 1983.

Baudrillard, J. (1990c) *Cool Memories*. London: Verso. First original language publication 1987.

Baudrillard, J. (1990d) *La transparence du mal: Essai sur les phenomenes extremes*. Paris: Galilee.

Baudrillard, J. (1992) 'A Seminar on Terrorism and the Media', in W. Stearns and W. Chaloupka (eds) *Jean Baudrillard: The Disappearance of Art and Politics*. London: Macmillan.

Baudrillard, J. (1993a) *Symbolic Exchange and Death*. London: Sage. First original language publication 1976.

Baudrillard, J. (1993b) *The Transparency of Evil: Essays on Extreme Phenomena*. London: Verso. First original language publication 1990.

Baudrillard, J. (1994a) *Simulacra and Simulation*. Ann Arbor: University of Michigan Press. First original language publication 1981.

Baudrillard, J. (1994b) *The Illusion of the End*. London: Cambridge: Polity Press. First original language publication 1992.

Baudrillard, J. (1995) *The Gulf War Did Not Take Place*. Sydney: Power Institute, University of Sydney. First original language publication 1991.

Baudrillard, J. (1996a) *The System of Objects*. London: Verso. First original language publication 1968.

Baudrillard, J. (1996b) *Cool Memories II*. Cambridge: Polity Press. First original language publication 1990.

Baudrillard, J. (1996c) *The Perfect Crime*. London: Verso. First original language publication 1995.

Baudrillard, J. (1997) *Cool Memories III*. London: Verso. First original language publication 1995.

Baudrillard, J. (1998a) *The Consumer Society – Myths and Structures*. London: Sage. First original language publication 1970.

Baudrillard, J. (1998b) *Paroxsym: Interviews with Philippe Petit*. London: Verso. First original language publication 1997.

Baudrillard, J. (1999) *Photographies 1985–1998*. Berlin: Hatje Cantz.

Baudrillard, J. (2000) *The Vital Illusion*. New York: Columbia University Press.

Baudrillard, J. (2001a) 'Police and Play', in G. Genosko (ed.) *The Uncollected Baudrillard*. London: Sage, pp. 61–9. First original language publication 1969.

Baudrillard, J. (2001b) 'The Divine Left', in G. Genosko (ed.) *The Uncollected Baudrillard*. London: Sage. First original language publication 1985.

Baudrillard, J. (2001c) *Impossible Exchange*. London: Verso. First original language publication 1999.

Baudrillard, J. (2001d) *Telemorphose*. Paris: Sens and Tonka.

Baudrillard, J. (2002a) *Screened Out*. London: Verso. First original language publication 2000.

Baudrillard, J. (2002b) 'Otherness Surgery', in *Screened Out*. London: Verso, pp. 51–6. First original language publication 1993.

Baudrillard, J. (2002c) 'Disembodied Violence: Hate, in *Screened Out*. London: Verso, pp. 91–5. First original language publication 1995.

Baudrillard, J. (2003a) *Passwords*. London: Verso. First original language publication 2000.

Baudrillard, J. (2003b) *The Spirit of Terrorism*. London: Verso. First original language publication 2002.

Baudrillard, J. (2004) *Fragments: Interviews*. London: Routledge. First original language publication 2001.

Baudrillard, J. (2005a) 'The Violence of Indifference' in *The Conspiracy of Art*. New York: Semiotext(e), pp. 141–55. First original language publication 1994.

Baudrillard, J. (2005b) 'Dust Breeding', in *The Conspiracy of Art and Other Essays*. New York: Semiotext(e). First original language publication 2001.

Baudrillard, J. (2005c) 'Telemorphosis', in *The Conspiracy of Art and Other Essays*. New York: Semiotext(e). First original language publication 2001.

Baudrillard, J. (2005d) *The Intelligence of Evil or The Lucidity Pact*. Oxford: Berg. First original language publication 2004.

Baudrillard, J. (2005e) *Cool Memories IV*. London: Verso. First original language publication 2004.

Baudrillard, J. (2005f) 'War Porn', in *The Conspiracy of Art*. New York: Semiotext(e). First original language publication 2004.

Baudrillard, J. (2005g) *The Conspiracy of Art*. New York: Semiotext(e).

Baudrillard, J. (2006a) *Cool Memories V*. London: Verso. First original language publication 2005.

Baudrillard, J. (2006b) *On Disappearance*. Unpublished paper presented in absentia, University of Wales, Swansea, 6 September.

Baudrillard, J. and Calle, S. (1988) *Suite Venitienne/Please Follow Me*. Seattle: Bay Press. First original language publication 1983.

Beard, S. and McClellan, J. (1989) 'Baudrillard', *The Face*, January: 61–2.

Belsey, C. (2003) *Poststructuralism: A Very Brief Introduction*. Oxford: Oxford University Press.

Boas, F. (1890) 'First General Report on the Indians of British Columbia: Tlingit, Haida, Tsimshian, Kotonaqa', in *Report of the British Association for the Advancement of Science 1889*. London: J. Murray, pp. 23–42.

Boorman, J. (dir.) (1981) *Excalibur*. Warner Brothers.

Borges, J.L. (1975) *A Universal History of Infamy*. Harmondsworth: Penguin.

Bracken, C. (1997) *The Potlatch Papers: A Colonial Case History*. Chicago: University of Chicago Press.

Browning, G.K. and Kilmister, A. (2006) 'Baudrillard, Dialectics and Political Economy', in *Critical and Post-Critical Economy*. London: Palgrave.

Butler, R. (1999) *The Defence of the Real*. London: Sage.

Caillois, R. (1961) *Man, Play and Games*. Glencoe, IL: Thames and Hudson. First original language publication 1958.

Callinicos, A. (1989) *Against Postmodernism: A Marxist Critique*. Cambridge: Polity Press.

Carrère, E. (2001) *The Adversary*. London: Bloomsbury. First original language publication 2000.

Chapman, R. and Rutherford, J. (1988) *Male Order: Unwrapping Masculinity*. London: Lawrence and Wishart.

Clastres, P. (1977) *Society against the State*. Oxford: Blackwell. First original language publication 1974.

Clutesi, G. (1969) *Potlatch*. Sidney, BC: Gray's Publishing.

Debord, G. (1967) *Society of the Spectacle*. English translation at www.marxists.org/reference/archive/debord/society.htm.

Deleuze, G. (1983) *Nietzsche and Philosophy*. London: Athlone Press. First original language publication 1962.

Derrida, J. (1978) *Writing and Difference*. London: Routledge and Kegan Paul. First original language publication 1967.

Derrida, J. (1992) *Given Time: 1, Counterfeit Money*. Chicago: University of Chicago Press. First original language publication 1991.

Durkheim, E. (1961) *Elementary Forms of the Religious Life*. New York: Collier. First original language publication 1912.

Durkheim, E. (1964) *Suicide*. London: Routledge and Kegan Paul. First original language publication 1893.

Durkheim, E. (1982) *The Rules of Sociological Method*. Basingstoke: Macmillan. First original language publication 1895.

Foucault, M. (1967) *Madness and Civilisation*. London: Tavistock. First original language publication 1961.

Foucault, M. (1970) *The Order of Things: An Archaeology of the Human Sciences*. London: Routledge. First original language publication 1966.

Foucault, M. (1977) *Discipline and Punish*. Harmondsworth: Penguin. First original language publication 1975.

Foucault, M. (1979) *The History of Sexuality, Vol. 1: An Introduction*. London: Penguin. First original language publication 1976.

Freud, S. (1977) *On Sexuality*. London: Penguin. First original language publication 1927.

Friedman, T. (2000) *The Lexus and the Olive Tree*. New York: HarperCollins.

Galeen, H. (dir.) (1926) *The Student of Prague*. Sokal-Film GmbH.

Gallop, J. (1987) 'French Theory and the Seductions of Feminism', in A. Jardine and P. Smith (eds) *Men in Feminism*. New York: Methuen.

Gane, M. (1991a) *Baudrillard: Critical and Fatal Theory*. London: Routledge.

Gane, M. (1991b) *Baudrillard's Bestiary, Baudrillard and Culture*. London: Routledge.

Gane, M. (ed.) (1993) *Baudrillard Live: Selected Interviews*. London: Routledge.

Gane, M. (2000) *Jean Baudrillard: In Radical Uncertainty*. London: Pluto.

Genosko, G. (1994) *Baudrillard and Signs: Signification Ablaze*. London: Routledge.

Genosko, G. (1998) *Undisciplined Theory*. London: Sage.

Genosko, G. (1999) *McLuhan and Baudrillard: The Masters of Implosion*. London: Routledge.

Genosko, G. (ed.) (2001) *The Uncollected Baudrillard*. London: Sage.

Grace, V. (2000) *Baudrillard's Challenge*. London: Routledge.

Gutting, G. (2001) *French Philosophy in the Twentieth Century*. Cambridge: Cambridge University Press.

Habermas, J. (1987) *The Philosophical Discourse of Modernity.* Cambridge: Polity Press. First original language publication 1985.

Hall, S. (1991) 'The Local and the Global: Globalization and Ethnicity', in A. King (ed.) *Culture, Globalization and the World System.* Basingstoke: Macmillan.

Hegarty, P. (2004) *Jean Baudrillard: Live Theory.* London: Continuum.

Heisenberg, W. (1958) *Physics and Philosophy.* Harmondsworth: Penguin.

Horrocks, C. (1996) *Introducing Baudrillard.* Cambridge: Icon.

Huntington, S. (1998) *The Clash of Civilizations.* New York: Pocket.

Ignatieff, M. (2000) *Virtual War.* London: Chatto and Windus.

James, I. (2000) *Pierre Klossowski: The Persistence of a Name.* Oxford: Legenda.

Jameson, F. (1991) *Postmodernism: Or the Cultural Logic of Late Capitalism.* London: Verso.

Jarry, A. (1996) *Exploits and Opinions of Dr Faustroll, Pataphysician.* Cambridge: Exact Change. First original language publication 1898.

Jarry, A. (1999) *The SuperMale.* Cambridge: Exact Change. First original language publication 1902.

Kellner, D. (1989) *Jean Baudrillard: From Marxism to Postmodernism and Beyond.* Cambridge: Polity Press.

King, A. (ed.) (1991) *Culture, Globalization and the World System.* Basingstoke: Macmillan.

Klein, N. (2001) *No Logo.* London: HarperCollins.

Klossowski, P. (1970) *La Monnaie Vivante.* Paris: Éditions Joëlle Losfeld.

Klossowski, P. (1997) *Nietzsche and the Vicious Circle.* London: Athlone. First original language publication 1969.

Lacan, J. (1977) *Ecrits: A Selection.* London: Tavistock. First original language publication 1966.

Lane, R. (2000) *Jean Baudrillard.* London: Routledge.

Leenhardt, M. (1979) *Do Kamo: Person and Myth in the Melanesian World.* Chicago: University of Chicago Press. First original language publication 1947.

Levy, A. (2006) *Raunch Culture: Female Chauvinist Pigs.* New York: Pocket.

Lyotard, J.-F. (1993) *Libidinal Economy.* London: Athlone Press. First original language publication 1974.

Malinowski, B. (1922) *Argonauts of the Western Pacific.* London: Routledge and Kegan Paul.

Marcuse, H. (1961) *One Dimensional Man.* London: Ark.

Marx, K. (1969) 'The Eighteenth Brumaire of Louis Bonaparte', in *Selected Works Vol. 1*. Moscow: Progress Publishers. First original language publication 1852.

Marx, K. (1995) *Capital: A New Abridgement*. Oxford: Oxford University Press.

Marx, K. and Engels, F. (1970) *The German Ideology*. London: Lawrence and Wishart.

Mauss, M. (1950) 'Essai sur le don: forme et raison de l'échange dans les sociétés archaïques', in *Sociologie et Anthropologie*. Paris: Presses Universitaires de France.

Mauss, M. (1979) *Sociology and Psychology*. London: Routledge and Kegan Paul. First original language publication 1950.

Mauss, M. (1990) *The Gift: The Form and Reason for Exchange in Archaic Societies*. London: Routledge. First original language publication 1924/5.

Mauss, M. and Hubert, H. (1964) *Sacrifice: Its Nature and Function*. London: Cohen and West. First original language publication 1898.

Merrin, W. (1994) 'Uncritical criticism? Norris, Baudrillard and the Gulf War', *Economy and Society*, 23, 4: 433–58.

Merrin, W. (2005) *Baudrillard and the Media*. London: Sage.

Moore, S. (1988) 'Getting a bit of the Other', in R. Chapman and J. Rutherford (eds) *Male Order: Unwrapping Masculinity*. London: Lawrence and Wishart, pp. 165–92.

Nietzsche, F. (1961) *Thus Spoke Zarathrustra*. London: Penguin. First original language publication 1883.

Nietzsche, F. (1968) *The Will to Power*. New York: Vintage.

Nietzsche, F. (1974) *The Gay Science*. New York: Vintage. First original language publication 1882.

Nietzsche, F. (1990a) *Beyond Good and Evil*. London: Penguin. First original language publication 1886.

Nietzsche, F. (1990b) *Twilight of the Idols* and *The Anti-Christ*. London: Penguin. First original language publication 1889, 1894.

Nietzsche, F. (1994) *On the Genealogy of Morality*. Cambridge: Cambridge University Press. First original language publication 1887.

Norris, C. (1992) *Uncritical Theory: Postmodernism, Intellectuals and the Gulf War*. London: Lawrence and Wishart.

Pefanis, J. (1991) *Heterology and the Postmodern: Bataille, Baudrillard and Lyotard*. Durham, NC: Duke University Press.

Plant, S. (1992) *The Most Radical Gesture: The Situationist International in the Postmodern Age*. London: Routledge.

Price, S. (1996) *Communication Studies*. Harlow: Longman.

Riesman, D. (1961) *The Lonely Crowd*. New Haven: Yale University Press.

Rosman, A. and Rubel, P. (1972) 'The Potlatch: A Structural Analysis', *American Anthropologist*, 74: 658–71.

Sahlins, M. (1974) *Stone Age Economics*. London: Tavistock.

Saussure, F. (1966) *Course in General Linguistics*. New York: McGraw-Hill. First original language publication 1915.

Shrift, A. (1998) *Nietzsche's French Legacies: A Genealogy of Poststructuralism*. New York: Routledge.

Sokal, A. and Bricmont, J. (1998) *Intellectual Impostures*. London: Profile.

Stearns, W. and Chaloupka, W. (1992) *Jean Baudrillard: The Disappearance of Art and Politics*. London: Macmillan.

Strathern, M. (1988) *The Gender of the Gift*. Berkeley: University of California Press.

Tarantino, Q. (dir.) (1991) *Reservoir Dogs*. Miramax Films.

Tarantino, Q. (dir.) (2003) *Kill Bill Volume 1*. Miramax Films.

Veblen, T. (1979) *The Theory of the Leisure Class*. Harmondsworth: Penguin. First original language publication 1899.

Walsh, J. (ed.) (1995) *The Gulf War Did Not Happen*. Aldershot: Ashgate.

Weber, M. (1949) *The Methodology of the Social Sciences*. New York: Free Press. First original language publication 1922.

Weber, M. (1970) 'Science as a Vocation', in H.H. Gerth and C. Wright-Mills (eds) *From Max Weber: Essays in Sociology*. London: Routledge, pp. 129–56. First original language publication 1948.

Weber, M. (1992) *The Protestant Ethic and the Spirit of Capitalism*. London: Routledge. First original language publication 1930.

Wheen, F. (2004) *How Mumbo-Jumbo Conquered the World*. London: Harper Perennial.

Index